CW00801982

FATTY

The strife and times of Paul Vautin

IRONBARK PRESS

FATTY

The strife and times of Paul Vautin

By Mike Colman

IRONBARK PRESS

Published in 1992 by IRONBARK PRESS
Level 1, 175 Alison Road, Randwick NSW
Reprinted 1992 (twice)

National Library of Australia
Cataloguing-In-Publication

> Colman, Mike
> Fatty: The Strife and Times of Paul Vautin.

> ISBN 1 875471 17 0

> 1. Vautin, Paul. 2. Rugby league football players —
> Queensland — Biography. I. Title.

> 796.3338

Editor: Larry Writer
Production: Geoff Armstrong
Design and Finished Art: Kylie Prats
Cover Photography: Ern McQuillan
Cover Design: Jayem Productions
Printed by: Globe Press

ABOUT THE AUTHOR

Mike Colman has been a journalist for 20 years, working on *The Australian*, the London *Sun*, the *North Shore Times* where he was editor, and the Sydney *Sun*.

He joined the *Sunday Telegraph* in 1989 as senior sportswriter and columnist. Colman has won six major awards for sportswriting, including the NSWRL Feature Story of the Year (twice), the NSWRL Print Media Award and the NSW Cricket Association Sheffield Shield Story of the Year (1990).

Colman was a senior member of the News Limited team at the recent Barcelona Olympics.

He lives on Sydney's North Shore with his wife Linda and daughters Matilda and Amelia.

Contents

WITH THANKS

A book such as this could not have been written without the enthusiasm and help of a great many people. The Vautin family — George and Leila in Brisbane and Paul and Kim in Sydney — were tireless in their support, spending countless hours reminiscing and retracing the past 30 years.

Wally Lewis, Wayne Bennett and Tosser Turner in Brisbane, Johnny Gibbs and Bob Fulton in Sydney, all took time out of their busy schedules to sit and recall the times they shared with their mate Fatty. Others, too numerous to mention individually, from Brisbane, Sydney and England, all were only too happy to add their comments and thoughts.

In order to provide fresh insight into the life and times of Vautin, I consciously steered clear of other books and the wealth of press clippings he and his family provided — with one exception. I found Robert Smith's excellent history of Manly-Warringah Rugby League Club, *The Sea Eagle Has Landed,* an invaluable source of reference.

And, as with everything I attempt, this book would never have been completed without the support of my own family.

— **Mike Colman**

AUTHOR'S DEDICATION:
To Linda

Introduction

When I sat down with the people at Ironbark Press to discuss the possibility of writing a book about Paul Vautin it was a case of 'why hasn't anyone thought of it before?'

The more I moved into the project I began to realise there was a lot more to Vautin than the character we see on the telly or the footballer we used to watch wearing the colours of Manly, Queenland, Australia and Easts. Like all interesting personalities, there is more to Paul Vautin than meets the eye.

Those who knew him as a boy speak of the sensitive kid who became the class clown to overcome his shyness. As a footballer he wasn't noted as the most diligent trainer but would never shirk his duty on the field, putting the most dedicated fitness fanatics to shame with his heart and stamina. He can cut an opponent to ribbons with his tongue and harsh wit, but is as dedicated a father and family man as you will ever meet.

In Paul Vautin and his alter ego Fatty, I found a mass of contradictions yet, I'm glad to say, he never ceased to surprise me — and always for the better.

Writing a book such as this is a daunting task. It requires teamwork and commitment from both the author and the subject. Having dealt with rugby league players for several years I was not always optimistic that Vautin's involvement would be what was required, yet he never let me down once. If I asked for him to make corrections to the manuscript, they were made — neatly written and delivered to my home. If he felt I had not captured an emotion or feeling adequately, he would offer to write it himself. I often had my doubts but sure enough, there he would be with a piece of paper in his hand: the words tuned, the sentiments spot on.

This was the side of Paul Vautin which made me glad I accepted the chance to write his story. The one who kept appointments, the one who would anguish on whether he had given a former teammate a big enough rap.

Of course Fatty was around the place too. He's the one whose hackles raised when he heard of a disparaging comment made by one of the many people I interviewed for the book. "Alright," he'd say, "he reckons that does he? Well I'll give it to him too." But he never asked that I leave out anything. Never suggested that an opinion or anecdote which painted him in a less than favourable light be cut.

"Warts and all," he used to say, "I don't regret a thing."

It was Vautin's suggestion that the book be a biography rather than a ghosted "autobiography". "I want other people to have their say too," he told me, "that way the readers can make up their own minds."

Fatty can be crude just as Paul can be sensitive. The louder Fatty asserts "I don't give a stuff what people say about me" the more you realise Paul does.

But in living, thinking and writing the story of Paul Vautin and his mate Fatty for the best part of a year, I found that one without the other was nothing. A sensitive kid from Brisbane would be crushed in the dog-eat-dog world of Sydney rugby league. An acid-tongued joker would soon wear thin on the media-fed public. Put them together and you had a winner. A small town boy who cared about who he was and where he came from, strengthened by the wit and sarcasm of the natural humorist.

It was Fatty who surprised me with his ability to recall and tell and anecdote with the style and timing of a nightclub entertainer. It was Paul who surprised me bright and early Easter Sunday with an Easter egg for my daughter.

We weren't friends when we embarked on this venture, I'm not sure we're friends now but I know I have respect for a fellow professional. When we had our first meeting he stressed that he wanted the book to be truthful. To be honest.

"I just want to know that when someone has finished reading it they'll know who I am. It doesn't matter to me whether they think 'gee, I don't like that bloke much' or 'I'd like to have a beer with him', as long as they know who I am."

Now that it's all over I think I know who Paul Vautin is.

I'll have a beer with him any day.

Mike Colman

Prologue

The TV newsreader looked into the camera, a picture of the footballer on the screen behind him, two words superimposed: Vautin Out.

"The 11-year career of Manly captain Paul Vautin appears over tonight after talks broke down on his new contract," he read. "He stormed out of today's meeting after only 15 minutes, claiming the Sea Eagles had offered a deal which almost halved his pay."

The screen danced with vision of the footballer arriving at Manly Leagues Club, head down, tight-lipped, as a reporter took up the story: "Vautin arrived at the Manly football club knowing his future was on the line but hoping to stay with the Sea Eagles. As Australian vice captain and with 11 years service to the club Vautin expected to be offered a contract on at least his present salary. Instead he was given a clear indication he was no longer wanted at Manly.

"Vautin's support for recently sacked Manly coach Alan Thompson and his criticism of club management hasn't helped his cause but Manly officials deny that was a consideration. Vautin left the brief meeting furious ..."

The film showed the footballer brushing aside reporters' questions and getting in his car. What it didn't show was him driving the 10 minutes to his home in nearby Cromer, his mind a blur, emotions haywire. As the television screen filled with footage of the footballer in his prime, scoring tries, holding a premiership trophy aloft or tackling, tackling, tackling, he drove on in a daze. At every red light, every stoppage in traffic, he would shake his head or smash his hand down on the dashboard.

Finally, as he neared his home he gripped the steering wheel until his knuckles whitened and shouted the words which had welled inside since the moment he walked from the office. "Why?" he screamed, "I haven't done anything wrong."

He turned into the driveway of his home where the red "Sold" stickers had been placed across the "For Sale" sign only days earlier, stopped the car, got out and walked through the front door.

And then it hit him with a cold, sickening finality. A career — no, much more than that — an almost familial attachment to the only club he had ever played with in Sydney — the only club he had ever *wanted* to play with was finished.

His wife met him at the door. She didn't ask the outcome of the meeting. She didn't have to. His face told the story as clearly as any of the newspaper headlines which would give the issue front-page prominence for days, weeks, to come.

He looked at her and shook his head. His eyes wide with the shock of how suddenly, how clinically, it had happened. "It's all over," he said. And then he started to cry like a little kid.

CHAPTER 1

Fatty And Paul

To understand Fatty you have to know Paul. In many ways they are very similar. They look alike, sound alike and even share the same passport. But, make no mistake, they are as different as the opposite sides of the Tweed River. One is a Brisbane boy, born and bred. He grew up in the suburbs where the cane toads' baritone lullaby would send him off to sleep on tropical nights. He learned to look someone in the eye when he shook their hand, to be polite and respectful to women. He learned there was something special about being a Queenslander. Something that other people — "Southerners" particularly — can't understand. Something intangible that even he can't explain.

He was shy, at times unconfident. He was, says a girl who knew him as a tongue-tied schoolboy, "the sweetest, most loyal friend you could ever have. The type of boy you'd like your son to be."

That was who Paul Vautin was, that is who he still is.

And then there's Fatty.

Fatty is the character you see on the telly. The one who sells garish Hawaiian-print shirts and Stubbies by getting pushed out of boats and impersonating bowling balls. The one who makes crazy bets on the air and dresses up in a tutu when he loses.

He's a brash kind of guy, never lost for words, which is why the scribes love him. They'll never go short of a good quote as long as Fatty is near a phone. He always says what he thinks, and hang the consequences.

His favourite expressions are "You're kiddin'" and "Give yourself an uppercut". He knows Paul Vautin well. Grew up with him as a matter of fact, but you'll never see them in the same room. Paul's wife Kim won't even let Fatty in the house.

They've come a long way, these two. Made some money, some headlines and an enemy or two. They've also made a lot of people happy. It hasn't always been easy. The road has taken the odd wrong turn and almost hit the occasional dead end since the journey began just over 30 years ago. But, for all that, it's been quite a ride — all started by a fella named George Vautin and his wife Leila, in a place called Everton Park.

He's a tough man, George Vautin. The footballers who came up against him in Brisbane and the bush will tell you. So, too, will his sons and daughter, but there is something about the railway worker from Bowen which doesn't need words as testimony to his strength.

Just weeks from retirement George Vautin still looked like he could mix it pretty well on a football field — or anywhere else for that matter. He exudes an underlying steel, doesn't speak for the sake of it, but when he does, he makes sense.

Life wasn't easy for George. An only child, his father died when he was seven, his mother six years later. He was raised by his grandmother and, at the age of 16, joined the railways. For a year he sweated it out in the Bowen rail yards, cleaning the locomotives until they gleamed before finally getting his chance as an acting fireman, shovelling coal on the old steam engines from sun-up to sundown. The work was an education in itself. It took George away from Bowen for the first time in his life. It showed him the wide expanses of the Queensland countryside from the cabin of a puffing loco, put money in his pocket and, most of all, built him up physically to excel at his great love — rugby league. In summer he fished, sailed and dived off the highboard with enough skill to win the North Queensland championship, but all were just fill-ins until winter came again and he could get back on a football field.

It is fitting that the first photograph George Vautin has of himself is as a wide-eyed four-year-old sitting in front of the Bowen Railways Rugby League first grade team of 1931. He is so small the photographer has him perched on two pillows so he is not hidden by the premiership cup he so proudly holds. Too young to be ballboy, George was appointed mascot. His father Harold, to whom George bears an uncanny likeness, was team manager. His Uncle Buck played five-eighth in the team and another uncle on his mother's side, Jim Parker, was second rower and the side's enforcer. "They called him the iron man," said George, "he was tough as they come."

That was a description they'd later use to describe George when

he followed his uncles into the team. A fullback in Bowen's successful Wilson Cup side of the late 1940s, he made his way to the
forwards when he moved to Brisbane five years later.

By all accounts George could have made his mark in representative football. He was an honest toiler in an era when Queensland
forwards were well represented in Australian sides. He liked the
hard stuff and had enough pace to back up for tries but an untimely
injury ruled him out of the Brisbane side to play Great Britain in
1954. That game proved George's only chance at the big time but he
has never dwelled on it. He had a successful career as a first grade
second rower with Brisbane Wests, playing under captain-coach
Duncan Hall, the 22-Test veteran, and against the likes of Brothers' Test captain Brian Davies. In his first year with the side, 1954,
they won the Brisbane premiership and he had two more seasons
before he gave the game away. By that time he had other things to
think about. Things like a wife, home and, before too long, four kids
including a red-headed bundle of energy named Paul.

With George's promotion from acting fireman to fireman in
1948 came a transfer to Hughenden. It was there, at a Christmas
dance, that he met former Townsville girl Leila Dallow who worked
in the office of the local town council. Leila was the daughter of a
train driver. Joked George: "She reckons she's been in the railways
longer than I have."

The couple were married the following year and, with another
transfer, moved back to Bowen soon afterwards. It was here, two
years later, that their first son Geoffrey was born. It didn't take
George and Leila long to realise all was not well with Geoffrey but
there was little that could be done in Bowen to help.

Today, they call it Down's Syndrome. There is any amount of
literature to refer to, doctors and social workers who specialise in
the condition and support groups to offer advice and physical
assistance. But all that is very much a recent phenomenon. When
Geoffrey was born the Vautins had no real family or professional
support to fall back on. George's only relatives were elderly, Leila's
hundreds of kilometres away, and specialised medical facilities in
Bowen almost non-existent.

George applied for a transfer to Brisbane so the Vautins could
be closer to the necessary medical back-up. The family moved to the
Brisbane suburb of Enoggera and it was while they were living

there in 1954 that Deborah was born and four and a half years later Leila gave birth to Paul at Royal Brisbane Women's Hospital.

It nearly killed her. Late in her pregnancy Leila was struck down with infected hepatitis. A month before the due date she was rushed to hospital and gave birth prematurely. When Leila was told she had given birth to a healthy red-headed boy she though she was delirious. "There had never been a redhead on either side of the family," she said, "I wouldn't believe it until I saw him myself and even then I thought it must have been because of the hepatitis affecting my liver. I thought it would go away after a while."

The red hair never did go away and despite all the odds Paul soon proved that he, too, was here to stay. With Leila suffering a highly contagious disease, the baby was immediately taken to a nursing home in Clayfield. Leila was not to see her son for six weeks and could only listen to George's descriptions of the newcomer to the family with disbelief.

Not that George was in a joking mood. He and Leila had just bought a new home in nearby Everton Park and, with the pregnancy seemingly going to schedule, had arranged to move in a month before the expected birth. As so often the case with the best laid plans, they soon went astray. When Leila was hospitalised and Paul arrived early, George was forced to take long service leave to look after Geoffrey and Deborah and supervise the move. For six weeks as Leila lay dangerously ill in hospital, George juggled his time between Enoggera, Everton Park, the Royal Brisbane and the nursing home at Clayfield, while at the same time caring for the needs of two young children.

It is a time which even today brings raised eyebrows and an involuntary shudder from both Paul's parents but finally, after nearly two months, the ordeal ended. Although still weak, Leila was allowed home. On the way from the hospital to take his wife to their new home for the first time, George pulled into the car park at the nursing home, went inside and returned with a small bundle.

Any doubts Leila might have had vanished immediately. Yes, the hair was as red as everyone had said but there were no doubts about parentage. There had been no slip-ups at the hospital — in fact name tags were superfluous: this kid had Dallow written all over him. From the first time she laid eyes on him Leila knew what people who have been struck by the facial resemblance have been saying ever since: hair colour aside, this boy was definitely his mother's son.

One of the first things Leila noticed about her newborn son was how quiet he was. "He was never any bother," she said, "never made a peep, but as he got older I realised he was very, very determined."

And inquisitive too. Paul remained very shy and quiet for much of his early life, but could still create a rumpus when he wanted to. When Paul was aged four, George and Leila took the family — by then enlarged with the addition of Russell, two years the junior — to Myers city store to see the Christmas decorations. "It was just days before Christmas and the place was packed," George recalled, "you can picture it, music, decorations and all the people getting in their last minute shopping. Somehow Paul managed to find the switch to the escalators and turned them all off."

With this, the excitement of the big trip to town soon took on a different turn. Paul took one look at George's face and headed off into the crowds with his dad in hot pursuit. "When we finally caught him two old ladies said to me, 'Don't you hit that child!'," said Leila. "Hit him? I wanted to wring his neck."

Neither party can remember whether young Paul did in fact cop a belting but chances are he didn't. Just an icy stare from George was usually enough to put the fear of God into Paul, and Leila had her own form of highly effective discipline. "I'll never forget the time I was in about the under-eights and we were playing a curtain raiser to a Brothers-Wests first grade trial at Corbett Park," Paul remembered, "and there must have been about 900 people there and we were standing around on the sideline waiting to run on, feeling very big time. Mum leant over the fence and told me to tuck my jumper in and I said, 'Nup'. I thought it looked pretty tough hanging out. She told me again and I gave her another 'Nup'. Next thing, she's walked straight onto the field, pulled my pants down, undies and all, and tucked my jumper in for me. There I was, 900 people watching, my shorts and undies down around my ankles and my little jelly bean sticking out for all to see. It's lucky I didn't grow up a poof — but the next time Mum told me to tuck my jumper in, I sure tucked it in fast."

By this time George had retired from football, two newspaper clippings and four photographs his only mementoes. Paul and Russell became his links with the game and his dream of having a son with whom he could share his love of rugby league became a reality. "I never thought I'd have a son play for Australia or anything like that," he said. "That's not why I wanted them to play. I never wanted to push them. It was just something that I knew about and could share with them, take an interest in and help them if they needed it."

From the first moment he could hold a ball, Paul became every bit as enthusiastic as his father. George would walk in the front door, dog tired after a day shovelling coal on the locos, and within minutes Paul would have dragged him into the backyard for a game or some tackling practice. "I'd hide around the hallway and as soon as he'd walk in I'd dive at his legs with a 'gotcha'," Paul said.

"I'd always have to go straight down the back to play a game," George recalled. "Me and Russell against Paul. He played hard, too, win at all costs."

When Paul was five George started teaching him the rudiments of tackling: where to put his head so he wasn't hurt, how to push an opponent backwards by driving forwards with his legs at the moment of impact. Rarely has anything a father taught his five-year-old son been put to such good use over such a long time. Whether playing for West Mitchelton under-10s, Padua College Ist XIII or in Test matches for his country, the basics learned in the backyard at Everton Park have remained the same. Vautin was coached by experts over the years — Frank Stanton, Bob Fulton, Jack Gibson and Wayne Bennett to mention a few, but even they would have to agree there wasn't much they could ever teach him about tackling.

And then there were those photographs. "I used to pester Dad all the time to get his photos out," Paul said, "and he'd have to show them to me over and over again. Then, when Mum and Dad went out I'd wait until I heard the car go up the road and head straight for the wardrobe where he kept the pictures and sit down on their bedroom floor looking through them. To see my dad playing football was just unbelievable."

George was always modest about his football career. The only story the kids ever heard was about the time Leila was listening to the radio and heard the commentator remark: "There's Georgie Vautin taking the ball up. He can't run out of sight on a dark night, but he'll do his job all day."

It was some 30 years later that Paul was to find there was more to his father's football career than plodding into the ruck with head down and bum up. On a trip to Brisbane in 1991 Paul accompanied George, Leila, Russell and his wife Robyn to a local restaurant. Midway through the meal Brian Biggs, an old team-mate of George from Wests' 1954 premiership-winning team, approached the group and introduced himself. After a few pleasantries he returned to his table, but Paul never took his eyes off him. When Biggs paid his bill and left, Paul jumped up and followed him into the carpark. "Excuse me, mate," he said, "I've always wondered, what sort of player was the old man?"

"Oh, he was tough, tough as they come," said Biggs.

It was a reply Paul had expected, but the next exchange was to shatter some long-held conceptions. "They say he was pretty slow," Paul said.

"What? You're kidding!" said Biggs, himself a pretty slippery winger in his playing days, "he was our leading try-scorer."

Even now, the secret out, George is reticent about his try-scoring prowess. "Well," he said when questioned about being top try-scorer in a premiership team, "that's what they say. I never counted them myself. When I came down from Bowen I was trialling for the second row spot and one time I found myself out in the clear with the ball so I looked around for someone to pass to. Duncan Hall pulled me aside later and said, 'Don't you have the guts to have a go yourself?' Another time I was out in the open and the old fullback in me came out and I kicked ahead. Duncan told me if I ever kicked again he'd cut my leg off. After that I just followed the other blokes around. They'd make all the breaks, I just had to catch the ball and put it over the line."

More times than anyone else in the best team in the competition, as it turns out.

Scoring tries was an art George never boasted about to his sons, perhaps for fear of sounding a bragger — the type of person Paul would one day dub a "Kenny Couldabeen" and avoid with alacrity. Instead, he just stressed the basics. Tackle the opposition, catch the ball when it comes and do your job for your team.

And that, in its entirety, became the creed which would take Paul Vautin to the top of the game.

The Kid From Enoggera

With George taking care of the football basics, it was left to a convent school at Enoggera to first take charge of Paul's general education. He did well at school, finishing top of his class, although one teacher was to tell George and Leila their son was "arrogant" when he refused to use the coloured rods then a vital teaching aid in mathematics. He preferred to add and subtract his own way and no amount of pressure from the teacher would make him do otherwise. It was the first but certainly not the last time Paul Vautin would dig in his heels and defy authority.

In grade four he was enrolled at Padua College, a relatively new school run by Franciscan fathers at Kedron. Padua was different from the more-established Catholic colleges in that it offered rugby league rather than rugby union. Father Alban Mitchell, who came up from Melbourne to establish the school in 1957 describes Padua's rugby league background as a "happy accident". "When I held the first meeting of parents to discuss the new school the hall was absolutely jam packed," he said. "The school was being established in a strong rugby league area and the parents had come along convinced that this interloper from Melbourne was going to come in and force their boys to play the dreaded Aussie rules.

"Of course I had no such intention. I've always believed that it isn't up to teachers to say what sport a child should play. It should be up to the parents and the children themselves. When they let me know they wanted to play rugby league, I was more than happy to go along with it."

The decision made, the hard part was trying to find someone to play against. "There was no Catholic schools competition," he said.

"Most of the other schools in the area played rugby union. We couldn't find any competition for the primary school boys so they ended up playing rugby union, but finally we entered the local high schools competition and played a very high standard of rugby league against them. I always thought it was a real stroke of luck, a happy accident. It gave the boys the opportunity to play the game of their choice, but at the same time enabled them to play against and mix with people from outside the Catholic school system. It was a very good thing all around."

Academically, Paul continued to do well at Padua's primary school and when his parents were invited to the school to discuss the results of an intelligence test they were given the fateful report: "Your son has a superlative IQ and a very strong will. That can either be a good or a bad thing. It's up to him."

With George still interested in the fortunes of his old club Wests, he and Leila would regularly take the children to watch the A grade team in action. It was never actually discussed but everyone took it for granted that when Paul and Russell were old enough, they would turn out for West Mitchelton, a Wests junior "satellite" club close to Everton Park.

President of "Wests Mitchy" was Frank Lind, a man who devoted his life to junior rugby league and had seen any number of promising youngsters go on to first grade and beyond. Future state players such as John Ribot, Norm Carr, Gary Prickett, Brian McDonald and Michael Hagan were West Mitchy boys who benefited from the interest shown by Lind, who nurtured them in the early years and who, as president of the Queensland Junior Rugby League, was instrumental in state under-18 sides being sent away on tours, thus providing an incentive to stay in the game.

Lind struck up an instant rapport with the little redhead from the first day he showed up to register with the club. He continued to take a great interest in him even though by Vautin's own admission, he was no star. "I struggled in those early days," he said. "I wasn't one of those kids who shine from the first time they play. I guess I was a bit of a late developer. It wasn't as if I was the first one picked or anything like that."

Precocious early talent he might not have had, but if they gave points for keenness, he would have been a world beater. "We had to buy him every book ever written on the game and he studied them like he was sitting for an exam," George said. "I had this old Meccano set and he'd keep at me until we got out all the pieces and laid them on the floor like they were players on a field. We'd go through all the moves and I'd push the pieces around to show him where everyone should stand in such and such a situation. And if we weren't doing that he'd want to be out the back tackling or playing against me and Russell."

Not that he had any shortage of real football. Throughout his primary schooling Paul would play rugby for Padua on Saturday mornings and league for West Mitchelton in the afternoon. With George now a train driver and often away overnight or sleeping days to prepare for night shift, Leila was in charge of transportation.

"I'd drive him somewhere to play rugby union in the morning, wait for him to finish, and then head right over the other side of Brisbane to watch him play rugby league," she said. "At one presentation night for the players I was given the award as 'The Mother In Waiting'."

It was in those early days that the Vautins first encountered Wally Lewis and his family. In years to come the two would form one of the closest on and off-field relationships in the game, but back in the 1960s it was very much a case of the star and the star gazer. From the first time he ran out for his Valleys club Wally Lewis stood out while Vautin, for all his love of the game, was a trier at best.

Not that such a little thing as quality of performance worried Leila, whose vocal support from the sideline proved almost embarrassing to the ever-tight-lipped George. "When Paul's team played against Valleys I'd be on one side of the field shouting my lungs out for Paul and Mrs Lewis would be on the other side screaming for Wally," Leila admitted, "the only difference was that she knew everything about football and I didn't know a thing."

Little by little, Paul began to become a more valuable member of the teams he played in. So important, in fact, that one coach was not above a little subterfuge to ensure the young backrower stayed eligible for his side. In those junior years teams were divided by weight, not age. When Paul's weight tottered on the cut-off point for the higher division his coach asked that he be weighed without underpants in a bid to keep him for another season.

But such signs of encouragement were few and far between. Paul remained the type of kid every team has but few coaches covet: a plodder. Keen, always there, but never the boy who'll win a match or make the junior rep teams.

When Russell decided he wanted to leave West Mitchelton to play with friends at Brothers, George and Leila moved Paul as well. By this stage he was playing league for his school on Saturday and for his club on Sunday. Russell playing for a different club would be a logistical nightmare for "The Mother In Waiting" so Paul was enrolled with the Brethren as well.

The move was to prove a learning experience on both sides. The Vautins found Brothers' reputation at the time as a cliquey club to be well-warranted and Brothers were to find that George Vautin was not one to back down when he felt he or his family had been wronged.

The first time George arrived to watch Paul play in his new colours he was surprised to see him wearing a winger's jumper. "The coach said I'm not good enough to play in the forwards," said an upset Paul.

"Fine," said George helping his son out of the jumper and leading him to the car, "if you're not good enough to play in the forwards you're not good enough to play in the team."

That night George received a phone call from the father of another Brothers player. "Don't worry about it, George," he said, "I know everyone at the club, I'll get him in the team."

George asked a few pertinent questions. "Are you the coach? Are you a selector? No? Well you don't have anything to do with it, then. 'Bye."

And that was that. Paul didn't play club football for the next two years, simply enjoying playing alongside his schoolfriends and, for once in their son's life George and Leila weren't particularly interested in whether he played football or not. The heady days of topping the class in primary school were now long gone. Paul had entered high school and a newcomer had arrived on the scene. A fella by the name of Fatty.

With the step up to high school, Paul changed. The painfully shy youngster who sucked his thumb and slept with a security blanket until the age of nine discovered the ability to make his mates laugh with his irreverent humour and classroom pranks. In short, he became the class clown.

Father Alban, then headmaster and the man who would coach Paul for two years in the school Ist XIII, remembers well the cheeky redhead and his ability to disrupt a classroom. "One day I was teaching him and he let out a cry and slumped forward on his desk," he recalled. "When he put his head up blood was spilling out of his mouth. I told two of his mates to help him out of the room and he half collapsed as they dragged him outside. About half an hour later they came back all smiles after he'd made a miraculous recovery. I later found out he'd bitten on a blood capsule he'd brought from a magic shop."

While this sort of high jinks was going on, George and Leila lived in blissful ignorance. "He stayed quiet as a mouse around the house," Leila said. "We just assumed everything was going fine."

Reality was to come gatecrashing in the shape of a letter from Padua. George and Leila were summoned to the school and informed of their perfect son's less-than-perfect secret life. It was the sort of larrikin wit which would make a character called Fatty a favourite on TV and radio and in wacky commercials but it wasn't winning too many fans in the Padua staffroom. Father Alban didn't mince his words. Young Vautin was a pest who specialised in disrupting the class and the class was loving it, egging him on to ever-bigger pranks. He was on his first and final warning: either he improved or he was expelled. Simple as that.

"It was totally unexpected, that was the worse thing about it," said George. "We simply had no idea of what was going on. One day we had this boy who we thought was going well and the next we were told he was going to get kicked out."

What was said that night when George and Leila got home can only be imagined, but it did the trick. Paul kept out of trouble enough to stay at school and while never hitting the heights as an academic, excelled at cricket, football and athletics and was popular enough with both pupils and teachers to be elected school vice-captain in his final year.

"There was always more to Paul than met the eye," said Father Alban. "There was this larrikin who could be pretty disruptive in class but I felt for all that he had a deep respect for the school and the Franciscan principles. It was something that a lot of the other teachers missed but I got to see that other side to him through coaching the firsts. Not every teacher would have died for him but I always liked Paul. I felt if you were willing to dig down beneath that brash exterior, he could surprise you."

Certainly he surprised his father and people around the Wests Mitchelton club when he finally made it back after the two-year break. When an old team-mate rang and asked him to make up the numbers for a club match, he was ambivalent. He had enjoyed playing football with his schoolfriends and wasn't sure if he wanted to commit himself to the grind of two matches a week. Finally George offered to drive him to the game. When Wests Mitchy kicked off, the father couldn't believe what he was seeing.

"When I walked off, Dad said, 'What's happened to you? You've had a blinder.' The coach came up and told me I'd done over 30 tackles. It was incredible. It was as if on that day everything clicked into place. For the first time I felt like I really knew what I was doing. I'd always loved the game but with that match I realised I could play."

"That's when things fell into place," said George. "He never looked back."

Father Alban noticed the change, too. "With adolescence you find some boys suddenly emerge as athletes," he said. "Paul was like that. He never stood out as a youngster but once he developed, we realised we had a talent on our hands. He had two distinct skills — the ability to tackle and the strength and pace to break through the defensive line."

And there was another thing which Vautin supporters will always refer to — the courage to keep coming back no matter how much punishment he had absorbed. Father Alban believes he saw that courage emerge in one of the first matches Vautin played for the Ist XIII. "We put him into the team when he was still in Year 11," he said. "He was one of the youngest in the side but still one of the most talented. Early in the season we were playing Kedron High, who always gave us a very hard match. On this day they realised Paul was our outstanding player and they targeted him. They really put a lot of work into him and I have to say he wasn't getting a lot of support from his teammates. They were giving us a pretty big hammering, it was about 15-2 at halftime and I remember thinking worse was going to come in the second half.

"Paul was pretty badly knocked around and when he limped off at half time I heard one of our supporters on the sidelines say, 'The redhead's finished.' The fellow he was standing next to said, 'I bet you he goes straight back on.'

"Paul came up to me and said he couldn't continue and I told him, 'Paul, if you go off, this team will decimate us. They want you off, that's why they've been chasing you. It's up to you, but as long as you stay on we can win this game. If you go off we're finished.

"He turned around and went back on and we nearly caught them. We didn't beat them, but the point is Paul went back out there and gave as good as he took. I went overseas soon after Paul left school and I never saw him play again but people tell me he kept that quality to the end. He'd always keep going as long as he could serve his team. I think that day was a turning point. If he'd given up then he might have seen how easy it is to stop trying when things are tough."

CHAPTER 3

Gun Lock Forward

The 1976 edition of the school magazine *The Paduan* says that Paul Vautin was awarded the Robinson Sports Store trophy as sportsman of the year. He was best and fairest for the First XIII, captain-coach of the First XI and ran with the athletics team.

His parents believe all that just about sums up why he never shone as a student. Sport was Vautin's life at school and he was determined to make it his livelihood after school. He joined the Commonwealth Bank as a junior trainee but in his dreams that was just a way to make some cash before becoming a professional footballer.

Unlike most dreamers, Vautin's aspirations soon became reality. After a year in West Mitchelton's under-17 team, Vautin did indeed become a professional.

Club president of Wests rugby league club was Hugh Kelly, a former Queensland representative player who would go on to become a long-serving Australian selector. Kelly's own sons played at West Mitchelton and he took a strong interest in the club. It was not long before news of West Mitchy's latest star reached him. "Frank Lind was always looking to help the West Mitchy boys get on in grade," Kelly said. "He told me about Paul and I watched him develop. When he got to the under-18s I suggested to our first grade coach Ron Raper that we place him on contract, he was such an outstanding prospect. Ron agreed and so we offered Paul the chance to make the same money in the under-18s that he would make when he came up to grade."

And with that, Vautin was a professional. He wisely resisted the temptation to pack in his job and live entirely on his football earnings. Astute move, that. The contract was worth $100 a year.

The money wasn't much, but the recognition that was starting to come his way was. Vautin started to make the local rep sides.

His coach in the under-17s and 18s was Rob Paynter, who had

a great rapport with his players, largely because of his youth. At 23, he was only five years their senior. West Mitchelton had a strong side but there was no doubting that the team's star was Vautin. He became a marked man.

"One day we were playing a new team called Pine Rivers," Vautin recalled, "and Rob got the word that they'd heard we had a gun lock forward and were out to put him out of the match. When we were getting ready to run out he handed me a jumper without any number on the back. I asked him where my jumper was and he told me he had this masterplan to outsmart the opposition. They wouldn't know who the lock was. I went right off at him. It was a big thing for me to wear that No.8 jumper and I wasn't too happy about being the only one in the team with nothing on my back but he reckoned it was a brilliant idea so I finally agreed.

"When we ran out the first thing their captain said was: 'That's him fellas, the one with the red hair and no number.' Nice one Rob."

Vautin ended the game with two tries and six goals. "After the game I just said, 'Great plan, Rob' and he was ecstatic. 'Yeah,' he said, 'I *knew* it would work.'"

Pine Rivers weren't the only ones noticing West Mitchy's gun lock. Wayne Bennett, who would later strike up a winning partnership with Vautin as coach of the Queensland State of Origin team, remembers him as one of the outstanding players in an outstanding era.

Then coach of the Brisbane Police Academy's under-18 team, Bennett believes the standard of that competition was unrivalled. "There were four players in the under-18s that year who I believe were probably the strongest we've ever seen together at that level," he said. "There was Vautin at West Mitchy, Wally Lewis at Valleys, Paul McCabe at Norths and Mal Meninga, who was a year younger but playing in that comp, at the Police Academy.

"For all four to come through in the same year was something special. Wally's team won the competition, we were second, Norths third and West Mitchy fourth, so you can see the influence those players had. There wouldn't be too many under-18 competitions with four players of that calibre running around."

As a late developer, Vautin only came to Bennett's attention in the last year of his junior football. He ran the rule over him when Police played West Mitchy. "He had a few wraps on him, people said he could play a bit, so I was interested to see him," Bennett said. "Before the game I looked out for him and I'd have to say I wasn't too excited. Here he was, this little dumpy bloke with the red hair. I thought, geez, how can he play?

"That game I came away thinking he had a good work ethic but he didn't do anything brilliant. I thought he was a good team player, but nothing outstanding as an individual. We played against him again that year and then the next when he went to Wests and I started coaching first grade at Souths. Let's just say Paul didn't feature in any of my team talks."

Perhaps not, but Vautin was featuring in the talks held by junior representative coaches. He was chosen for Brisbane and Queensland junior sides alongside Lewis and McCabe and on one occasion, with Lewis overseas with the Australian schoolboys rugby union team, captained the Brisbane under-18 side on a tour to Nowra and Group 7.

It was here for the first time that the fledgling Fatty's leadership qualities surfaced. When subtlety, insight and diplomacy were needed, officials soon learnt that Vautin was not the man. The team was coached by Lewis's father Jim and the story of young Fatty's delicate handling of a potentially embarrassing situation has become folklore.

According to a player on the tour, the boys had been sitting around in a pub one afternoon shooting the breeze talking about footy and lying about women when it came time to get on the bus. Jim Lewis summoned the troops and did a quick headcount, only to find one of the players was missing. Just then the hotelier called Jim aside and gave him some rather delicate news. The missing player had been seen sitting down in a toilet cubicle with a Playboy magazine and was definitely not just reading the articles.

Realising the implications and embarrassment to the player if he was confronted, Lewis called Vautin over and quietly suggested that he check out the situation and report back.

Ever the responsible, diplomatic captain with his players' interests at heart, Vautin sneaked into the bathroom before bursting out seconds later, his red face ablaze and screaming in a voice that could be heard back in Brisbane: "He is, he is ... HE'S KNOCKIN' THE EARS OFF IT!"

But for all his humour and larrikin wit, there was no doubting that Vautin took his football very seriously. His mother was often stunned by the depth of his feelings for the game. "If his team lost he'd walk straight in and lock himself in his room for hours," she said. "We couldn't believe how seriously he took it. After every game he'd sit down at the dining room table with an exercise book and write down everything that happened. How the game went, who did what, how Paul played and how he could improve."

The hard work paid off when Vautin was chosen to represent Queensland under-18s in a three-match series against NSW. With Lewis taking the contentious lock spot, Vautin was moved to the second row. The second match of the series was curtain raiser to the Australia-Great Britain World Cup final in Sydney.

"There was a plane strike on so we had to go down in two 10-seaters," he recalled. "In those days they were like bi-planes and a lot of us hadn't been in any sort of plane before, let alone one of those little things.

"It took us four hours to fly down, and there was no food, no drink and no toilets. Blokes were pissing into empty drink cans. It was shocking. Wally was the big world traveller, he reckoned he'd been everywhere so he spent the trip trying to scare the crap out of everyone else.

"He'd be saying things like, 'Geez, that wing doesn't look too good, should it be shaking like that?' and everyone would be looking around saying, 'What wing? Where?' Then he was saying, 'Geez that pilot doesn't look to good. Does he look alright to you? How you going, mate? You feeling okay, you *look* crook. Been eating prawns or something? Don't worry, I can fly a plane, I'll fly it for you.'

"The planes landed about 1.10 and we were due to run out at half past one so we had to change in the bus. It wasn't really the perfect preparation.

"Our coach was old Herb Steinohrt who was about 80. Lovely bloke, but he didn't have too much of an idea then. They had blokes like Geoff Bugden, Graeme Wynn, Steve Folkes, Peter Tunks and Steve Ella and were coached by Jack Gibson so we were right up against it. It was 20-nil after about 15 minutes.

"I remember standing under the posts waiting for them to convert a try and some bloke in the crowd yells out, 'Hey, No.9, your head's on fire!'

"I looked over and Wally was standing next to me and he just broke up. He still reminds me about it 15 years later.

"Just before halftime our centre went off and Herb moved Wally into the centres and put the reserve on at lock. He's just got out there and their halfback runs 40 metres from the scrumbase and scores under the post. At halftime Herb's looked around and grabbed Wally. 'That man ran from the scrumbase,' he says. 'Lock forward, lock forward, you should have chased him. What were you doing out there in the centres?'

"Wally's told him, '*You* put me out there, you silly old goat!' "

Herb nodded and got back to business with a "Yes, yes, quite so, right." He then gave the young Queenslanders a taste of what many were to learn with a vengeance as they got into the senior ranks. "Okay," he told them, "we can't beat them, so I want you to go out and kick them, punch them, bite them, anything you can do to anyone in that filthy blue jumper, you do. We hate that bloody jumper. Don't you forget it, we hate them!"

To see 80-year-old Herb Steinohrt shaking his fist with true hatred in his eyes made a lasting impression on young Vautin. "He was that old he could hardly walk, lovely bloke, wouldn't hurt a fly," he said, "and here he was telling us to kick, bite and gouge. It made me realise just how much feeling there was in interstate football."

That wasn't the only thing Vautin learned on that trip. The young Queenslanders were billeted in a Kings Cross hotel and that night Vautin, Lewis and two teammates headed out for a look around. As they walked down the main street of Sydney's centre of sleaze, a lady of the night stopped them and beckoned to Vautin. "Hey you," she said, "you with the red hair, you want a girl?"

Vautin's sincere answer brought howls from Lewis and a look of sheer disbelief from the prostitute. "Umm... why?" he asked.

"She just walked off shaking her head," Vautin said. "Well, I was just a little country boy, I didn't know what was going on. Wally had to explain it to me. I was shocked."

Vautin was learning fast — on and off the field. At the presentation night after the 12-match representative season, he was declared Brisbane under-18 Player of the Year, with Lewis runner-up. He accepted the engraved gold watch with pride, but admits there could have been some politics involved. "Wally's dad was coach," he said. "It would have been a bit embarrassing if he'd won it. Still, I wasn't complaining. If they wanted to give it to me, I was only too pleased to take it."

The year ended with Vautin again on tour, this time with Wests' first grade side. Ron Raper had called him up to grade to sit on the bench in some of the team's last games and used the end-of-season tour to introduce him to the players who would be his teammates in the coming season. Although Raper would leave the club, to be replaced by Don Oxenham the following year, he helped Vautin settle in and gave him a run in the tour match against Townsville.

When he hit the big time the next year, Vautin didn't get a pay increase but he did move out of home, to a house which he and his fellow renters dubbed Legend's Lodge. Every beer can drunk in the house was displayed on a makeshift trophy shelf and Vautin's two-door Monaro LS took pride of place in the garage. It was bachelor heaven for the upwardly mobile — if somewhat underpaid — football star.

Vautin was one of only four players to play all 21 first grade games for Wests that season. His colour photograph featured as a pin-up in the Brisbane program and soon became a collector's item — ("Mum and I have both got one") — and another Vautin portrait graced the cover of Wests' annual report.

"Paul Vautin was unquestionably the success of the year, coming straight into first grade, and showed he has the flair and ability to bring the crowd to its feet," wrote coach Oxenham.

He ended the year as a force in the competition, a non-stop tackler and explosive runner who had progressed well under the influence of established first graders such as Norm Carr and Rod Bradshaw. As team goalkicker he could have been more consistent but he still won $500 as Wests' Player of the Year. It was the biggest cheque he had ever seen. Oxenham predicted a bright future for Vautin at Wests. He was half right. Vautin *would* have a bright future, but not at Wests.

"He wanted to live somewhere else, he wanted to *be* someone else," said Hugh Kelly. "The committee were shocked when I told them, but I urged them to let him go. I told them we might lose in the short term but there was no way we'd lose in the long term. No matter what we did, eventually Paul was going to go to Sydney and I wanted him to go with our blessing. In a way he'd outgrown us. He had to find out just how good he was and I was determined not to stand in his way."

CHAPTER 4

Travelling South

Fate comes in all shapes and sizes. For Paul Vautin it was the shape and size of a football, thrown on an August afternoon in 1978 by Wests hooker Gary Prickett. If Prickett had decided to pass to someone else, had he put down his head and gone himself, or if Paul had done the unthinkable and dropped the ball, things would have been a hell of a lot different.

There would still be a Paul Vautin of course. He'd probably be working for the Commonwealth Bank in Brisbane, maybe coaching Wests reserve grade in his spare time. His cupboard at home in Everton Park would be full of best and fairest awards and maybe even a Queensland jumper.

But there wouldn't be a Fatty.

There wouldn't be Lowes ads or television contracts, he wouldn't have a radio spot, write newspaper columns or have books written about him. He'd just be Paul Vautin. All if not for that pass.

Norm Carr's Wests were in the knockout semi-final against premiership favourites Valleys, spearheaded by the veteran Ross Strudwick and whiz-kid Wally Lewis. At the beginning of the '78 season not even Wests' most one-eyed supporters would have given them any chance of making the four, but here they were at Lang Park, up against the top side in the competition, and giving the game a real shake.

And then, midway through the second half, came the moment that changed Paul Vautin's life forever. Prickett took the ball on Wests' 22-metre line and passed to Vautin. What happened next was over in seconds but for Vautin the moment is never far away. Mention that try and he can recall every step, every move, as he ran 75 metres to the tryline.

He saw the try replayed many times over the next few weeks but never took a copy. Video recorders weren't standard issue in 1978 but perhaps it's just as well. No video could do justice to Vautin's memory of that try.

Ask him about it and the eyes shine, the face creases into a smile and the dial that has sold a thousand pairs of pyjamas takes hold. It's classic Fatty. "I took it from Gary on our 25," he said, "and beat the cover. Then I went round Strudwick. Alan Mills was the Queensland fullback and he came up. Straight past him, too quick mate. They had a winger called Mick Neill. He came across and dived at me about 15 metres out. No worries, he bit the turf and I scored next to the post to put us in front. You wouldn't want to know. Our bloody kicker missed the conversion."

The try was the most spectacular of the season. TV commentator George Doniger's call made it even more so. "He's round Strudwick, Mills won't get there ... go son, go ... you little beauty!"

With the conversion unsuccessful, Valleys came back to win the match 17-10 and it was a dejected Vautin who sat at home watching Valleys take on Redcliffe the next week.

When Wally Lewis ran 40 metres from the scrumbase to score, commentator Ross Lawson enthused, "Oh, Lewis, that's the try of the year, that one!" Pig's arse, thought Vautin, it doesn't come close.

And it didn't. At season's end Vautin's try was judged the best of the year and he won the princely sum of $200.

Wayne Bennett, who was in the crowd, says that was the first time he recognised that Vautin was something special, more than just a good team man. Wally Lewis had an even better view. "I remember that try pretty well," said Lewis. "Fatty and I were always pretty competitive because we were both playing lock in those days and when he scored I thought, 'bugger it, Vautin's scored'. I looked at the replay when I got home to find out where I'd been at the time.

"He still gives me a hard time about it and I have to laugh because my memory of it is not quite the same as his. Let's just say I think it might have become a better try in his mind as the years go on. Still, it *was* a good try and he showed a lot of pace to score it. That was the thing about Fatty and me when we were young, we could both move. We ended up as slow as a wet week but when we were kids we could match just about anybody. Over the first 30 metres Fatty was terrifically quick. Whether he was quite as quick scoring that try as he likes to think he was I couldn't say but good luck to him. The only thing I was dirty about was that it cost me 200 bucks."

And in 1978 $200 was not to be sneezed at. "It was a lot of money in those days," Vautin said, but the try brought the spirited 18-year-old a lot more than $200. It brought him a new life.

Within days of the match the phone rang. Cronulla Sutherland calling. Would Paul be interested in playing in Sydney? Would he like to fly down and talk it over? Would he what!

At that time on his three-year contract at $100 a year. Just the idea of flying down to Sydney on his own was an adventure.

He told Hughie Kelly of the offer. "Just have a listen to what they say," said Hughie. "Don't sign anything, ask for some time to think things through."

Vautin was met at the airport and taken on a tour of the Cronulla area. He met the club directors and later that night, over dinner at the club bistro, Cronulla made their offer. Three years, at $6000 a year.

He nearly choked on his prawn cocktail. "I thought, 'Shit, this is unbelievable' — $6000 — I'd never even dreamed of that sort of money first up."

If he was excited, his parents were downright shocked. "The old man fell off his chair," he said. "We didn't know what to do. That was huge money, but for some reason I just wasn't too keen on Cronulla. Dad said to hang on a bit. He said you never know. One club was interested, someone else might come up with an offer, too."

The next club to enter the market was North Sydney. Paul McCabe had just come to terms with the Bears and asked Vautin if he was interested in joining him. Vautin told him of the Cronulla offer. "Don't do anything," said McCabe, "I'll get Tommy Bishop (the North Sydney coach) to come and see you."

Within days, the former English halfback was knocking on the door and sitting across the table from Vautin, his parents and Hughie Kelly. The negotiating team had worked out their strategy earlier. Hughie would do the talking and nobody else was to say a thing. Above all, show no emotion, no matter what was offered.

Bishop got straight down to business. "We'd like to have you join us, lud," he said. "How's $7500 sound?"

To be truthful, it sounded pretty bloody great but no-one was letting on. The four of them sat stonefaced, nodding and shrugging as if this sort of offer came over the Vautins' dining table every night. Underneath the table it was a different story. Vautin sat furiously kicking George's shins with excitement.

Kelly asked for a quiet word and led the way into the backyard. After a quick pow-wow he advised Vautin to sign. "We'll stick a six-thousand-buck transfer on you," he said. "It shouldn't be any problem."

"No problem at all," said Bishop, as Vautin signed the contract. "I'll sort it out at tomorrow night's committee meeting and we'll see you as soon as you can get to Sydney."

The next night the talk wasn't quite so positive. "I'm sorry, lud," Bishop said down the phone. "The committee won't pay the transfer on an unknown. I can't tell you how bad I feel." Vautin had a fair idea.

"I was devastated," he said, "I'd set my heart on playing with Norths. Paul McCabe was going there, Tommy Bishop seemed like a good bloke. I didn't know what to do. I wasn't keen on Cronulla but I was only 18. I thought I could stay with Wests for another year, maybe get another offer, but when you're that young you think you'll never get another chance."

Re-enter Hughie Kelly. Unbeknown to Vautin, the Wests president had contacted his old mate, Manly club secretary Ken Arthurson.

"We'd known each other for years," Arthurson recalled, "I'd always said, 'Hughie, if you see someone who's something special, let me know.' Sure enough, he rings me and tells me about this kid who can get through 40 or 50 tackles a game, every game. I said, 'Sure Hughie, sure,' but he kept at it. Finally I said, 'Okay, if you're fair dinkum and he really can tackle like that, send me a video of a few of his games and I'll have a look. By the way, what's his name?"

Arthurson scribbled down the name Vautin on his pad and within days a pile of videos arrived on his desk. He picked up the first on the pile and sat down to watch this tackling machine in action. The first tape was Wests versus Valleys, knockout semi-final.

Unbeknown to Arthurson, Kelly had wound the tape onto the second half. To this day, Arthurson believes Vautin scored his try after a minute of play. "I'm sitting down thinking I'm going to see this freak tackler and the first thing I see this redhead's broken through, the ruck and scored a superb 75-metre try. I'm thinking, 'Forget the other kid, I'll take this one.' Then, when I check my notes, they're the same kid. I nearly fell off my chair.

"I thought, 'Geez, if he can tackle *too* I've seen enough. I got a contract up to Hughie in the next mail. I never did look at any more of those videos."

And Vautin never spoke to Arthurson, or anyone else at Manly for that matter. Kelly's recommendation was good enough for him. Manly offered $6000 and paid the transfer fee to Wests without blinking. Kelly asked just one other thing. "I said to Ken, 'Listen, he's a good kid, promise me you'll look after him,'" he said.

Replied Arthurson: "Hugh, it goes without saying." The papers were signed. Vautin was a Sea Eagle, and couldn't have been happier.

"I guess if I had a favourite Sydney team in those days it was Wests because I liked the way they played that biff and barge type of football but my all-time favourite player was Terry Randall," he said.

"I remember that year Manly drew the grand final against Cronulla then went on and won the replay on the Tuesday just playing on heart and memory. I was playing squash with a mate and I kept running upstairs to see how the game was going. The guts they showed that game was incredible, then they got seven players on the Kangaroo tour. They were the team to be with, I couldn't believe my luck."

Manly director Doug Daley, head of the Commonwealth Bank's staff department, organised a transfer to the Brookvale branch from January 10, 1979. Paul Vautin was on his way.

Rugby League Week's Queensland correspondent Lawrie Kavanagh was quick to interview the latest Southern recruit. It was the shy, quietly-spoken Paul Vautin who admitted in that article he was going to Sydney to play reserve grade and learn from the established stars but perhaps there was a more confident Fatty holding his tongue in the background.

"I said that about playing reserve grade but deep down I don't think I ever meant it. I was going to Sydney to make it. You never know how you'll go until you get into top company but I remember thinking, 'Hey, I'm young, I'm strong, and I can play. Why *shouldn't* I make it?' I was never cocky but I guess I always had every confidence I was going to do okay."

But for all that, Vautin had no illusions about his time in Sydney. At a boozy farewell party in the backyard of Legend's Lodge, he lurched from group to group telling his friends not to make any long term plans without him. "It's only for three years," he told his mates. "It's not as if I'm going forever. Hey, I'm a Brisbane boy. I'll be back in three years."

Again half right. Vautin has never been anything but a Brisbane boy, but he has yet to make his way back home.

The next morning, feeling worse for wear, he loaded up the Monaro at his parents' home and headed south. As he drove up the street, he gripped the steering wheel a little more tightly and looked around the familiar sights, really noticing them for the first time in years. "Geez, eh?" he thought, "I'm really doing it." And off he headed for Sydney, taking the big step into the unknown. If he wondered what his parents' thoughts were at that moment he wouldn't have had to travel far to ask. They followed behind him in the family sedan.

The first night they shared a motel room in Armidale. When Sydney came into view the next day, the convoy changed configuration. George and Leila took the lead in the XY Falcon and the Monaro brought up the rear. "Dad had been to Sydney before, he sort of knew his way around," Paul said, "I didn't know anything about the place. I'd been there with the under-18s and once when I was 12 and we all stayed in a caravan at Lane Cove. Apart from that it was what I'd seen in books and on *Skippy*. Dad and Mum went first, with the *Referdex* open on Dad's lap."

Until then Sydney and all that it represented was just a dull ache in the pit of Vautin's stomach. When he let himself dream of playing alongside the likes of Randall and Graham Eadie the heartbeat would quicken but the reality always seemed just that little bit out of reach over the next hill. When the two cars hit Warringah Road and Vautin saw the ocean for the first time, reality finally arrived. "I saw the water and I thought this is okay. Matter of fact, I thought this is going to be *fantastic*," he recalled.

"I started looking around for the first time and really taking everything in. I thought to myself, 'I wonder where I'll be living?'

I even looked up into the hills and thought, 'Hey, I wouldn't mind living there.'

Just over 10 years later Vautin did, indeed, end up living on that hill, in a magnificent split-level home at Cromer Heights. Saltwater pool in the backyard, two cars in the garage and the trappings of the best that sport can bring on show in every room.

But on that afternoon in 1979 he would have been satisfied with a pitched tent and the guarantee of a few games in first grade.

The Vautins drove straight to Manly Leagues Club and walked to the reception desk. "Err, I'm Paul Vautin," he told the receptionist. "The club has just signed me and I'm supposed to meet the directors."

"Yes Paul, we've been expecting you," she said and a few moments later a distinguished-looking gentleman walked through a door with hand outstretched.

It was Doug Daley. Ironically, 12 years later, the man who first welcomed Vautin through the door would be the one to point the way out. Then there would be no smiles and handshakes.

The introduction to the board proved a nerve-racking experience. "Like being a model," Paul recalls. Daley led the three Vautins into the boardroom where they stood staring at a wall of 16 faces. After some wooden introductions came the first words from one of the directors. Paul has forgotten the identity of the speaker, but he'll never forget the comment. "You're a lot smaller than we thought you'd be."

Hardly a statement to reassure a nervous 19-year-old on his first day in the big smoke. Not to be outdone, he tried to stand taller, puffed out his chest, and said, "Umm, I play at 13 and a half stone."

Obviously when the chest went out other parts of the anatomy went with it. Thinking the 13 and a half stone could be better distributed, Ken Arthurson asked with concern: "Have you been doing any training, Paul?"

"Sure have," Paul replied eagerly, "I set up a circuit around home and I've been running a three-mile time trial every couple of days."

"Good, what time are you doing it in?"

"Twenty seven minutes Ken," he said proudly.

To his credit, Arthurson's face didn't betray what he must have been feeling.

"Hmmm, that's very good," he said, even though at that stage Manly players were expected to run three miles in under 20 minutes. The first training run Vautin attended, the squad was set a two-mile course to be completed within 12 minutes as a warm-up.

But that ordeal was still days away. In the meantime the Vautins had to survive three nights at the local pub, the Brookvale Rex, cloistered in a room directly above the resident rock band, which belted out Rolling Stones cover versions until the early hours, much to Leila's discomfort. "Mum wasn't too impressed," said Vautin. "But we didn't want to say anything about the accommodation, we didn't want to make a fuss."

Arthurson had organised for Vautin to stay with his secretary Pam Parker and her family at their home in Mona Vale. "Some families brought home stray dogs," said Pam. "We used to bring home stray footballers."

The Vautin convoy duly arived at the Parker home, George and Leila met Pam and her husband Harry, had a cup of tea and headed off. "I walked them out to the car said goodbye and that was it," said Paul, "for the first time in my life I was on my own."

Pam and Harry Parker had never seen a game of rugby league before Pam began work as Arthurson's secretary in 1975. Migrants from England where Harry had been a keen soccer fan, they took to the game and its players with a vengeance. "Harry thinks soccer is boring now," said Pam who still works with Arthurson at the Australian Rugby League. "He can't watch it. He's at the football every weekend with me and our kids Damon and Kyra. Damon was a Manly ball boy. It's a real family thing with us and that's why Mr Arthurson likes to put the new players with us. The big thing they miss when they come to Sydney is family and a home atmosphere."

Vautin and fellow recruit Jim See moved in with the Parkers the same day. Vautin stayed a couple of months before finding a flat of his own. Jim See was still there two years later, finally moving out when he transferred to Cronulla.

Pam Parker became a surrogate mother to the young players, watching them get accustomed to the area and the pressure of big-time rugby league. She remembers Vautin as a quiet, very polite rookie, but with an underlying steel. "You could tell he knew what he wanted out of rugby league," she recalled. "He'd obviously set certain goals and nothing was going to stop him. He appeared shy at first but there was something about him, that driving ambition that some players have.

"I've come into contact with a lot of young players over the years and somehow you can tell the ones who are going to make it. They have this hunger, this drive. You can see it in their eyes."

Paul and the Parker family have remained on good terms. "If he sees me in the street we'll always stop and have a chat," Pam said. "He's still the same person he was back then. Nothing has changed."

Vautin's overriding memory of the stay is less emotional, more culinary. "They were a great family," he said. "Pam and Harry are two of the best people you could ever meet. They treated me like a son but one thing I'll never forget about staying there was baked beans. We had it every meal. Baked beans for breakfast, baked beans for lunch and baked beans for dinner. If we were having a roast we'd have baked beans on the side. At one stage I think we had baked beans with ice cream. It was a baked beanathon. Just as well I love baked beans."

Not that he had too much time to worry about the menu back in that summer of '79. He was too busy trying to keep up with the super-fit Sea Eagles.

His first training session came the day after moving into the Parker home and he admits it nearly killed him. "Arko drove down and introduced me to Frank Stanton," Vautin remembered. "I just stood there in the background in awe. I was looking around and thinking, 'Gee, there's Terry Randall, there's Graham Eadie, there's John Gray and Russel Gartner. These guys were the ones I'd seen on TV and read about in the papers. I just stood there staring."

And just as he was watching them, they were watching him. "We were a pretty tight club in those days," said John Gibbs, Manly's Kangaroo halfback who is still one of Vautin's closest friends. "Most of the blokes had been around for a while or come up through the juniors and it was pretty rare for a young player to be imported into the club. We might get some big names from other clubs who everyone knew about, but when we heard a kid was being brought down from interstate or the country, we pricked up our ears. You knew that if Ken Arthurson was bringing someone in, they must have a fair bit of ability.

"There has always been all this garbage about Manly players being aloof or up themselves. It wasn't like that at all. If someone was a good bloke, they were welcomed in just like that. That's how it was with Paul. I suppose I was a white-haired boy around the place. I'd just come back from the Kangaroo tour and was pretty well-known about the place, but Paul and I hit it off straight away. From about the second training run we started what has become a lasting friendship."

Graham Eadie, the legendary fullback then at the peak of his career, remembers waiting to clap eyes on the latest recruit from Queensland. "You'd hear around the club that they'd signed a new bloke from somewhere and you'd be interested to have a look at him, see what he looked like and how he shaped up. To see what his nickname was going to be as much as anything else," said the man known as Wombat.

Vautin's nickname didn't take long in coming. One of the most resilient players — and greatest characters — in Manly history is Fred Jones. Premiership-winning captain, veteran of 298 games for the club and a colourful personality to say the least, Fred was coaching the club's reserve grade side in 1979.

Fred had no time for airs and graces. The blow-waves and beefcake calendars of rugby league 1990s-style are certainly not his go. To Fred Jones, a spade is a bloody shovel. Ken Arthurson still laughs when recalling the time Jones captained Manly in the club's first grand final for decades. Addressing the players after their final training on the eve of the match, Arthurson spoke of how much a win the next day would mean to the club, the district and him personally. He spoke of loyalty, service, sacrifice and discipline as the keyed up players made a silent vow to give their all for the Sea Eagles the next day. "Now," said Arthurson when he'd finished, "I'd like to buy you all a drink before you head home."

He led the way to the Time and Tide Hotel and ordered the players' choice of lemon squash, soda water or lemonade, then turned to the team leader. "What's yours, Fred?"

Jones looked straight at the barmaid. "Schooner of old and a packet of Rothmans, thanks luv."

When Jones was introduced to then-Prime Minister Malcolm Fraser after a match the politician asked him what he did for a living. "I'm a wharfie," said Jones.

"Oh, really?" replied the PM. "I have a lot of friends on the wharves."

"Yeah?" said Jones, "I've never met any of them."

This then, was the man who would label Vautin with a name which would prove the final cut-off from his past. While the metamorphosis would take a few years to become complete, the nickname marked the end of the shy, reticent young man from Brisbane and the birth of a confident, opinionated media star whose capacity for speaking his mind would win him a legion of fans — and a few enemies — from one end of the country to the other.

Tradition would dictate it probably should have been Bluey, or Bloodnut or Ginger, but Fred Jones has never been a traditionalist. As he walked up in his faded footy shorts and thongs, face creased into a well-worn smile and teeth safely back in the car, he took one look at the newcomer and said, "Ullo, who'th thith little fatty then?"

Eadie, jogging past, remarked, "That'll stick." Little did he know how well. "Welcome to Manly ... Fatty."

The Cheeky Red-Headed Bastard

Frank Stanton remembers the newcomer well. "He was a cheeky little red-headed bastard — still is, nothing's changed." The affectionate description of Vautin was built up over a year's coaching and more than a decade of mutual admiration but as he eyed the Queensland recruit for the first time that hot summer's afternoon, he thought of him only in terms of the contribution he could make to Manly.

Although he would later coach at Balmain and North Sydney, Frank Stanton was Manly to his bootlaces. The man they would refer to as "Biscuits" as a player and "Cranky Franky" as a coach made his first grade debut for the club as a 20-year-old and was overseas with the Kangaroos only three seasons later.

As a player, initially a centre and then halfback, Stanton was noted for his pluck, strength and fitness. As a coach he was noted for his discipline. His iron fist was behind the first Kangaroo team — the '82 side — to go through their tour of England and France undefeated and he drove Manly with the same single-minded approach, resulting in premierships in 1976 and 1978. Like all successful coaches he was always hungry for more success and on the lookout for new talent to help him achieve it.

"We needed a bit of new blood," he recalled. "We'd had a very hard campaign in winning the premiership in 1978, followed by the Kangaroo tour, and the wear and tear was starting to show. We'd also lost Ian Martin, who'd played lock in the grand final, so the opening was there for a talented player, preferably a young bloke with ability who would be with the club a long time.

"I didn't have much input into the recruiting, that was Ken Arthurson's job, but I had faith in his judgement and if he thought this kid was worth a go I had no doubt he would be a good footballer.

"I remember he was a good goalkicker but that wasn't a problem for us, we had Graham Eadie filling that role. What we needed was a forward who could make a bit of an impact and Paul certainly proved to be that.

"When he arrived at training that first night he was a quiet sort of bloke, just looking on at first. You never would have picked him as the sort to make a name for himself in the media, but as I got to know him I felt he had a pretty high IQ. I found him a good kid to coach. He listened and worked hard. When he arrived his fitness level wasn't up to the required standard but he put in the effort and came up with the results. I never had any problem with him at all."

And there was another thing. Until the arrival of Vautin, Stanton had been the club's most famous red head. He took one look at the recruit's flaming mop and immediately saw a kindred spirit. "Once I saw he was a red head he always had half a chance with me," he laughed. "I had to look out for him, I knew what he was going to cop."

If Stanton was giving out favours on that first training run, somebody forgot to tell Vautin. The coach called his players together and mapped out a five mile warm-up run. "Out there, up the creek, around and back," he announced, pointing into the distance, towards what Vautin assumed was Gosford.

Honed to peak fitness by his gruelling three mile run around Legend's Lodge, Vautin set out with the rest — and found himself trailing off within minutes. "Don't worry about it," said a friendly voice at his shoulder. "Stick with me, we'll go alright."

The fellow plodder, a long blond-haired bloke, introduced himself as Rick Chisholm and the two made it back towards the starting point just within sight of the leading pack.

Sucking in his breath as he slowed to a walk, Vautin felt relief. "Hey," he gasped, "that wasn't too bad."

"No, mate," said Chisholm, dragging him along by the jumper, "that's only halfway, we've got to go around again."

Not for the last time in those early weeks, Vautin looked to the heavens. "Strewth," he thought, "how fit are these guys? I'm never going to keep up."

At the end of the run, Stanton pulled him aside for his first word of fatherly advice. "Listen, son," he said, "Rick's got a lot of talent but he's not the best trainer in the world. I'll be wanting you to finish ahead of him from here on."

Vautin took the hint. Running alone around the streets of Brookvale, he managed to improve his condition, but never came close to the awesome fitness of the likes of Randall or Stephen Knight. "I came last in every run," he said. "I found it very hard. It was nothing like anything I'd been used to. I guess it just wasn't my go. I tried hard, but I was never a long-distance runner.

"I did better in the sprints. We'd do a set of 10 and for the first four or five I'd be right up there, then I'd trail off as the fitness told. It was pretty demoralising. No matter how hard I tried I couldn't keep up. It got to the stage were I was really worried about making a fool of myself when I finally got to play a game. I just couldn't see how I'd keep up."

The chance to find out came a week before the first official trial match. As premiers, Manly were invited to take part in an annual round robin tournament at Newcastle. Big things were expected of the team and there was pressure to perform. To not win the two-day tournament would be a major embarrassment for Manly while at the same time the other clubs, including two strong local teams, were pumped up to Test match proportions in their desire to knock off the big names. When the squad of 20 to travel to Newcastle was read out, Paul Vautin was the last name on the list. Just to be in the company of Randall, Eadie, Krilich, Gartner and co was a huge thrill but it quickly soured.

The first day, as Manly fought through their preliminary rounds, Vautin sat on the bench like a wallflower at the school dance. Stanton, eager to experiment with as many combinations as he could, moved players on and off throughout the day. To an increasingly-demoralised Vautin it seemed everyone in the squad had run on except him.

It was a deflating experience. The newcomer to the club had been unable to make a positive impression on the training paddock and now seemed denied the chance to show what he could do on the field as well. The butt of good-natured ribbing about his performances in the dreaded distance runs, he was determined to gain the respect of his clubmates the best way he knew — by playing football and playing it bloody well. He felt he just needed a chance but for that day at least, chances didn't come his way.

At the end of the day Manly were safely into the next afternoon's final against Queanbeyan Blues. The Manly players were happy, relaxed and looking forward to a few ales and the enjoyment of each other's company. Many had grown up together and as teammates through the juniors, some had toured and played alongside each other for Australia. Vautin felt very much the odd man out. As the others set off for dinner or drinks, he disconsolately headed to his room. Brisbane, Wests and the Try of The Year never seemed further away.

As he passed Stanton's room he heard his name being mentioned in conversation. Inside, Stanton, team captain Krilich and his deputy Alan Thompson were finalising plans for the next day's game. "I heard Frank say something about Vautin and the old ears pricked up," he said. "I wasn't going to eavesdrop, but you wouldn't be human, would you? He was telling them that he'd brought me along because of Arko and he was going to have to give me a run, just to keep onside with the boss.

"I heard him say, 'Look, I'll just stick him on for the kick-off, let him play a few minutes then call him off and we can get on with business.'

"It was funny, I didn't get upset or feel real nervous or anything. I just went back to my room and said to myself, 'Righto, Frank, I'll show you.' I slept really well, woke up feeling good. Matter of fact, I couldn't wait to get stuck into it."

Everything went perfectly to plan — Vautin's, not Stanton's. He was chosen in the run-on side and stayed there the entire match. The local ref evened things up early by sending off Ian "Magilla" Thomson and Wayne Springall and it was 11 versus 13 for most of the game. In Brisbane-like heat Vautin was in his element, tackling, running the ball up hard and following halfback Steve Martin through the gaps to take off on a couple of long runs.

"Someone told me I did 35 tackles in the second half," Vautin said. "We won by a couple of points and saved Manly some red faces. It wouldn't have looked good for the premiers to lose their first hit-out of the year. As I walked off Frank looked at me and said, 'Well done, son.' I'll never forget it. I felt 10 feet tall."

If Stanton was retaining his famous scowl even in victory, Fred Jones wasn't so reticent. Teeth in his back pocket, beer can grasped firmly in one hand and a Rothmans in the other, he pushed his way through the exhausted players and sought out the kid he'd labelled a fatty only a few weeks before. "Jethus, thun," he lisped, as much in relief as praise, "you really *can* play!"

In the next day's newspapers Arko did what any self-respecting club secretary would do under the circumstances — called it the greatest debut since Bobby Fulton. "The best debut since ..." It's as much a part of the new season as the first blast of a referee's whistle or the headline proclaiming a player will die in the new year heat, but with the luxury of hindsight Arthurson stands by his statement.

"I make no secret of the fact that as far as I'm concerned, Fulton is tops. I don't put anyone in his class — and not just as a Manly player," Arthurson said. "I believe he's as good a player as ever played the game. But just below Fulton there is another level of player. I put a player like Graham Eadie in that class and it didn't take me long to put Paul Vautin in that class as well. The quality that Paul had in abundance was courage. I saw it then and I saw it time and time again over the years.

"In those first few months with the club he proved he was something special. It's always a source of enormous pride for me when I see someone I brought to the club go on and achieve success. There was no doubt in my mind he was going to do that the first time I saw him play in a Manly jumper."

If Vautin needed any further evidence that he had broken the ice it came on the bus trip home. Exhausted, he fell asleep and Eadie and Russel Gartner drenched him in beer. It was probably only a few cents worth of stale ale but it represented a hell of a lot more. It meant he was accepted.

That first performance earned him some respect, certainly attention, but no fairytale start to Sydney football. With the core of Manly's grand final winning side available, Vautin was graded in reserves for the first match of the season against St George at Kogarah.

While George and Leila waited anxiously in Brisbane for news of their son's premiership debut, his surrogate mother Pam Parker and her family travelled across town to lend support. "Oh I was nervous for him," Pam recalled. "I mean, he was still living with us then, he was like part of the family. It was a very personal thing for me, I just wanted him to do well. It was pretty nerve-racking."

Vautin took the field with his new teammates, the St George kicker put up the first ball of the season and young Paul Vautin called "mine" as he got underneath it, ready to make his first mark on the big time. The ball hit him on the chest and went straight to ground. The referee blew his whistle for a scrum. On the sideline Stanton winced and shook his head. Pam Parker sank into her seat. "I thought, 'Oh you poor little soul,'" she said. "I felt so sorry for him but I never said a word. I don't know if he even knew we were all there. To this day I've never even mentioned it."

From that inauspicious start, things improved — they had to. Vautin played soundly in a beaten team, hit the upright with an attempted goal from the sideline and, as would become his trade-mark, tackled everything that wasn't wearing maroon shorts. He was happy enough with his first match — catching the kick-off aside — and obviously impressed the hard-to-please Stanton.

Vautin and his reserve grade teammates sat on the bench watching as an eager St George team took the premiers apart in the first half of the main game. At the break, Terry Randall held up a hand which had ballooned to Christmas ham proportions, and the team doctor shook his head. There'd be no more Igor that afternoon. Stanton called over his red-headed mate. "Fatty, you're on."

Vautin couldn't get out there quick enough. Stanton's parting words as the team trooped back on gave him an added boost. "Listen son," he said quietly, "you've got a chance here. Make the most of it."

And he did. The Sea Eagles couldn't make up the deficit but Vautin did his best to make sure the scoreline didn't get any worse. He made 15 tackles in the half and the next week, with x-rays verifying that Randall's hand was broken, the team read out to play Newtown included: "No.10, Paul Vautin ..."

He controlled his emotions, gave a self-conscious half-smile as the regulars like Eadie, Thompson and Krilich welcomed him to the team, went through the drills with the rest of the side and waved them goodbye in the car park — then ran across the road to a public phone box, dropped in some coins and shouted before the STD beeps had even finished: "Hey Mum, guess what ... I've made it!"

Back home the Brisbane papers mentioned how the local boy had made good. An interested reader was Wally Lewis. "I was always very interested in how any Brisbane player went in Sydney because I wanted to go there myself," he said. "But I was even more interested in Fatty for a number of reasons. First-off, because he was my age and played the same position, and, second, because I felt we were about the same in terms of playing standard. Before he went to Manly I got a call from a bloke I knew saying North Sydney were interested in signing both me and Paul. He said they'd pay me $6000 which was an absolute fortune. Obviously my first question was how much they'd offered Paul. He said the same. That's the way people looked at us in those days. There wasn't a struck match between us.

"When I read about him making first grade I rang my father and told him. He said, 'I'll bet you he goes very well. The test will be how he goes the next week.' He was right on both counts."

Henson Park on a cold, wet Sunday isn't a place many football-ers would hold dear in their hearts but for Vautin it conjures the warmest of memories. He won man of the match in his debut, Manly won 10-6 and it was the newcomer from Brisbane who scored the winning try. It was no Lang Park 75-metre job but it gets longer with each telling. Halfback Steve Martin stood one side of the ruck, feinted to the open to draw the defence and threw a long pass to an unmarked Vautin on the blind. The Fatty who had been bagged for his times at training showed his pace over the shorter distances to outstrip Jets fullback Phil Sigsworth on a 40-metre sprint to the corner.

When Sigsworth joined Manly years later Vautin would remind him of that race. "Geez, Siggy, you haven't got any faster, remem-ber that time I outran you to score at Henson Park?" Sigsworth, whose career included a few moments he would probably rather forget, would answer: "I don't remember it, Fatty", so Vautin would eagerly relive the moment for his old opponent — and anyone else who happened to be within earshot.

Vautin filled Randall's big shoes for the next three weeks and when the Kangaroo star returned from injury Stanton had some news which shocked not only Vautin and the Manly club, but the entire rugby league community. When the team to play Penrith was announced, Vautin held his spot. The revered Randall was named in reserve grade. The next morning's papers were full of it. Radio and television stations led with the item on their nightly sports bulletins. Former Manly player and journalist Peter Peters wrote Stanton had paid Vautin "the ultimate compliment". The game was to be memorable for another reason as well. It was the first time Vautin appeared in a televised match. For years he had sat at home in Brisbane watching the Sunday night replays of the games called by former Manly star Rex Mossop. He had imagined what it would be like to play in such a match alongside the likes of Eadie or Krilich and now, here he was, playing in the second row beside the hulking presence of dual international Stephen Knight. It was a schoolboy's dream come true.

As the players were getting ready for the match Mossop strode into the dressing room with his camera crew, straight up to where Vautin and Knight were changing. "Okay, fellas," he said, "get your shirts off."

"Eh?" said Vautin.

"Get your shirts off," repeated the then-undisputed king of televised rugby league, "you're the new Manly second row pairing, I want a shot of you together to start the telecast."

Stephen Knight immediately pulled off his shirt, revealing a torso and arms which belonged more in a bodybuilding magazine than a Penrith Park dressing room. A former rugby union star who divided his time between the beach and the gym, the part-time model had a body most men — and women — would kill for.

"Come on son," repeated Mossop to Vautin, "we haven't got all day." Reluctantly, the 18-year-old from Brisbane with the pink skin and nickname of Fatty stripped off his shirt and lined up alongside the man they called The Body — much to the amusement of his teammates in the background.

Vautin repaid Stanton's trust with another winning try but the experience was soured by what happened when he raced home to watch the replay. Imagining all his mates back in Brisbane doing the same, he sat down in front of the television in nervous anticipation as the theme music and opening credits faded away. And then, there they were, filling the screen. A stunned Vautin, stripped to the waist looking like a stunned, rather podgy pink rabbit staring into the headlights of a car, alongside Knight, a tanned, relaxed, Adonis, muscles bulging, teeth shining brilliantly.

"All I could think of was, 'God, please let there be a blackout in Brisbane," Vautin said.

"Steve was unbelievable, the best physique you ever saw, but a real gentle giant. A great bloke to play alongside, though. That was his first year in the forwards after an illustrious career as a centre or winger, and sometimes he'd get a bit lost or really shagged out. He'd come up to me on the field and say, 'That's it, Fatty, I'm stuffed, I can't go on', and I'd tell him how well he was going and where to stand and things. It was good for me because it made me feel an important part of the team, helping this big-name international, and he'd encourage me. We'd gee each other up when things got tough. It worked both ways." Vautin and Knight formed a good partnership on the field but off-field Vautin could never quite match up to Knight's awesome physical standards.

"He and Magilla Thomson used to belt the punching bag in the gym and I'd get a nosebleed just looking on," he said. "It was scary. One would hold the bag and belt the absolute stuffing out of it, then the other one would have a go. I'd just stand there with my mouth open. Sometimes one of them would say, 'Hey, Fatty, want a go?' but I'd just answer, 'Oh no, thanks guys, I'll be right' and go back to my little weights or trying to pick up the medicine ball. At night I'd dream I was them and wake up belting my pillow."

But even though he'd never have the physique of Knight or aggression of Thomson, there were no complaints about Vautin's performances on the field. When Randall did come back into the side after the Penrith match it wasn't instead of Vautin, it was with him. Randall took his old second row spot, while Vautin moved back to lock.

"It was probably then people really began to pay attention," Vautin said. "I started getting a fair bit of press. People started recognising me as a part of the team, not just as Randall's replacement. It was exciting but I kept a level head, I knew I was only there as long as I did my job, so I got out and did my work every week. I didn't worry about the attention, just got out and did the hard stuff."

Even though the Manly side contained one of the most punishing defenders of all time in Randall, Vautin soon got a reputation as a tackling machine. It was something that would stay with him throughout his career — perhaps to the detriment of his attacking capabilities. Those who watched Vautin closely in his years with

Manly believe at times he was a victim of his own honesty as a tireless defender.

"I think there were times in the later years when some of the guys would think, 'Well, we've got Fatty to do the tackling, I won't have to worry about it,'" said John Gibbs. "He wouldn't get upset about it, he'd just keep tackling his heart out but I think it got to the stage where he thought that was his role. It worked against him a bit in the end, I think he might have lost a bit of faith in his own ability to run with the ball. It was always very disappointing to me that we didn't play more together because we knew each other so well. I always thought that if we'd had more of a chance we could have turned into a really good attacking combination but it wasn't to be."

Gibbs' career was cut short prematurely through injury. A Kangaroo at 22 and one of the most exciting players in the game with the ball in his hands, Gibbs still tried to exhort Vautin to use his attacking abilities after he had been forced from the game. As sideline commentator for radio station 2UE he had the chance to stay close to the action. "Whenever we were calling a Manly game I'd make sure my microphone was turned off and give him a bit of advice," he admitted. "If he was close to the sideline or walking into the sheds at halftime I'd say, 'Hey, Fatty, they're a bit soft on the blind,' or, 'They're dropping back for the kick'. I was always trying to get him to put his head down and have a go. When he ran with the ball he could really move. That Fatty business was never really warranted. He had plenty of pace but I think I always had more faith in his ability as an attacking force than he did."

Stanton, who was to coach Vautin for only one season, was another who recognised attacking capabilities but saw them pushed further to the background as his career went on. "There was no doubt he was a good defender," he said. "But I felt he could have been developed as a running forward. I wasn't there after that first season of course, but I seem to remember Arko mentioning that he needed a player to take over the role that Terry Randall had filled so well. I guess that's how it turned out but there is no doubt Paul had the ability to play another kind of football. You saw it when he played State of Origin. It was probably only there he really had the opportunity to express himself in attack and it was good to see. He thrived on it."

But back in 1979 there was no thought of State of Origin or anything other than the hard slog Manly were facing each week. The arduous campaign of 1978 and the strain on the seven Kangaroos who had played virtually non-stop for a year was taking its toll. The '79 Sea Eagles were a far cry from the eager, injury-free outfit which had embarked on the premiership the year before. They had been there, done that. Put simply, they were stale.

When woodenspooners Norths beat them at Brookvale to record the Bears' only win of the season, Stanton knew his champion side was a long way from recording back-to-back premierships. Partly blaming himself for laxity creeping into the side, he decided to bring some of the famous Stanton discipline to the fore.

"They didn't call him Cranky Franky for nothing," Vautin recalled. "He was a good coach, bloody hard, but with a good football brain. He'd work out little weaknesses in the opposition and coach us to exploit them in the years before that became what coaching was all about. But if he had the shits, or sensed any slackness in the joint, look out.

"After that loss to Norths he realised he needed to pull us into line. As soon as we arrived at training that night I knew we were in trouble."

Stanton greeted his players thin-lipped. "Into the corner," he barked and set them a circuit of 20 x 400 metre sprints — to be completed in 60 seconds each. For once Vautin wasn't the last man home.

Englishman John Gray, noted for his sleight of hand rather than greyhound speed and agility, kept up for the first few, then halfway round the track looked helplessly at his teammates and with a plaintive "Fookin' 'ell," promptly passed out.

When the disciplinarian Stanton announced he was leaving at the end of the season, there were those who welcomed the change, but not Vautin. He responded to the former international's coaching and was one of the few people in the club who could get away with giving him a bit of cheek.

It took a few months, but the larrikin Fatty finally started emerging from behind the quiet veneer. Those who had shared a drink and joke with him like Gibbs and Magilla Thomson knew there was more to the newcomer than "Yes sir, no sir and who do you want me to tackle sir?" The others, like Eadie and Stanton, were soon to find out.

Trying to halt a mid-season slump, Stanton called an early Friday meeting. All players were seated in front of the blackboard like errant schoolkids when in stormed Fatty, half an hour late and straight from Friday afternoon bedlam at the bank. "When Frank was on the warpath, nobody said much," remembered Gibbs. "You just sat there and listened. That was the way he was that afternoon and there we all were, right on time, with blokes like Eadie and Randall and Krilich sitting there like kids. If Frank said three o'clock, he meant three o'clock and in came Fatty, halfway through. I remember thinking 'Uh oh, the kid's gonna get it now.'"

If looks could kill, Vautin was a dead man. "Don't you apologise for being late?" snapped Stanton.

"Not to red-headed pricks like you!" snapped back Vautin, happily taking his seat.

"That was when we knew there was more to him than we thought," said Eadie. "A lot of people weren't all that fussed on the way Frank went on, but nobody ever said anything about it. The way Fatty treated the situation was right. Working in the bank there was no way he could get there on time and he wasn't going to apologise for it. He always called a spade a spade and he handled the situation his own way. If ever you ask any of the players that year to tell you something about Fatty, they'll tell you about that incident. We just couldn't believe it."

Stanton for one, remembers it well. "Nobody ever spoke to me like that," he said. "We had a fairly disciplined set-up. I stared at him for a second or two then burst out laughing. I had to walk out of the room."

Stanton returned a few minutes later, looked at Vautin and started laughing again. It was another five minutes before the meeting restarted, much to Vautin's embarrassment. "It left a few mouths gaping, I can tell you," said Stanton.

As the Manly players and Sydney football public were starting to learn more about this character rapidly becoming known by his nickname alone, so too was Vautin learning more about big-time rugby league. The unspoken view that he had almost been afraid to share with anyone else — that he was good enough for Sydney — was being proven week in, week out. As each challenge appeared, he was almost surprised at how regularly it would be pushed aside.

"I'd have to say I found it easier than I thought it would be," he said. "I'd seen these guys on TV and read about them in the papers since I was a kid. I had some idea that they were like supermen and the games would be harder, faster and tougher than anything I'd ever played before. And it wasn't like that. Once I overcame the problems with training, I suddenly realised it wasn't any tougher than playing in Brisbane. They were footballers, just like us. Fitter maybe, but no better, a lot of them."

It was a lesson Vautin helped teach his Queensland teammates in State of Origin campaigns to come, often to the Blues' cost. Each game he played that year taught him more about survival and success at the highest level. From Stanton he learned about self-discipline and preparation, from Krilich and Thompson he learned about captaincy, and from Randall and Eadie the single-minded pursuit of excellence. But perhaps the most important lessons came from a man who played way out on the wing, Tom Mooney. From Mooney he learned how to win.

"I think I was always determined, I always had the will to win, but Tom was something else. I never saw anyone as determined as he was, anyone as willing to lay everything on the line in order to win," said Vautin. "There were times when we'd be in trouble, stuck on our own line making hard work of getting out of trouble and Tom would run in from the wing and grab the ball from dummy half. He'd actually shove someone out of the way and yell out, 'Give me that bloody ball, you pack of sheilas' and charge off from dummy half and strain and push for every centimetre. It would always take two or three of them to put him down and as he was playing the ball, he'd be turning around to us saying, 'See, that's the way you take it up.' It would always give us a lift, you'd see all the forwards pick up their workrate and charge onto the ball with new spirit."

Commentator Rex Mossop would often say no-one liked scoring tries as much as Tom Mooney and few wingers were as good at it. In 1979 Balmain's Aboriginal sensation Larry Corowa had finished the season leading the try-scoring lists, three tries ahead of Mooney, with Manly still to play their last game against grand final-bound Canterbury.

"There was some prize up for grabs and it was a pretty big

honour to finish top try-scorer in those days," Vautin recalled. "I remember when we got into the dressing room before the game Tom was bent over putting on his boots and someone called out, 'Hey Tom, you only need four tries to beat Larry'. Everyone laughed until Tom sat up. He had this look on his face that just shut the room right up. He said, 'Don't bet against me' and there's no way any of us would have. By the time we ran on he was like a machine. He scored four tries and won the award."

Mooney was a huge influence on the young Vautin, often inviting him to his home at Bronte for a meal and a talk about football. It was all part of his education about what Sydney rugby league was all about but he admits nothing that had gone before could have prepared him for his first match against Wests.

"It was right at the end of that Fibro-Silvertail shit and almost from the first game the other guys in the team were saying, 'Just wait till we play Wests, Fatty. Wait till Les Boyd and Dallas Donnelly get a hold of you, then you'll know about it.' I wasn't real worried, more interested. It was a big thing at the time and I couldn't help wondering what it must be like."

He found out midway through the season, with Manly facing Wests at Brookvale on the end of a three-match losing streak. The tension in the dressing room was obvious from the moment he walked in. "Guys were wandering around geeing themselves up, saying stuff like, 'Come on, give it to Boyd, belt Ray Brown,' all that sort of stuff. Ian Thomson came up to me and said, 'Don't worry about Dallas, he'll be mouthing off, but I'll take care of him.' I said, 'Err, sure Magilla, if that's the way you want it, no sweat.'

"When we ran out it was mayhem from start to finish. We're waiting to kick off and blokes are mouthing off at each other across the field. Les Boyd is staring at someone and calling his mother a slut and blokes' eyes are rolling around in their heads. I'm just standing there thinking, 'What the hell is going on here?' Then we kick off and everybody is straight into it. After about 20 minutes Max Krilich got king-hit after he played the ball and it was all in. Max stood up and Dallas hit him and down he went again. Magilla's got Boyd down on the ground by the throat and he's just belting him into submission. Dallas is sent off, Steve Knight is sent off, and I'm still standing there with my mouth open thinking, 'Ohhhh, so this is what they've been talking about all year'."

The game was a win to Wests, yet another disappointment in a dismal year for the defending premiers. They won only 11 of the 22 games, although the performance of Vautin, who played in all but two first grade matches, was a face-saver for Arthurson and his committee. Early in the season Arko took his newest recruit aside and congratulated him on his form. He also had a quiet word about his dress sense.

In those days Paul Vautin didn't do advertisements for Lowes but he could have bought his entire wardrobe there for under $10. His pre-match ensemble consisted of a pair of thongs, stubbies and T-shirt. He might have played for the "silvertails" and boasted a North Shore address, but his heart was very much back in Brisbane and Legends Lodge. Finally Arthurson could stand it no longer. "You're in the big time now, Paul," he said. "Playing for the best club in the country. These clothes you're wearing ... how about lifting your standards a bit, eh?"

Vautin might have been from the bush as far as his teammates were concerned, but he knew enough not to upset the boss. The next week he proudly turned up at Cumberland Oval wearing thongs, boardshorts and a T-shirt — with a collar.

Arthurson gave up on the newcomer sartorially, but not as a player. With half the season gone he promised he would re-assess Vautin's contract if his good form continued to the end of the season. "Come and see me," he said.

If the offer had been meant as an incentive, it did the trick. Vautin continued to win man-of-the-match awards and tackle himself to a standstill week after week. The first hint that his name was being mentioned in higher circles came when Tom Raudonikis, writing a newspaper column on the eve of the City-Country clash, forecast that while the City firsts team picked itself, there could be a new face in the City seconds. "Paul Vautin has been playing in the back row for Manly like he's been there all his life," he wrote. It put the seed in Vautin's mind. "Gee, I wonder if..."

City coach Stanton stoked the fire further, pulling Vautin aside at training and telling him not to be surprised to hear his name read out by the City selectors.

It wasn't to be the last time Vautin would be on the wrong side of a selector's red pen. True, there was an new face in the seconds, but it wasn't Fatty's. "Don Prior," he said. "He played three games for Souths. Who is he? What happened to him? Could make a good question for Trivial Pursuit."

A representative jumper would have been a worthy reward for an outstanding debut season, but Vautin could still be well pleased with what he had achieved. At year's end he confidently knocked on Arthurson's door. "Paul," the affable club secretary said, leading him to a chair, "Paul, you know, this is just between us, but you were our best player this year. I can't tell you how pleased I am with the way you've gone. You've become almost like a son to me. Now, what can I do for you?"

"I was thinking $15,000, Ken."

"What?! Listen son, we've got internationals getting less than that. One swallow doesn't make a summer you know. I'd love to give it to you, but how would it be if the other fellows found out. Now, like I said, Paul, you had a good year — a great year. You made me proud, enormously proud. How are your parents by the way? Lovely people…"

Vautin did get his $15,000 but now knows he could have got $20,000. "He always robbed me, but in the nicest possible way," he said of Arthurson. "You'd say to yourself — he's not going to get me this year, go in there ready to fight him and come out thinking he was the greatest bloke in the world and you were the best footballer ever to play for the club. You were halfway home before you realised you'd been fleeced."

Arthurson remembered it slightly differently. "Well, Paul does have that ability to tell a good story," he said. "Yes, he did a fine job for us and he was very handsomely compensated. He made good money, but he deserved it, he was a great player, made me very proud. You know, he was like a son to me…"

While Arthurson's "son" was giving good service to the club Vautin's real parents were determined not to be left out. "It was very frustrating for us," said Leila. "We'd watched nearly every game he'd ever played and here he was playing first grade and we couldn't see him. It wasn't like it is now, they didn't show all the matches on television and we didn't even get the live radio broadcasts in Queensland."

But they did get them in NSW, so every time Manly were featured in a radio game Leila would cook up a batch of scones, fill the thermos and George and she would drive south for a few hours until the car radio picked up the match. "We'd find a nice spot in the shade, open the car doors and have our coffee and scones then when the match was over we'd drive back," she said, "one time we drove all the way down the coast and the match wasn't broadcast."

Another time when a Manly crunch game against Wests at Lidcombe was being shown live on television in NSW George and Leila booked into a motel at Ballina for the weekend. No sooner had they sat down to watch the game than Paul hobbled off with an ankle injury. "It wasn't always easy being so far away," Leila said. "We always tried to ring him on the morning of a match to wish him luck. My phone bill was $250 for the first three months after he left."

And with growing fame and public recognition came added pressures. Russell Vautin, who had been a promising player himself until outed for life by a legitimate Wally Fullerton Smith tackle, often found it hard to cope with his older brother's success. For years if anyone asked him if he was Paul Vautin's brother, he would answer stonily, "No."

George Vautin, while full of pride at his son's achievements, was also very sure to keep things in perspective. "Sometimes people would come up to me and say, 'Are you Paul Vautin's father?' I'd say, 'No, he's my son.' There's a difference."

A Seaside Romance

The assistant manager led the way to teller's cage No.9. "Paul," he said, "this is where you'll be working, and this is who you'll be sharing with. Kim McGurgan, meet Paul Vautin."

He took one look, and his mind was made up. "I just looked at her and thought, 'Geez, I'm gonna marry this sheila,'" he said. "It took me six years, but I did. She wouldn't wear me at first, but I couldn't keep my eyes off her. I liked everything about her, the way she looked, the way she talked, the way she moved. Marrying Kim was like winning a grand final, a goal you set for yourself and work at until it happens. There were times when I was at pretty long odds, but I got there in the end."

There were a few minor hitches on the way, but on that first day in his new job at the Dee Why branch of the Commonwealth Bank, Vautin's luck was very much in.

He'd been with Manly only a few weeks, but off the field as well as on, his life was starting to take shape. The rough edges on the boy from Brisbane were steadily being smoothed off. On the football field it was by watching the likes of Krilich, Mooney and Randall. Off the field more often than not, it was by listening to their advice over the dining room table. "They all looked after me pretty well," he said. "I was only a kid and they were almost like father figures to me. People like Wombat Eadie and Bruce "Goldie" Walker, Tom Mooney, Alan Thompson and Krilich. They'd all have me round to their homes for dinner and make sure I was getting along alright. They'd all been around a while and been through what I was going through and they helped me along the way when I needed it. They kept me focussed on the job and it was appreciated."

The "one-season wonder" is a well-known phenomenon in Sydney rugby league. Vautin was determined not to become another example, and people like Eadie, who had known the pressures of stardom at an early age, were there to help. "Wombat used to tell me not to take too much notice of what was written about me in the papers or what people were saying at the bar. After a couple of good games early I used to get a few people slapping me on the back and wanting to buy me drinks. I remember Wombat pulling me aside once and saying not to get carried away. He said, 'Those blokes buying you a beer won't be around if you have a bad game. Don't take it to heart, but they'll be off buying someone else a beer.' He was right. I never took any notice of the Billy Backslappers after that. It was good getting noticed and seeing my picture in the papers but I knew it would only last as long as I was playing well. I learned to become my own judge. If I knew I'd gone alright and if my coach and teammates thought I'd done my job, that was what mattered."

While the married players like Mooney, Walker and Krilich were eager to invite Vautin home for some home cooking and sage advice, there were still plenty of young single Sea Eagles happy to show him the sights of Sydney.

After three months with the Parkers, Vautin moved into a flat on his own, advertising for a flatmate and ending up with a local character named Humphrey. When the lease ran out he was offered a room at Ian Thomson's home at Harbord, an offer he made the most of for the next three years.

The two forwards became the closest of mates during those days although early on in the partnership Thomson did have misgivings. A few days after Vautin moved in Thomson went up to Frank Stanton at training.

"Hey Frank," he said, "I'm a bit worried about Fatty."

"What's up?"

"Well, I looked in his room this morning and he's got about 200 magazine centrefolds stuck on the wall."

"So? What's wrong with that?"

"Mate, they're all of racehorses."

It was during that time he first became aware of the double-edged sword of being a public name. A spurned admirer took to telephoning and dropping around at all hours, day and night. Early one morning the situation reached an inevitable conclusion. By their own admission, Vautin and Thomson were two young men who needed their beauty sleep. The front door was opened, words exchanged, the lady evicted and the door slammed shut. Half an hour later, the banging on the door restarted, only this time it was the police.

Vautin and Thomson were both charged with assault and the story was all over page one in the afternoon tabloids. When the two housemates arrived at court for their committal hearing, the press were waiting. "It was like something out of *Witness For The Prosecution*," Vautin said. "The cab dropped us out the front, then we walked around the side and there were all the reporters and photographers and cameramen. Someone yelled out, 'There they are' and they all started running towards us.

"Magilla said, 'Geez Fatty, what'll we do here?' I said, 'Try a bit of this' and stuck my hand up over my face like I'd seen them do in *Perry Mason*. We pushed our way through like the Great Train Robbers. If it wasn't so serious it would have been funny."

The pair were charged and sentenced to appear at a later date, but in the interim the charges were dropped and Vautin never heard anything more about the incident.

It was a rare piece of spice in an otherwise rather tepid social life. By this time Paul's heart was very much pining for his co-worker Kim, but there was a slight problem. Aside from the fact that, in his words "she couldn't stand the sight of me", she was also very much involved with another man. Paul resolved to play the field — without much success. "I was throwing out plenty of lines but I wasn't getting too many bites," he admitted.

And to make thing worse, his new flatmate proved to be the Casanova of the northern beaches, with the girls quite literally climbing over Vautin to get to Thomson. "We had deadlocks on the doors but girls would be calling around for Magilla at all hours," Vautin recalled. "The sheilas knew they couldn't get in through the doors but they figured out that we couldn't lock my window so they used to get in there, climb over my bed and through to his room.

"I couldn't get anywhere with women and here I was, every couple of nights I'd hear the window open and some gorgeous sort would tread on my face and out of my life. It was driving me crazy."

Luckily there were other distractions, usually provided by Johnny Gibbs, who had become Vautin's closest mate.

Like W.C. Fields' first wife who drove him to drink — "the only good thing she ever did for me" — Gibbs introduced Vautin to the pastime which would become a major part of his life — the punt.

"When I came to Sydney I didn't drink much and didn't have a bet. Gibbsy did his best to change that. I never became much of a drinker, but I sure do like a punt," Vautin said.

Every Saturday the two Manly stars could be seen at the track, covering more territory running between the bookies than they did on the training paddock. The day would finish with a steak at the Frenchs Forest Black Stump. It was a schedule set in stone and while a Saturday game might preclude them from a visit to the races, it would never stop them having a bet. By the time Gibbs was forced to give up playing the game two years later, the pair knew the locality of every TAB between the peninsula and the major league fields of Sydney. Even more, they knew precisely how long it would take to drive between each betting shop on the way to the grounds, enabling them to place bets before each race as they made their way to the game. It was a practice which would cause some problems in years to come, but it was one which helped cement a friendship which remains one of the strongest in rugby league.

When Vautin found his work at the bank made it hard to attend training, it was Gibbs who found him a new job — but not before team captain and successful plumbing contractor Max "Thrower" Krilich had offered a helping hand. "For a couple of weeks after I left the bank I didn't have a job and Thrower asked me if I wanted to work for him," he remembered. "He said he was working on a house and needed a labourer. Nothing too strenuous, he said. I asked him if I'd get paid. 'Well paid,' he said, 'don't worry about that, you'll be very well paid.'

"I said okay, and when I got there it turned out it was his own house. He smiled, patted me on the back, handed me a shovel and pushed me down this trench. I never saw him smile again for four days. He nearly killed me. When I got out of the trench at the end of the day I couldn't stand up straight. I was working 10-hour days and at the end of the week I stuck out my hand for some dough.

"He says, 'What did we agree on again?' I said, 'We didn't agree on anything, Max, you just said I'd be well paid.' 'Oh yeah, right,' he says and hands over some cash. When I unrolled it and got the moths out, it was 120 bucks. I was killing myself for about three bucks an hour. I said, 'Max, you're kiddin'. He says, 'What are you on about? That's good money, and I didn't even take out what you owe me for the pies I bought you for lunch.'

"He was the tightest bloke ever. I remember one day he got me to work with him clearing a drain for a real estate agent. We got the electric eel up the drain and the agent is giving Max a hurry-up. Max says: 'I'm doing my best, champ' and just then this enormous Richard the Third comes flying out of the drain and lands on the side of Max's face. The estate agent is standing there in shock and Max stands up calmly with this giant blob hanging off the side of his face, and says, 'See this mate, I don't get shit on my face for nobody. This just cost you an extra $20.'

"It was then I decided being a plumber's mate wasn't for me. Needless to say when Gibbsy came up with the groundsman's job at Mona Vale Public School where he was working, I jumped at it. I was still there four years later."

Gibbs, who was teaching at the school, said he learnt a lot about Vautin during the time they worked together. "People always used to go on about how much energy Paul had on the field. They used to wonder how he could get through the amount of work he did and still be going strong at the end of the game," he said. "Well, having worked with him, I know. It was because he rested all week at work. He did nothing.

"The only time he ever got out of his little room under the building was to mow the lawn — and it was a sit-on mower."

Vautin admitted he wasn't overworked at the job but says he had an eager conspirator in crime. "I used to spend a lot of time doing the form," he says, "and even when I was on the mower I'd have the old earplug in listening to the races, but Gibbsy was no Mr Chips himself. Whenever the midweek races were on I'd stand in the playground under his classroom window at precisely 2pm. He'd set the kids some tricky sum on the blackboard then sidle over to the window and stick his head out like he was looking at the view. The kids would all be doing their work and the two of us would be there listening to the race cheering under our breaths."

The job was not without its hazards though, with the school principal often on the prowl. "The principal was a very good bloke but I think he was always a little concerned about the fact that he could never find me," Vautin said. "This little room I had under the building had one of those bolts on the outside of the door which was supposed to be pushed across if I wasn't in there. The boss was always wandering down there looking for me, so I'd hide down behind the work bench where I could listen to the races. He'd come down, stick his head in to see if I was there and when he couldn't see me, he'd go back out and push the latch across. There was only a tiny little window pretty high up in the wall so I had to wait until school was out and stand on some boxes yelling for one of the kids to let me out."

The job was to provide the perfect environment for a race-mad footballer who liked to conserve his energy for match days but it came only after a hard year juggling training, working at the bank and settling in to a new life. For while each day Vautin felt more at ease in this strange land Queenslanders refer to simply as "down South", there was still something eating away at him. His confidence was growing both on and off the field, he no longer needed the "Referdex" open on the front seat of the Monaro to find his way to the local shops, but, for all that, he never felt totally at home.

One night, as he and Gibbs downed a few beers at the Harbord Diggers Club, he was approached by a pair of staunch Manly supporters, Ron and Pat Wheatley. Pat, who recognised the distinctive red mop she had been gazing down at from her regular seat at Brookvale Oval for the past few weeks, walked over and introduced herself. "How are you finding life in Sydney?" she asked the club's latest import. "Fine," he said, but with typical openness admitted he was missing his family and friends. And Leila's home cooking.

"The poor kid was so homesick," Pat said. "I really felt for him. I told him I was cooking a roast the following Tuesday night and he was welcome to come around if he wanted to."

"That'd be great," Vautin said, scribbling the Wheatley's Allambie Heights address down on the back of a drink coaster. He went that Tuesday and has been back just about every Tuesday since.

"For 14 years it's been part of my life," he said. "Every Tuesday I'd go there and have dinner and talk about footy and everything that was happening. Pat and Ron became like foster parents to me. They had four kids of their own and I watched the little ones grow up. I'd share things with all of them the same way I'd be sharing them with Mum and Dad and my family if it had been in Brisbane. Now it's not just me. Kim and the kids come with me. Every Tuesday night, like clockwork."

Right: Baby Paul at six months, with his dad, George.

Below: He was a little Fatty, even in the early days, as shown in this toddler shot of Paul tackling a fence at home.

Below right: The first photo of Paul Vautin footballer — proudly sporting the outfit of the West Mitchelton Under 8's, his first team ... but sans boots.

Above: The first team shot, with Paul (second from the right in the back row), obviously enjoying the moment as he poses with the premiership-winning West Mitchelton Under 10A's of 1969.

Right: Just a freckle-faced kid, Grade 4, Padua College.

Left: The teenage Paul Vautin, a first grader already, with Wests (Brisbane) in 1978 — his first season in first grade.

Below: Long hair and loose ties were the fashion. Paul, vice captain of the school, 1976.

Above: The Brisbane Under 18 team of 1977 contained two players destined for greatness whose careers would cross again and again in the years ahead. Paul Vautin is on the left in the back row and third from the right, back row, is his captain, Wally Lewis.

67

Above: Iron man Terry "Igor" Randall was an early hero and inspiration for the young Vautin. Here Randall receives the treatment from Easts' international Royce Ayliffe, while Fatty looks on.

Left: Vautin and Paul McCabe had plenty to talk about after the Redfern Oval match against Souths in the 1983 premeirship. The two star backrowers both played at prop this day.

Left: The young Sea Eagle, 1983.

Below: It's try time for Fatty and a spectacular photo resulted. V Cronulla at Brookvale, 1981.

The clearly visible shoulder pads give the year away. It was 1985 — the only season of his life that Fatty Vautin wore the shoulder protectors, to help with a slow-healing injury.

Above: A flying Vautin tackle, brilliantly portrayed as he nails Penrith's Warren Fenton in the 1985 semi-final play-off at the Sydney Cricket Ground. Tony Melrose is the player in the background. Penrith reached the semis for the first time by winning 10-7.

Below: Ouch! Paul Vautin's noggin connects with terra very firma, thanks to this tackle by Parramatta's Paul Taylor.

Clockwise from top left, four Manly champions: Frank Stanton, Max Krilich, Terry Randall and Graham Eadie.

Clockwise from top left:
Mark Broadhurst, Tom
Mooney, Fred Jones,
Johnny Gibbs, Alan
Thompson. Each
contributed to the making
of Paul Vautin, footballer.

Right: Paul's head is in some danger of being detached from the rest of the Vautin torso, thanks to the vigorous fitness test being applied by the Penrith giant Mark Geyer in a match in 1988.

Below: "C'mon fellas, lift yourselves!" Captain Fatty does his bit behind the line after a Penrith try in the tight semi-final play-off against Penrith in 1985.

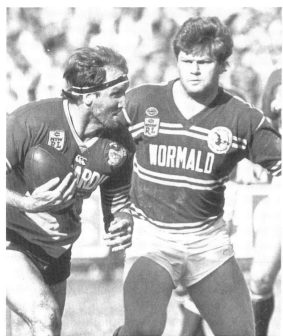

Left: Vautin and the Parramatta champion Ray Price were fierce rivals — but Vautin's respect for the indestructible Price was sky high.

Below: Vautin looks left for support as St George's Tony Trudgett tackles him in a match at Brookvale in 1983. Looming on the right is the formidable and ferocious Les Boyd.

Left: A quick handshake and a smile as the opposing grand final captains of 1987 meet at the GF Breakfast. Vautin respected Canberra's Dean Lance as a "lovely bloke and a real hard man."

Below left: Vautin ploughs ahead in the grand final of '87. Hooker Steve Walters is the Raider on the left.

Below: They called Canberra's Sam Backo "Big Sam". Paul Vautin finds out why.

Right: Left to right, Prime Minister Bob Hawke, a proud Paul Vautin, the treasured J. J. Giltinan Shield and Noel Cleal. Grand final day, Sydney Cricket Ground 1987.

Above: How sweet it was! David Ronson (at back, left), Mick O'Connor and Kevin Ward (with shield), Paul Vautin, Mark Pocock and coach Bob Fulton (right), Cliff Lyons (kneeling) and ball boys Lee Thoroughgood (left) and Brett Fulton on Manly's happy grand final day, 1987.

Above left: "Are you fair dinkum, ref?" Paul Vautin, 1987.
Above right: Vautin, bruised and exhausted after a match against Balmain
in 1983. He had played a Test for Australia (against New Zealand) the
previous day.

Above: Boxing Day 1988 and Vautin is playing for St Helens in the
traditional post-Christmas match against Wigan at Knowlsley Road.
Wigan's Denis Betts is on the right and Ged Byrne in the background. Wigan
won, 18-11.

Above: Why is this man laughing? Even Paul Vautin can't answer that question. He has just played his last game for Manly, the 10-all draw against Balmain in 1989 and his emotions are closer to tears than cheers.

Above left: A relaxing spa after a game at Brookie in 1988. Right: A knee injury suffered against Illawarra in 1988 had Vautin in trouble, and in pain.

79

Of course some nights Paul might ring and say he can't make it, and there are times the Wheatleys cancel but usually by the next week it'll be business as usual.

"I remember one night when he was still living with Ian Thomson he rang to say he was sick and couldn't make it," Pat recalled. "He sounded dreadful, said he'd been sick as a dog for a couple of days and that he'd try to make something out of a can for tea. I told him he'd do no such thing. I packed up the roast, the sweets and everything, put it all on the backseat of the car and Ron and I drove around to Harbord and gave it to him there. Well, I mean, it's just what any mother would do, isn't it?"

There are other things a mother would do too. The Wheatleys became Paul's shoulder to lean on as he suffered the physical and emotional knocks that come with a career in first grade rugby league. They spurred him on when he was down, sat proudly in the stand at the Sydney Football Stadium as he played for Australia and sent telegrams before big matches. They even supported Queensland in the State of Origin. "Our kids reckoned we were turncoats," Pat said. "We'd sit there going for Paul and they'd all be cheering for NSW. That was hard."

What wasn't hard was standing behind Vautin as he was released by Manly in the most sensational of circumstances in 1989. Manly supporters all their lives, Ron and Pat immediately turned in their season passes and never attended another Manly match.

And Pat, for over 20 years a member of the club, sent her badge to chief executive Doug Daley, with a note. "Just a short one," she said, "telling him what to do with it."

Ron wasn't quite so demonstrative. He kept his club membership, but makes no secret of his feelings. His allegiance is very much to Paul Vautin first, Manly second.

That chance meeting at Harbord Diggers and the roast dinner which followed opened up a whole new world for both Ron and the homesick kid he now calls either "Bluey" or, simply, "The Redhead". They have become the closest of mates, speak on the phone at least once a week, own a promising racehorse together and "go bush" on country shooting expeditions as often as possible. "He's like another son to me," said Ron, "and I mean that, I'm not just saying it. After 14 years he just walks in, goes to the fridge for a drink if he's thirsty, and we're just the same at his house. Like family. That's just the way it is. He's a terrific bloke to be with, great company. We've been getting away shooting up at Yeovil on the back road to Dubbo for years. That's when we really get away from it all, when we really have some laughs."

There was the time Dale Shearer drove his brand new Holden ute into a creek; the time they went with Trevor Gillmeister in their old jeans and T-shirts to the Yeovil Rugby League Club annual dinner and found themselves guests of honour at a mixed black-tie function for 300 at the town hall.

"The redhead had to give a speech," Ron Wheatley said. "Everyone was dressed up for the biggest night in their lives and there's Bluey in his jeans and sandshoes. He carried it off though. We left at 3am. Gilly found his way back to camp at 6."

Then there was the time Dale Shearer wandered off in the bush and got lost, then reappeared three hours later from exactly the opposite direction. "Don't ask me how he did it," said Ron. "I was surprised enough that the redhead got back in one piece, he'd get lost in a revolving door. But when Shearer didn't show up I started to worry. I could see the headlines — 'Football Star Lost In Bush'. My young fella let off a shotgun blast every half hour and Shearer reckoned he just followed the noise. Thing was he was last seen heading north and he walked into camp from the south. I've never been able to work that one out."

But most of all there are stories about Vautin's overwhelming fear of snakes and spiders. "You can't stand in front of Bluey in the bush," Ron said. "If he thinks there's a snake behind him he'll run right over the top of you. Shearer's always throwing little spiders at him. Once he sees one he's quicker than Carl Lewis."

And it's not just spiders. Vautin is scared of just about anything that can't wear shoes. "He's hopeless," Dale Shearer recalls. "He won't sleep in a tent he's so scared of something getting him. Spiders, wild pigs, snakes, anything. He reckons there's always something out there after him. I remember one night it was so cold, we had a fire on and we were still wrapping anything around us we could find — newspapers, sugar sacks, you name it. It was freezing but Fatty still wouldn't sleep outside with us. He slept in the car. It must have nearly killed him."

Ron says the night he "bumped" Vautin at the Diggers was one of the luckiest of his life. One story he tells sums up why. "I've been with Telecom for 35 years, never had a day's compo in my life, then I rolled a forklift and broke my leg," he said. "When I got home from hospital I was lying there and heard someone mowing the lawn. I pulled myself up to the window to see what was going on. I've got three sons of my own, but who do you think it was? The redhead."

From the very first Tuesday night the Wheatleys' dinners became a weekly opportunity for Vautin to offload, sit back in a family environment and pour out his heart about football, the pressures of living in Sydney and, more and more, about his co-worker Kim McGurgan.

It was a sad, sad story. Paul was desperate to attract Kim's attention but, unfortunately, he let Fatty lead the way. Unsure of how to make this girl notice him, he fell back on his experiences in Brisbane. The quiet, shy youngster had suddenly become the most talked-about boy in class when he started acting the fool. It had worked at Padua College, Kedron, why not at the Commonwealth Bank, Dee Why. He never actually resorted to a blood capsule, but tried just about everything else. Looking back on it now Paul realises he was obnoxious, boorish and often downright disgusting. As he put it, "I set out to charm her off her feet. It didn't quite work."

Kim is equally blunt. "He was uncouth, a hillbilly. In fact he was pretty awful. He seemed like such a kid, I felt so much older and more mature than him."

Finally admitting defeat, he dropped the facade and became himself. And all of a sudden Kim decided this Paul Vautin wasn't such a bad person after all. They became friends. It wasn't exactly what Paul had hoped for, but it was as good as he was going to get.

"She had this bloke," he said, "and as I got to know her better, I got to know him too. I was determined not to like him, but pretty soon I was friendly with him too. We used to have dinner together every now and then and I found he wasn't a bad guy. Kim and I got to be real close friends, but that was it. I had too much respect for both of them to try to make it anything but that."

When Kim left the bank and married her boyfriend, Paul resolved himself to the fact that this was one grand final that he was never going to win. "Then all of a sudden a while later I bumped into Kim's mother at the bank," he said. "She banked at the branch and we used to have some very long and meaningful conversations like, 'Yes, Mrs McGurgan, will that be 10 twenties or 20 ones?' Obviously she thought I was a pretty good guy because she told me Kim had left her husband and was living back at home. The bank closed at three, I was around there at five past."

For the next few months Kim and Paul became even closer friends as she tried to work out her feelings. Eventually she decided to give her marriage a second try. "I thought that was the end of it," Paul said. "My hopes were dashed again and I thought this time it was for good. I went out and met another girl, who just happened to be named Kim as well. For a while there I thought she might be the one."

And then came another phone call. Kim's marriage had broken up once and for all. For Paul it seemed like all his Christmases had come at once. Here he was, the boy from up north who couldn't get a girl with not one, but two, beautiful women. He had a choice to make, but like the kid in the lolly shop, was in no hurry making up his mind.

"I thought, 'How good's this?'" he recalled. "I kept telling myself that I'd break it off with one of them but I guess I just never got around to it. Neither one of them knew the other one existed. It was hard, but I kept them away from each other for three months. The best thing was that they were both called Kim. Every time the phone rang I'd pick it up and say 'Hi Kim'. They'd ask how I knew it was them. I'd say just a lucky guess."

Paul's double life with the two Kims was eventually discovered. Unbeknown to him, they met and compared notes. One night at 11pm there was a knock at the door. "It's a friend of yours," shouted Magilla.

"I thought, 'beauty, who is it? Gibbsy?'" Paul remembered. "Then I walked out and there was the other Kim. I said, 'Hi,' and she just reeled off and gave me an absolute gobfull, then walked off. I stood there with my mouth open for a few minutes but it dawned on me pretty quickly what had happened. Oh well, I thought, no worries, I've still got Kim McGurgan. Think again Fatman. She wouldn't talk to me either."

From being the man about town with a choice of two ladies, Paul suddenly found himself back on the bench, with the nearest he got to female companionship being the nights a girl would climb over him to get to Thomson.

"I was ringing Kim McGurgan every day but she'd hang up," he said. "When I was forced to make a decision about them I made it easily but I thought I'd blown it. I couldn't get near her. Finally I wrote her a four-page love letter. I really poured out my heart to her and waited for the response."

And waited and waited.

"Eventually I had to ring her," he said. "It must have made some impression. At least she didn't hang up straight away. I said, 'Did you get my letter?' She said, 'Yes.' I said, 'Well?' She said, 'Well what?' I thought, 'This is terrific.' I said, 'Look, I'd like to see you again.' She said, 'I'll think about it,' then she hung up. I was making real progress."

From that rather shaky start, the romance blossomed again. As Paul put it, they "courted" for about three years before being married on Australia Day, 1985. A happy ending, but not without another hiccup — this time caused by best man Johnny Gibbs.

By this time Vautin was working at Moby Dick's nightclub for some extra cash in summer and had decided to hold the wedding reception there as well. Overlooking Whale Beach, Moby Dick's has magnificent views and is a favourite social spot for the locals. Vautin was employed picking up glasses and, ironically for a man who would rarely throw a punch in more than a decade of first-class football, as bouncer.

Thanks to his reputation as a rugby league hard man, Vautin was rarely asked to demonstrate his fistic skills — or lack of them — but the weekend before his wedding, he got an urgent call from the manager. "Quick," he said, "there's some lunatic making trouble downstairs. Go and throw him out."

"Is he a big guy?' Vautin asked. "Maybe we should call the cops."

"Nah," said the manager, "he's only little."

"Righto," said Vautin, following the manager downstairs, his voice suddenly a few octaves deeper. "No worries, I'll murder the little arsehole. Where is he?"

The manager pointed out a very angry blond chap, obviously the worse the wear.

"Hang on," said Vautin, "that's Gibbsy. I can't throw him out, he's my mate. He's going to be my best man here next week."

The manager remained unimpressed so Vautin tried to smooth things out. "Hey Gibbsy, do us a favour willya? I've got to get married here next week. Go home, eh?"

Gibbs, who had been close to coming to blows with another drinker, suddenly turned his attention to Vautin. "What kind of mate are you? I was just about to beat the crap out of this bloke," he said, shaping up, "now I'll beat the crap out of you instead. Come on, put 'em up, put 'em up."

It took all Vautin's soon-to-be-famous oratory skills to talk Gibbs out of fighting him, the other patron or the manager and get him outside in one piece. The next day he went to Gibbs' home expecting another argument but instead was greeted with a tip for the daily double. All was right with the world and the following week he and Kim were married with Gibbs by his side.

It had taken a few years and at times he was, as he says "a million to one" but he'd done it. He'd won his first grand final.

CHAPTER 7

Fatty The Eagle

Vautin had come a long way in his first 12 months in Sydney football. He started the year in a hotel room above the band at the Brookvale Rex and ended it in one overlooking Waikiki Beach.

Despite their poor performance in the competition, the Manly players travelled to Hawaii for an end of season trip. The two week holiday gave Vautin the chance to travel for the first time and strengthen friendships with his new clubmates. It also gave him the opportunity to see two of the legends of rugby league close up.

In Hawaii at the same time were rival clubs Cronulla and Western Suburbs. Cronulla's reserve grade coach of the time was Billy Smith, the former St George halfback noted for his cool head on the field and his wild ways off it.

Early in the trip the Manly players headed to the other side of the island to visit a plush golf club. "We travelled for a couple of hours to get there and as the bus got within about two kilometres of the course the driver said, 'what the ...' and pulled over," Vautin recalled. "We all stood up and looked out the windows. Coming towards us was a golf cart driven by Billy Smith. He was crouched over the wheel with this determined look on his face and a glass of beer in one hand. Right behind him were two police cars with their lights flashing and sirens on. It was one of the funniest things I've ever seen. We never did find out what it was all about."

Another night Vautin and a couple of teammates walked into a favourite nightspot, the English-style pub The Rose And Crown. "As we walked in, Dallas Donnelly was at the bar," he said. "He turned around, took one look at us and yelled out, 'Manly poofters — let's bash 'em.' He was pretty disappointed when someone told him to shut up and have another beer. I wasn't. Dallas with a few under his belt wasn't a pretty sight."

The trip had a disastrous end when a burglar broke into the

room Vautin was sharing with Wayne Springall and stole the pair's money and passports. As the rest of the touring party checked out, it was feared Vautin and Springall would have to stay until new passports could be arranged through the Australian consulate.

"We didn't have a cent between us so we weren't too fussed on being stuck there while everyone else went home," Vautin said, "but luckily Arko got in touch with Michael MacKellar who was the local member back at Manly, and he got it sorted out."

Vautin got back to Sydney in time for the start of training, but after a few weeks must have been wishing he'd stayed in Hawaii.

The year was always going to be a watershed year for Manly, and Vautin in particular. After his success of the previous season, big things were expected but the pressure was on. Stanton, who had taken a personal interest in his fellow redhead's progress, was gone, replaced by another former Manly international, Allan Thomson. Then there were the signings of the three Wests stars Les Boyd, Ray Brown and John Dorahy.

Arthurson created a furore which would rage for years by snaring the three internationals from the Magpies. Wests' coach Roy Masters would use the coup to motivate his "Fibros" against the "Silvertails" for as long as he was with the club. Arthurson was accused of trying to buy a premiership at the expense of the battling Magpies and Boyd and Brown — who could fill every position in the pack — would put enormous pressure on every Manly forward.

There were reports that the signings of the three former opponents created a division within the Manly ranks but Vautin denies it. "We all thought it would be good for the club," he said. "There was no doubting they were all great players. We knew it would put pressure on for spots but there was nothing wrong with that. We all wanted to win a premiership and we thought these would be the guys who would help us get it."

It wasn't to be. The year was a disaster both for the club and Vautin personally, but he believes the problems were much deeper than a few noses being out of joint because three top players had been signed in the off-season. "For me it all started when the word got out that Frank Stanton was leaving," he said. "When they told me the new coach was Allan Thomson, I had to ask, 'Who's he?' I'd never heard of him. They told me he was a real tough forward, a top defender, and because of that everyone said I'd go real well. He was my type of guy. It didn't quite work out that way. Even Terry Randall told me he was a real tough nut, so I knew there must be something to it, but it just never worked out.

"Thomson never got the respect of the players the way Frank did. Not many of us had ever seen him play so the fact that he was a tough bastard on the field didn't mean much, and tactically he wasn't in Frank's class."

The injection of new blood into the side didn't help either. Arthurson and the committee had gone out on a limb buying the Wests players. It had cost them big in terms of both money and public expectation. Manly supporters demanded instant results, supporters of other clubs were combined in their condemnation of the Silvertails' cheque book forays.

It put the former Wests players under enormous strain. Estimates of the size of their contracts were bandied about and opposition crowds delighted in baiting them over any mistake or fumble. With demands for instant success from management and fans the established Manly players were not given the luxury of time to settle in with the newcomers and unfortunately for Thomson, it all passed on down the line to the coach.

"The bookies had us favourites to win the comp and that put pressure on everyone," Vautin said. "You had to feel sorry for Thomson in the end. Our forwards used to cop a bagging. People said there were a whole lot of stars but no ticker. That's rubbish. We had one of the best packs going around. I believe what we didn't have was a decent coach. It all blew up in the end but at first everyone was pretty happy when the Wests guys came into the side. It was pretty funny really. A few months earlier these blokes had really given it to us at Lidcombe and here they were arriving at training ready to play alongside us. Boyd was obviously the one everyone was wondering about because on the field he always went on as if he hated our guts. It didn't take long to sort that out. He'd been on a Kangaroo tour with a lot of the guys and they all liked him. Pretty soon we all did. He was a real funny guy. Off-field he was so quiet you could hardly hear what he was saying, and he looked so disinterested you'd swear he didn't care about football at all. Then as the game got closer he turned.

"He had that quiet country twang in his voice and he'd come up to me before the game and say, 'You ready Fatty? You ready? You gonna give it to 'em Fatty?' and I'd just say, 'Yeah, sure.' That sort of stuff never really got to me, I never needed any special psych-up but Boydy and some of the guys in the team would go bananas. About 2.30 on match days his eyes would start spinning and by 3.00 they'd be doing cartwheels. He'd go on the field and just scream at blokes. Theirs and ours. He'd be telling the opposition what he was going to do to them and telling our blokes what the opposition was going to do to them and what they were going to have to do back.

"In the dressing room before the game I'd just sit there watching them, shaking my head. Magilla and Boydy would stand there slapping each other across the face. And I mean really whacking each other. Then Boyd would turn to Terry Randall and start shouting at him like: 'You're a cat, Igor. They're gonna give it to you, Igor. You gonna give it back to them? You tough enough Igor? Are ya, are ya?' Every now and then he'd look over at me and just look away. I always got the feeling he thought there was something wrong with me because I didn't get into all that stuff. Like he felt I was a second-rater or something.

"One time Magilla and Randall belted each other so hard before the game they ran out bleeding."

More often than not that season the aggression was wasted. Manly never clicked, although there were some times when Boyd was simply awesome. "Of the three of them I always thought Boydy was going to be the best value and that's how it turned out," Vautin said. "I used to like playing with him and sometimes he was sensational. One time when we played Penrith he was unstoppable. The first half he turned in was the best I've ever seen from anyone. He absolutely smashed them. In the end they wouldn't run the ball up and when he had it he was like a bowling ball skittling them all out of the way. It was like watching a cartoon."

When Boyd played hard and within the rules he did a great job for his team but unfortunately for him, and Manly, all too often his aggression spilled over into violence. His sickening elbow to the jaw of Queensland prop Darryl Brohman in the 1983 Origin series saw him suspended for 12 months. Two games after his return he was again sent off and suspended a further 15 months on a charge of eye gouging Canterbury hooker Billy Johnstone. In his nine seasons in first grade Boyd was sent off eight times and suspended a total of 138 weeks. In his five seasons with Manly he played only 75 games.

"Les was his own worst enemy," said Vautin. "When he was copping those big suspensions he'd come up to training the night after the judiciary and you'd say something like, 'Bad luck, Boydy', and he'd say, 'Aw, they're trying to get rid of me, they're trying to force me out of the game.' I have to say I didn't have a lot of sympathy. He only had himself to blame. All the signals were there. Everyone knew what was happening. The league had made a decision to clean up the game and you either woke up to yourself or you didn't. Bob Cooper got that big suspension and Dallas Donnelly got one, so blokes starting thinking, 'Hey, what's going on here?' Their livelihood was at stake, they realised there were certain things you just couldn't get away with if you wanted to keep playing. You had to cut the rubbish out. But not Boydy. He just couldn't help himself."

As a player noted for his hard but fair play — in 13 seasons he was sent from the field only once, to the sin bin for a professional foul — Vautin was a big fan of the clean-up campaign headed by judiciary chairman Jim Comans. "I thought he did a great job," he said. "When I came to the club it was the tail end of the Manly-Wests feud. No-one went into a game against Wests feeling scared but you knew you were going to cop it. You really took your life in your hands."

The "feud" fuelled by Masters and his "Them versus Us" analogy began when the two clubs ventured to Melbourne for an exhibition match in 1978. As a promotional vehicle, the game was a disaster. Only 1200 fans showed up and what they saw was rugby league at its worst. The game developed into 80 minutes of brawling mayhem. When the fulltime whistle went, the cause had been set back 20 years in Victoria but for Wests coach Roy Masters, a realisation had dawned.

Just as Douglas Jardine had once detected a glint of uncertainty in the eye of Don Bradman when facing a high-pitched ball, Masters believed he had seen the Manly forwards buckle under the onslaught during the Melbourne "friendly". Jardine developed Bodyline. Masters developed the Fibros versus Silvertails.

Spurred on by Masters' rhetoric about the unfairness of their contrasting backgrounds, the poor, underprivileged Magpies would whip themselves into a frenzy at the prospect of taking on those high falutin' millionaire pretty boys from Manly. It was a recipe for violence and that was just what it produced. In the four years following the Melbourne match confrontations between the two clubs would result in six players being sent off and another two cited for foul play.

Finally the league decided enough was enough. The violence permeating the game, and in particular the much-publicised Wests-Manly powder keg was harming the image of rugby league and effecting development at both junior player and spectator level. The final straw was a segment on the top-rating TV program *Sixty Minutes* showing two Wests players being dragged apart by teammates when their pre-match face slapping got out of hand. Comans was given the job of cleaning up the game and Vautin for one applauded his appointment.

"It meant you could get on with playing football and not have to worry about any rubbish," he said. "It's a tough game and you expect to cop a bit but there are some things which are not on. When we played Wests in those early days you knew it was a pretty fair bet you were going to get hammered off the ball. It wasn't like we all went to training saying, 'We'd better watch it, we're playing Wests on Sunday.' We weren't scared of them, just wary. You had to have eyes in the back of your head and if you got off the field with everything intact and where it had been went you went on, you figured you'd done pretty well."

Not that all the violence surrounding the confrontation was as unsubtle as an elbow to the back of the head or thumb to the eye. Manly's gentle giant Steve Knight, a former Magpie himself, was twice sent off against Wests. "You couldn't get Knighty mad by belting him," said Vautin. "You had to say something to him, something that really dug deep. They'd obviously done their home-work."

Vautin was no fan of Masters' psychology: either the Fibros versus Silvertails spiel or the face slapping and pre-match wrestling it inspired. "For a start that sort of thing never worked with me and, secondly, I thought it was very limited." he said. "It might work once but surely it couldn't work twice."

The game changed markedly when Jim Comans arrived on the scene. Masters headed from Lidcombe to St George with its lavish leagues club known as the Taj Mahal. Eventually Wests-Manly games started resembling football matches rather than a cross between tag team wrestling and demolition derby. Families started returning to rugby league, players such as Vautin could concentrate on playing and the knucklemen could either knuckle under, or get forced out. Paul Vautin had played at the end of an era and survived. Les Boyd had not.

"In the end I got the feeling he was almost relieved when he was forced out of the Sydney competition," Vautin said of Boyd. "It was as if he hated it and all the trappings that went with it. He was a country boy at heart, he hated the city and the media attention and the pressure. Some people love it, but he couldn't cop it at all. You'd almost swear that deep down he wanted to get rubbed out. Sometimes when I was playing with him I thought he hated the game, but years later he was still playing back home in Cootamundra. Maybe that's all he ever wanted. It wasn't football he didn't like, it was everything going on around it."

It took Boyd nine seasons to get home. For a while it looked like Vautin wasn't going to be around for anywhere near as long. After the rave reviews and solid performances of his debut season, 1980 started out in direct contrast. Maybe it was the mental letdown of having proven to himself that he could make it, maybe it was over confidence, or maybe it was too many Big Macs in Hawaii. Whatever, Fatty was very much living up to his nickname when he turned up for pre-season training. All the hard work of the previous year went out the window when Thomson named the squad for Manly's first trial to be held at Boyd's home town of Cootamundra. Vautin, a stone overweight and back to his old position at the tail of all training runs, was not selected to make the trip.

It was a huge slap in the face for everyone's rookie of the year and almost as big a shock to Arthurson who had just doubled his pay. The club secretary soon called his young protege in for a chat. His words were short and very succinct. Pointing to the calendar on the his desk, he said simply: "See that Paul? It's not 1979 any more, it's 1980."

The redhead took the hint. For the second year running he put the hard work in on the training paddock and worked his way into the top side. In a team which couldn't seem to get its act together he was more than welcome, his workrate and enthusiasm often embarrassing his more illustrious teammates. He was glad to be back in first grade but 1980 is a year neither he nor anyone else in the team would like to remember. Almost fittingly, it ended disastrously for him.

Midway through the season Manly travelled to Lang Park for a midweek KB Cup match against Combined Brisbane. It was Vautin's first trip back home since moving to Sydney and he wanted to make a big impression, especially against old adversaries such as Wally Lewis and Mal Meninga. Things didn't go to plan. In keeping with Manly's year, the locals were putting the cleaners through the southerners when Vautin went in to tackle Meninga. His hand hit the big man's boot and immediately he knew he'd be playing no further part in the game. By the time he'd been helped to the dressing room he was in agony. It was a depressing moment for Vautin as he slumped against the wall in the visitors' dressing room. He had come back to Brisbane with dreams of a hero's welcome, now here he was in a beaten team with his hand swollen to the size of a Sunday roast.

It was then that a dressing room attendant called out that someone was at the door to see him. "Okay," Vautin shouted, and in walked his brother Geoffrey whom he hadn't seen for two years. Now in his late 20s, Geoffrey had moved to a hostel in the country, returning home on weekends and holidays. He had boasted to anyone and everyone at the hostel of his brother's visit to play at Lang Park until finally a carer had agreed to bring a group down for the game.

"Paul," he said, sitting down on the bench next to him and gently taking his brother's shattered hand, "sore, sore hand. Hope it gets better."

And with the delighted roars of the Lang Park crowd echoing above them, Geoffrey Vautin sat comforting his younger brother as the tears welled in their eyes.

Later that night it was George who took Paul to a 24-hour medical centre for attention. When the doctor came out after having seen the x-rays, he asked: "What happened, did someone smash you with a hammer?"

Thinking back to the sight of Mal Meninga bearing down on him Vautin could only reply, "Yeah, sort of" before hearing the news that he would be out of action for six weeks. He made it back into first grade against Balmain but the end of a disappointing season was inevitable. Manly played ninth-placed Cronulla in the last match of the minor premiership. If the Sea Eagles won they were in the play-offs. They lost 35-12 but such was the feeling in the team there were few tears shed.

"Most of the players were glad the season was over," said Vautin. "The commitee wasn't too fussed though. They sacked the coach."

The knives had been out for Thomson almost from the start of the competition rounds. There were even rumours that Manly had attempted to buy out Stanton's contract from Redcliffe and bring him back midway thorough the year. Eventually it was Ray Ritchie, yet another home-grown international, who took up the reins and Arthurson moved quickly to add more starch up front to the club by signing Parramatta's Geoff Gerard and Kiwi international Mark Broadhurst.

Although he packed down with his boyhood hero Terry Randall and alongside the likes of Boyd and Ian Thomson, Vautin rates Broadhurst the toughest man he ever played with at Manly.

"You couldn't hurt him — and there were plenty who tried," he said. "No matter what sort of punishment he had to cop he'd take it and keep coming back for more without complaining. For some reason Ray Ritchie never really went for him and he spent a fair bit of time in second grade. I couldn't believe it. I thought he was a sensational player. He should have been a superstar at Manly."

Cabdriver Ritchie, who played on the wing in the 1957 World Cup was, like Stanton and Thomson, a Manly man through and through. The difference with his predecessor was that he knew the Sydney competition well, having coached the reserve grade side with some success.

Vautin always admired Ritchie for his enthusiasm and devotion to the club, but their relationship proved a stormy one. "Ray wasn't a bad bloke," he said. "He was one of those guys who would do anything for Manly. He was always working for the club in some capacity or other. He was a funny bloke. He had these sayings he used all the time. He used to say stuff like, 'I'd commit my mother to a lunatic asylum if it meant getting two points from Sunday's game' or 'You can lead a camel to the well but you can't make him drink.' One of his favorites was 'dropping the ball is like pissing into the wind.'

"He just loved the place but right from the start he gave me the impression he didn't like the way I did things. The way I went about my job wasn't necessarily wrong, just different to the way he wanted things done."

The first clash came early in the season. In round four Manly travelled to Penrith Park. Had it been a Sunday it would have been just another day at the office for the Manly players but the game was scheduled for a Saturday and as far as Vautin and John Gibbs were concerned, not just any Saturday. It was Doncaster Day.

The pair stopped at every TAB between Brookvale and Penrith, placing their bets for the early races. Came time to get ready for the match, their bodies might have been in the dressing room but their minds were very much at Randwick — and their heads buried in their sports bags. "We had our trannies in our bags and were listening to the race," Gibbs admitted. "The other blokes were getting psyched up but we were taking as long as we could to get our boots on so we had a reason to have our heads down around our knees. It was like: oops, this boot isn't tied up properly, I'd better do it again."

Manly lost the game 28-10 but Gibbs managed to shine, taking one radio station's man-of-the-match award. It wasn't enough to save the whole team from the wrath of Ritchie at the next training run.

"We were standing around before training and Ritchie was giving it to us and up pipes Les Boyd with, 'Ray, how can we be expected to win when two players are listening to a race before the game?'" Then Gibbs said to Boyd, 'You worry about your game and I'll worry about mine', and that was the end of it but Ritchie wasn't too impressed."

Vautin sensed that, so far as his relationship with Ritchie was concerned, the writing was on the wall. "Nothing was said about it then but I got the feeling that wasn't going to be the end of it. You could say we didn't see eye to eye," he said.

The feeling that Ritchie wasn't one of his biggest fans was borne out emphatically towards the end of what had been a good season for both Vautin and the team. "My hand had mended well and I went straight back into first grade from the start of the year," Vautin recalled. "All the problems of the previous year were over and the side was going real well. We all thought we could go all the way. Canterbury were one of the big guns and we blitzed them with about six games to go. It was a pretty impressive performance and

I was looking forward to getting stuck into Souths the next week.

"On the night before the game a few of us went around to Krilich's place for a game of cards. There was Thrower, Alan Thompson, Goldie Walker, Peter Peters and a couple of others. It was a pretty quiet night and we headed off early. Then the next morning I woke up sick as a dog with the 'flu and had to pull out.

"Ritchie brought Mark Broadhurst up from reserves and moved Goldie back from the second row to lock and they won by about 20 points. I was right the next week so I expected to go straight back into the side but when I arrived at training Ritchie pulled me over and asked how I thought they went.

"I said I thought they went well but then he started going on about how well everyone played and how he didn't want to change the team. He's saying: 'Goldie had a blinder Paul, Broadhurst had a blinder.'

"I said, 'Yeah, that's great Ray, but I've played the last 17 games in first grade.' He just says, 'Well, you're not in.' So I told him to go and get stuffed and stormed off home." Vautin would not play first grade again until May the next year. "Now let this be a lesson to all the kiddies at home," he said, "Never tell the coach to get stuffed." It was to be a lesson hard learned. "He wouldn't even put me on as reserve," he said, "I think he just didn't like my attitude."

The team went on to make the finals for the first time since Vautin had joined the club and he wasn't part of it. He sat morosely on the sideline as Newtown — led, significantly, by former Fibro Tom Raudonikis — got stuck into Manly from the opening scrum. The brawl that followed was reminiscent of the pre-Comans era at its worst. And in the thick of it was Mark Broadhurst. "They gave Broadhurst everything they had and he still kept coming back," Vautin said. "His jumper was red with blood but he still played a great game. That match summed up Mark Broadhurst to me. He was as tough as any man I ever saw on a football field."

But even Broadhurst's mettle up front wasn't enough. Newtown won 20-15 and the Manly players started thinking about next season. When Vautin started that season in reserve grade, his career was looking shaky, to say the least. As had happened before, it was Arthurson who stepped in to push him back on the rails. "I was in reserve grade and going nowhere," Vautin said. "I was trying, but the motivation wasn't there. I was really just going through the motions. Ray put me on a couple of times as a reserve but I wasn't ever a chance to make the side. Finally Arko called me in for a chat."

Arthurson's luck was finally starting to change. The disasters of 1979 and '80 were far behind the club. His expensive gamble of buying the Wests stars was paying off and adding the starch of the rugged Broadhurst had given the Sea Eagles forwards credibility. The team had made the final in 1981 and was showing all the signs of going even further in '82. Arthurson could have written Vautin off as a promising youngster who never realised his potential and forgotten about him. That he didn't is testimony to his undoubted genius as a club administrator.

"He called me in and asked what the hell was going on," Vautin recalled. "I told him that all I wanted to do was play first grade and I didn't think there was any chance that was going to happen as long as Ray was coach."

Arthurson deliberated for a few seconds before speaking. In that short time Paul Vautin's career was probably in the balance. "Okay Paul," he said, "I want you to promise me something. If you get back into first grade I want your word that you'll give it everything you've got, that you'll get back to being the player we all know you are."

Vautin gave his word and the next week, for the first time in eight months, heard his name read out in the first grade team. Ironically it was to be against Canterbury, the team he had last been selected to play against in the top grade. True to his word, he gave it everything and made a team high 37 tackles.

"The first person to come up and say well played was Ray," he said.

It was to be the start of one of Vautin's most rewarding periods in the game. Before the season was out he would have represented his state and his country, won man of the match in a KB Cup final victory and played in a grand final.

He also snared another large contract, thanks to some typically straight answers to a reporter's questions in the aftermath to the KB Cup win. "I wasn't even in the team to run on but Boyd pulled out at the last minute and I went in off the bench," Vautin said. "It was a great night. We beat Newtown to win the cup for the first time and I won the best player award."

In the euphoria of the winner's dressing room, *Daily Mirror* league writer Ian Hanson congratulated Paul and asked about his future. "Oh, I dunno mate," he replied. "I'm not signed yet and I'll see what's on offer. You've got to do the right thing for your future, haven't you?"

The next day the *Mirror* splashed on the story that Manly's cup hero would quit the club if he didn't receive a major pay increase. "Arko nearly had kittens," Vautin said. "The phone was ringing off the hook while I was still in bed. I told him what I've always believed, that if someone asks me a fair question, I'll give them a straight answer. That's what happened with Hanson. Arko told me I'd better come in and have a talk."

In the meantime Vautin got another call. From Jack Gibson, coach of premiers Parramatta and a legend in the game. He and Paul had never met but the coach had obviously been watching the progress of the Queenslander with interest. "He was pretty impressive, really," said Vautin. "He had this funny slow way of talking but it was very flattering that he was interested. I got off the phone thinking, 'this is alright.' He didn't beat around the bush."

Vautin takes off Gibson's drawl as he remembers the exchange. "Jack Gibson here Paulll ..."

"Yeah Jack."

"We'd like to have you come to Parramatta, Paulll. What are they paying you there? Well, we can do better than that, Paulll. Where are you living, Paulll? Well, we can get you a nice house on the river. You know Parramatta River, Paulll?"

"Can't say as I do, Jack."

"Aw, it's a real nice river, Paulll. What sort of job you got Paulll? We can do better than that, Paulll, you're smarter than that aren't you?"

"I'd like to think so, Jack."

"Well, we can fix that up. What sort of car you drive, Paulll? You like cars?"

And so it went on, with Gibson's offer finally totting up at $47,000 a season, huge money by 1982 standards.

One of the first people Vautin told was Ron Wheatley. "I told him to sign as soon as he could, before Gibson changed his mind," Wheatley said. "But he told me he couldn't think of playing for anyone else. He said Manly was like his family. I told him he was mad. I've been around those Manly blokes all my life. I knew what they'd do to him in the end."

Vautin went to his meeting with Arthurson late in the season with Gibson's offer still ringing in his ears. He didn't hide it from Arthurson, telling him straight off what he would have to beat. Arko went into his act. "Paul," he said, "now I'm talking to you now as a father talking to his son because that's what you are to me Paul, a son ... Paul, the type of money you're talking is just crazy. Now, I've got a set amount here Paul. An international gets $30,000. No more, no less."

The money was an important issue, but no more so than the chance of playing under Gibson. Vautin was back in first grade under Ritchie but their relationship had progressed only slightly since the clash at training a year earlier. There were rumours that Ritchie would not be renewing his own two-year contract with the club. Vautin told Arthurson he could not make up his mind until he knew who would be coaching. The answer he received was a tonic. After swearing Vautin to secrecy Arthurson confirmed that Ritchie would not be returning. His place would be taken by Bob Fulton.

"Why, I was just speaking to Bozo this morning," he said. "Put the phone down as you walked in the room, as a matter of fact, and you know what we were talking about Paul? You. Bob is very, very interested in what you're doing, Paul. He's got big plans for you, son. Very big plans."

"That changed everything," Vautin said. "I never wanted to leave Manly and now Fulton was going to be coach. He was a legend and I thought he was a good coach too. He'd had some good results at Easts without a lot to work with. It changed things a lot."

But there was still that money on offer.

Arthurson started playing dirty. "When did you last go to the beach Paul," he asked.

"This morning."

"Really, and tell me Paul, how long did it take you to get there? Three minutes? Four? You can't get to the beach in five minutes from Parramatta, Paul. What are you going to do, swim in Parramatta River? You'll get typhoid."

Again Vautin brought up the money.

"Okay," Arthurson said, "here's what I'll do. I'll give you $70,000 for two years and we'll advance you the money for the second year up front on one condition, that you put it into a home unit. I don't want you to leave this game with nothing to show for it Paul. Now, that's $70,000 up front."

"I signed on the spot," Vautin said. "I was as happy as Larry. Bob Fulton coaching and $70,000 for two years. It was only when I was in the car that I started thinking, hang on, he's done it to me again. I was dropping 24 grand. Still, in the long run it didn't matter. I was still where I wanted to be, I was looking forward to being coached by Fulton and I did end up buying that home unit. There was no use worrying about the money. You couldn't put it over on Arko no matter how hard you tried."

The new contract was vindication of the faith Arthurson had shown when Vautin's future had looked less than bright only months earlier. The year had progressed better than probably even Arko had imagined possible. All it needed was a grand final win and a spot with the '82 Kangaroos announced that night to make it perfect. It was not to be. What should have been one of Vautin's greatest memories in rugby league turned out to be a day he and his teammates would rather forget.

"It's probably easy to look back at things years later and say what could have happened and what should have happened but there were a few things going on around that game that just weren't on," he said.

"We hammered Parramatta 20-nil in the major semi and went straight into the grand final. We had that week off but Ray ran us every day. I remember a couple of nights before the grand final it was absolutely pouring but he had us out there running our rings out. It was madness. It was my first grand final and I should have memories of the feeling of excitement and the build-up but all I can remember is running round in the rain.

"And he wouldn't tell us what the team was going to be. It was getting closer and closer to the match but we still weren't sure who was going to be in the pack.

"Boyd hadn't played in the semi and Goldie had an absolute blinder but Ray just wouldn't say which one would be playing."

Vautin believes the late decision on the team's make-up contributed to an uncertain build-up — as did the rumours about why it happened.

"The players were in the dressing room ready to run out when Ritchie told Goldie he wasn't in. To my mind he had been our best player against Parramatta. He deserved to be there."

Neither Vautin nor Krilich believes Manly could have beaten Parramatta in that match but the incident still raises high emotions among the players of the day. "Parramatta were a champion team, there's no doubt about it," Vautin said. "That backline — Sterling, Kenny, Cronin, Grothe, I don't think any backline has ever come close — except maybe Manly in '87. We all played badly for some reason. Maybe we played our grand final two weeks before, but the way the team was selected left a lot to be desired.

"It probably didn't make any great difference to the team on the day but it made a hell of a lot of difference to Goldie Walker," said Krilich.

The match, won by the Eels 21-8, was an anti-climax for Manly who had played brilliantly in beating Parramatta in the major semi-final. The Sea Eagles had ventured to the Sydney Cricket Ground to watch the Eels perform a similar demolition job on Fulton's Easts in the final. "We knew then we had a real game on our hands but we just didn't fire on the day," Vautin said, "it was hopeless."

And things were going to get a lot worse before they got better. After making his Test debut against New Zealand earlier in the season Vautin was considered a certainty for the Kangaroo tour. "He was in everyone's side," said Wally Lewis. "I'd told him we'd see each other on the plane and he said he was hoping. I thought he was a very good chance. He'd done everything the selectors had asked and done it well. In my opinion he had the runs on the board."

And in the opinion of most other judges too. "All the scribes had me in their side," Vautin said. "You don't like to tell yourself you're in, but you can hope."

The night had started off badly when John Gibbs got into an argument with a doorman who refused to allow his mother into the official dinner back at the club. "It was horrible," said Leila of that evening. She had driven down from Brisbane with George for the match. "Everyone was very disappointed with the way the game had gone and then we were sitting there waiting for them to announce the Kangaroos. It was just a terrible night."

Club president Roy Bull climbed onto the stage to read out the names of Manly's tourists. "First up, he announced Max Krilich was captain and called him onto the stage," Vautin said. "He was saying how proud the club was of Max and while he was talking Max looked over at the piece of paper with all the names on it. He looked up and caught my eye at the back of the room and shook his head. That's how I knew. I felt like someone had smashed me in the face."

When the names were read out George pushed away his plate. "I couldn't eat another bite," he said. "I would have been sick."

It was a depressing end to what had been a marvellous year but Vautin could not afford to dwell on it. As a professional sportsman he had to throw himself back into his work and unlike the year before, the future looked very, very bright. He had a new contract in his pocket, he was earning more money than ever before and one of the most important influences on his career was about to enter his life: the Prodigal Son, Bob Fulton.

Bozo's Back!

Bob Fulton was, is and probably always will be, Manly's favourite son. Signed by Arthurson from Wollongong in 1966 as a 17-year-old, "Bozo" became the embodiment of the Manly style of backline play. Superbly fit, strong, fast and with uncanny timing and anticipation, he *was* Manly for a whole generation of Sea Eagle fans. So much so that in the early 1970s, when the church on Manly Corso erected the placard "What would you do if Jesus came to Manly tomorrow?" someone wrote the answer, "Move Fulton to five-eighth and play him in the centres." To many, this was blasphemy. At the time Fulton was doing fine in the centres and shouldn't be moved for anyone.

Arthurson has never made any secret of his admiration for Fulton. To be ranked in the second echelon of Manly players — where he puts Vautin — is praise in itself.

Fulton scored a field goal in the club's initial first grade premiership win in 1972. A year later he was in the centres in the grand final against Cronulla and scored two tries to be the difference between the sides. Three years later Manly were there again, finishing 13-10 over Parramatta, with Frank Stanton coach and Fulton captain.

And then the unthinkable. After 213 first grade games, 510 points and 11 years, Fulton left Manly. Millionaire businessman Kerry Packer, an Eastern Suburbs supporter and great fan of Fulton, made an offer too good to refuse. Even Arthurson, a man renowned for his skill with a pen and cheque book, was powerless. Fulton rang him from Packer's office with the unsigned contract sitting in front of him.

"What's he offering, Boze?" Arthurson asked. Then, hearing the answer, offered: "Take it." He knew when he was beaten.

But now, seven years had passed. Fulton had achieved great success with Easts, moving from captain-coach to fulltime coach and taking the Roosters to two minor premierships and the 1980 grand final. If Arthurson harboured a dream in the twilight of his career as Manly secretary, it was to see Fulton return to Brookvale — and this time, Arko wouldn't be denied.

For Vautin, the return of Bozo signalled the start of a virtual second career. "I was excited about him coming — just about everybody was," he said. "He'd had good results at Easts with some pretty ordinary sides. Paul McCabe had played under him at Easts and he told me he was a good coach. Hard, but good. Macca told me Fulton used to really bash 'em up at training. He'd call runs at two in the afternoon or midday and everyone had to front. It sounded a bit different to what we were used to and that's how it turned out. He really turned the whole joint around."

Manly had achieved respectable results over the previous few years but Vautin believes that was through the talent of the individual players rather than any master plan. Fulton proved the ultimate professional and the majority of Manly players responded.

"There were some blokes who didn't like him. They reckoned the place was cliquey and if you weren't in Fulton's gang you wouldn't get anywhere. I never saw it. The fact of the matter is when you are young you don't care about any of that crap. All you want to do is play football. It's only when you get old and angry that you can be bothered listening to all the talk that goes on around the place."

Fulton brought a number of top players with him from Easts, players such as Noel Cleal, Kerry Boustead, Ian Schubert and Dave Brown. He also brought a professional outlook to coaching that swept right through the club. "Every Tuesday he'd have us in there watching the video of the previous game," Vautin said. "Ray Ritchie used to show us the video but we'd be falling asleep. Bozo didn't show us the whole thing, he'd have it all cut down into certain points. If he got you to watch something, there was a reason. It wasn't just sitting down and watching the thing for the sake of it.

"We trained bloody hard, everyone was really fit, but we had fun too. Bozo was a shocking bagger. He'd give everyone a hard time, but it was done in fun. One time we were watching the video of this game against Balmain. Phil Sigsworth scored a 30-metre try and there was a very good shot of him running right towards the camera. Now Siggy didn't have any teeth. He used to take his falsies out before the game, so in this video he looked about 108 years old. He was running towards the camera with his mouth open and it was all gums and wrinkles. Bozo must have shown that try in slow motion about six times. Everyone was killing themselves laughing and yelling out comments and Siggy was sitting up the back swearing and yelling back. It was all good fun, it made for good harmony."

On field the Sea Eagles were having a super year, and none better than Vautin. Early in the piece Fulton pulled him aside. "Listen Fatty," he said, "they tell me around here you're just a tackler but that's bullshit. When I was at Easts I used to tell my blokes to watch out for you because you had a good step and could make things happen. We used to think of you as a danger man."

It was the confidence booster Vautin needed. He played 38 first grade games that season and rates it the best club season he ever had. "They whinge these days that there are too many games in the season," he says. "They should have been around in '83. We had 14 clubs and 26 games. For the first three weeks of the comp we'd play our Saturday or Sunday match and then have to back up again on either Tuesday or Wednesday to get through all the games."

And later in the season there was the midweek cup which, if successful, meant another five games. Manly were successful. And ironically, that was the club's problem. Going into the season the club had 15 internationals on its books. By winning the midweek competition and making it to the grand final of the Winfield Cup, plus having so many players take part in minor representative matches, State of Origin and Tests, the physical demands were enormous.

When Fulton returned to Manly, he brought with him the allegiance of Packer and while rumours that Packer was paying Fulton's salary were never confirmed, he did offer as much support to the players as possible. In the basement of his Park St, Sydney, headquarters, Packer had built the country's swankiest health club, The Hyde Park Club. On Monday mornings the battered Manly players would head for the club to recharge their batteries. But not to the main area, where the rank and file members worked out. Oh no, the Manly boys were given access to the inner sanctum, the private gymnasium complete with spa and sauna, which Packer reserved for himself and special guests.

"Sometimes it was all we could do to get in there a couple of times a week," Vautin said. "Sometimes we couldn't train at all we were so knackered."

The toll was high. Long-serving Manly and Kangaroo skipper Max Krilich was forced out of the game with a bad neck injury. Such was Manly's depth that his place was taken by another Kangaroo, Ray Brown. "That summed up the club," Vautin said., "Ray was an international playing in reserve grade, but he wasn't alone. Our reserve grade was a fantastic side. We had blokes like Brown, Ian Thomson, Goldie Walker and Ian Schubert. They'd all played for Australia and they couldn't get a regular run in firsts. That kept everyone on their toes, kept us all going."

And how. The team played some sensational football and recorded huge wins. "It was probably the best side I've ever coached," Fulton said. "We absolutely blitzed some sides."

With Krilich out the captaincy reverted to five-eighth Alan Thompson who, with Krilich, remains the best club captain Vautin ever played under. "They were different styles of captains," Vautin said. "If someone scored a try against us when Max was captain, he'd get us behind the posts and call us everything under the sun. Thommo was different. He'd say, 'Well, they scored that because of so and so. Now from the kick off, let's go back, punch three down the blind, do an XY move and kick into the left hand corner."

The combination of Fulton and Thompson brought out the best in some players. Graham Eadie, after average seasons in 1981 and '82, had a superb year and young halfback Phil Blake proved the sensation of the year. "He'd come along the year before, but in '83 he was just unbelievable," Vautin said. "He topped the try-scoring list with 27, daylight second. He was just a freak. They showed a tape of 10 of his tries at the Dally M awards that year and they were amazing. They just don't happen that way now, and the defence wasn't that bad. He was just too quick."

That was Blake's greatest moment. He never again captured the brilliance that he showed in his first year under Fulton, a fact that still puzzles Vautin. "I like Phil," he says, "he's a good bloke, but he was always a disappointment to me. Having seen him that year, I thought he could have been anything but he just never went on with it. He should have played for Australia at the very least. He had pace, skills, he was tough in defence but he just never kicked on. He had one good year for Souths but apart from that, he just never looked like the same player again."

Another anchor for the side was Easts convert Dave Brown. "He was the rock, there was no tougher man than him," Vautin said.

On the other side of the scrum was Geoff Gerard. Vautin had respect for the former Parramatta prop, but it wasn't shared throughout the club. "We had a function at the end of 1984 after Jethro had left the club and some of the lower grade blokes were mouthing off about him. Apparently they didn't have a very high opinion of him. They called him Softprop, but I thought he was good. He did a top job for Manly that year."

As the season neared its end, the Manly team sent out each week often bore little resemblance to the one which had started the season. Krilich was gone, Boyd was gone and, at the business end of the year both props were out for extended periods. Fulton had no alternative but to play Vautin and McCabe in the front row in a three-match sequence which included the KB Cup Final.

"The first one was against Norths at Brookvale," Vautin recalled. "Their props were Don McKinnon and Steve Mayoh — both the size of a block of flats." Manly won 54-16. A few days later it was the cup final, won 26-6 over Cronulla and then a win over Souths.

"I was loving it," said Vautin, "front row is a very simple game. You just have to stay in the middle and tackle. That suited me fine. People ask me what I reckon was the best game I ever played for Manly and I say that KB Cup final. For some reason it was one of those games when everything went right."

Despite his mastery of the position Vautin returned to the second row, but that did not signal an ease of pressure on the players. "It was a very emotional time for us," said Vautin. "It was like we were getting up in the morning and saying 'geez, here we go again,' but Bozo never let up on us. The training had to drop back a bit because sometimes we couldn't get a fit 13 along, but mentally, he kept us on the job the whole time. He'd be telling us, 'Here's where you're going right, here's where you're going wrong!'"

Manly won the minor premiership by 10 points, and entered the final series warm, if not red-hot, favourites. The judges believed the Eagles would be too classy for a Parramatta side chasing three in a row, but before that question would be settled, Vautin had a few other competitions to appear in.

Throughout the season he had been mentioned as a possible Rothmans Medal winner. By the time the winning post was in sight he had firmed from a possible to the best of probables. One afternoon paper quoted him at 2-1. Although not a regular at awards nights, he was contacted by a club official and told he'd better be there. "All the tipsters in the papers reckoned I was a good thing," he said, "some blokes had me winning by 10 points. I don't usually go to those things. They're a bit of a wank if you ask me, but this official reckoned it would be embarrassing for the club if I won and wasn't there."

So Vautin rented a dinner suit and got along to the Sydney Hilton, thus beginning one of the most embarrassing nights of his life. Throughout the evening, his name was mentioned by everyone near a microphone, his hand shaken raw by well-wishers. All eyes were on him as presentation time drew closer and then ... nothing.

"As the night got closer and there was all this publicity I started thinking, 'Geez, I'd better win this or I'm going to look like a bit of a goose,'" he said. "Right on both counts. I didn't win and I looked like a goose. At the end of the night they put up this leader board and after every round they'd take off one name. I didn't even rate a mention on the thing. It was one of the great wastes of time."

After Michael Eden had won the medal and made his acceptance speech, printed sheets with all the votes issued were placed on every table. Vautin did not bother to look but Dave Brown, who was sitting next to him did. "Hey Fatty," Brown said drolly, "you got five votes. Well done."

Vautin's answer is not repeatable, but he did win back lost pride a week later at the Dally M Awards. Unlike the Rothmans Medal which is voted for by referees, the Dally Ms are decided by the working press and, in one category, by the players themselves.

Vautin won the categories Second Rower of The Year, Representative Player of the Year and, to him, most importantly, Players' Player of The Year.

"That was the one I was really happy about," he said. "With sportswriters, well, I know it can go in phases. One minute everybody is saying, 'This bloke is great,' the next they've all decided he's a dunce. With the players' player award it was different, it meant I could play a bit."

For good measure Vautin rounded off the season with the NSW

Rugby League Writers' Association Player of The Year Award. All were great compliments and are still displayed proudly in Vautin's home, but the real honour was a few weeks up the track. As they had the previous year, Manly beat Parramatta quite easily in the semi-final and progressed straight through to the grand final. Vautin says the preparation was perfect, but it wasn't to be his — or Manly's — day.

"You couldn't fault the lead-up," he said. "Bozo was great, we knew who was in the team unlike the year before, and the training went perfectly. Bozo was very controlled, very professional. They tell me that when he first started at Easts he used to be into the 'Get out there and bash 'em' stuff, but by the time he came back to Manly he'd got past that. It was more 'You'll beat these blokes if you do this, this and this ...' That suited me just fine. I was never into that forced motivation stuff. With Bozo it was tactics and discipline."

That might have been so, but no amount of tactics or discipline was going to help Vautin. A few months before the game, he had bought a home unit at Queenscliff and George and Leila drove down to stay with him and watch the grand final. At 5pm on the night before the game, Vautin suddenly began to feel off colour. He went to the bathroom and found there was a large lump in his groin. He was obviously suffering some infection. For four hours he sat in front of the television willing it to pass, but with his parents starting to wonder about the trips to the toilet every two minutes, he finally had to admit defeat. He went to another room and rang Fulton at 9pm.

"G'day Fatty," the coach said, "how ya feeling?"

"Pretty good Boze, except for one thing ..."

"Yeah, what's that?"

"I've got a big lump in my groin and I'm feeling crook as a dog."

Once Fulton could be convinced this was not a practical joke, he told Vautin to be at the club doctor's home in five minutes.

"I'll be back soon," Vautin told his disbelieving parents and headed of into the night. The doctor gave him a shot of penicillin and some antibiotics. Vautin spent a sleepless night, with one eye on his groin and the other on the clock. At 7.30am Fulton was on the phone.

"How ya going?" he asked.

"Fine," Vautin lied.

"Look, I've been talking to Arko and he's a bit concerned ..."

"Shit," thought Vautin, "they're going to leave me out."

"But we've decided we'd rather have you half fit than anyone else, so even though you're not 100 percent we're going to go with you."

Vautin says the infection didn't affect his performance but Manly were never in the hunt. "We just struck a Parramatta side which had arguably six of the best players in the world," Fulton said.

"There was a howling gale blowing and even though it was 12-nil at half time I still thought we were handily placed. We scored soon after half time and I thought we were going to go on and win but a couple of our blokes made mistakes and that was it. People say we were certainties in '87 but I thought we were just as good things in '83. Parramatta just came out and showed us how good they really were.

"The test in a situation like that is to ask how many of the Manly side would you put in that Parramatta side? I reckon maybe about half. It was that close but they did better on the day."

Vautin says Manly were never in the hunt after an atrocious start. "In the first five minutes McCabe threw a long pass to no-one and Brett Kenny scored under the posts for 6-nil," he recalled. "Then they made a big break down the blind and we saw something we never expected ever to see: Graham Eadie missed a tackle on Eric Grothe. It was one of the tackles you wouldn't expect anyone but Graham to get.

"Soon after halftime they put up a bomb and three of our blokes watched it bounce straight back into Kenny's arms. We came back with a try to make it 18-6 but that was as close as we got. There were plenty of tears shed in the dressing room after that one, but the fact was we'd only lost five times all year and three times were against Parramatta."

After two years sitting disappointed in the stand George Vautin vowed never to watch his son in another grand final. "I'm a Jonah," he said.

For the Manly players the defeat was a shattering end to a superb year, but there was still one more fixture to be played before packing up the boots. The team had agreed to a promotional match in Darwin and at least one member of the touring party was giving it the importance of an Ashes decider. "With a few weeks left in the season we noticed that Bozo was really getting involved in the training," Vautin recalled. "He was busting a gut in the fitness stuff and we had to ask him what he was doing."

"I'm getting ready for Darwin," came the reply.

Sure enough, when the match against Darwin had been on for a few minutes a familiar blond head was seen warming up on the sideline. Fulton's last game had been in 1978 but he launched himself into the match like an 18-year-old.

"He came on like a tornado," Vautin said. "He was running around everywhere, getting up blokes, throwing himself into the tackles."

At one stage Fulton called Vautin to run off one of his passes. "Fatty," he screamed, "run into the hole." Vautin took one look at the Darwin forwards lurking nearby and quickly relayed his own message. "This isn't 1968 and there's no bloody hole," he shouted back, "now start acting your age."

A few minutes later, a Darwin player made a break in centre field and set off for the line. Vautin turned half-heartedly and jogged off in pursuit. "I thought, 'What the hell, it's 45 degrees, we're ahead by thirty and it's a friendly game.'" he said. "I was in no hurry, then this blur of blond hair burst past me and took off after him. He got him too. Pulled him down a couple of metres out."

As Fulton climbed to his feet and stood in the marker position he looked up at the approaching Vautin. "That's the way you do it, Blue," he beamed.

The match might have been a triumphant swansong for Fulton but it nearly ended the career of Vautin. He suffered a torn hamstring late in the match and was forced to pull out of the upcoming Queensland tour of England. He had hoped the rest might have been enough, but if anything it got worse with time. By the time November came around, he couldn't walk. Finally Fulton sent him to Dr Neil Halpin. "Neil was the doctor who saved Mitchell Cox's career," Vautin said. "When Mitchell was with Norths he went through a period where he just couldn't play. He'd been going to doctors for months and taking antibiotics but nothing seemed to work. Neil took one look at him, diagnosed hepatitis and had him back on the field in a matter of weeks.

"It was the same with me. In January everyone was training but

I couldn't even jog. Neil put me in hospital and stretched the hamstring under a general anaesthetic. In two weeks I was running three-quarter pace and I played my 100th first grade game in the first match of the season."

Years later when he was playing with Easts, Vautin was talking to Halpin and thanked him once more for saving his career. "That's alright," the doctor replied. "By the way, I never told you how I did that, did I?"

"No."

"We lifted the leg right above your head. You know, there was a one in 10 chance it could have snapped altogether and you would never have played again."

"Neil," said Vautin, "I'm very glad you never told me that."

Halpin got Vautin back on the field for 1984, but it proved a disappointing year. Just as he was hitting form he broke his cheekbone playing in a Test match against Great Britain and was sidelined for eight weeks. He came back in time for the semi-finals but Manly exited in the worst of ways. After leading South Sydney 14-nil after eight minutes, the Rabbitohs came back and won 22-18. The reputation of Manly as a team that faltered at the business end of the season gained momentum.

It had been a different Manly which had embarked on the 1984 season — a Manly without Arko. Before the beginning of the season Arthurson announced that he was taking up the position of executive chairman of the NSW rugby league and chairmanship of the Australia rugby league. After 33 years with the club, 21 as club secretary, the loss of Arthurson was a huge blow. He was replaced by John Tenison, but Manly were losing much more than a club secretary, they were losing their most steadying force, an institution, and for Vautin and Fulton in particular, the void was great.

"I think Bozo was really stunned," Vautin said. "They both had a lot of time for each other. Arko used to call Fulton his son and Bozo said Ken was the greatest influence on his career. Arko was keen to get Bozo back to the club and I think Bozo thought it would be like him and Ken against the rest. The two of them working together. It all started off so well. We absolutely romped in the Club Championship and I think Bozo felt a bit let down when Arko left after just one season — I know I missed him.

"In all the time I played in Sydney I never came across a club administrator who came close to him. He was the best by a country mile. Up against him the others were just cardboard cut-outs. One of the best things about him was he could make you feel like you were the best player in the club and there's nothing like a bit of praise to make a guy try harder.

"I remember after the games he'd come down to the dressing room and pull you aside. He'd say, 'Paul, mate, dead set you were the best player on the field today by miles. I don't know who got man of the match but I know who won my vote. You did the club proud today.' You'd go off to have your shower feeling 10 feet tall. Then someone like Max Krilich would come in and say, 'Hey, you know what Arko just told me? He reckons I was the best on the field by a mile.' You'd say, 'What? He just told me that too!' Turns out he would have gone around telling everyone the same thing. He used to go up to my parents when they were down and say, 'George, you must be very proud of that son of yours. He was our best player out there today.' They'd come up all smiles and I never had the heart to tell them he said that to everyone in the room."

By the end of the season Arthurson had been joined by all of the premiership winning team of 1978, the team which Vautin had joined when he came to the club. The last game of the season signalled the end of an era for Manly and, in a way, for Vautin. He had come into the side in 1979 an innocent 19-year-old and looked on in awe as the four giants of the club went about their work. Terry Randall, Graham Eadie, Max Krilich and Alan Thompson were, to Vautin, what Manly was all about in his first five years with the club.

"As far as I was concerned, they were the greatest," he said. "There are other legends in the club of course, going right back, but these were the ones I played with and when they were all gone at the end of '84 it was like starting all over again. They had been there so long, they meant so much to all the other players. It was strange to think they wouldn't be there any more. As far as Manly were concerned they had given great service but, personally, they had all been a great help to me as the years went on.

"I'd always idolised Randall. He was the player I used to pretend to be in the backyard footy games, the one I most looked out for when Manly were playing on the telly. It was really strange to arrive from Brisbane and then a few weeks later be packing down alongside him. He was a real quiet sort of bloke. I'd never say we got to be friends but we got on okay and I thought we worked pretty well together. I remember packing in the scrum with him. I'd put my arm around his back and you could just feel the strength coming through. I like to think some of it rubbed off. He was a very tough bloke. He never stopped trying. His last year was in '82. He only played about four games all season but he was there in the grand final. It was sad we couldn't win it for him. He hung his boots on a peg in the SCG dressing room and left them there. He walked out and never looked back.

"Max got forced out because of a neck injury he got in a Test match. He was a great leader and an underrated player I reckon. He was totally fearless, courageous. It didn't matter how badly he got smashed, it never worried Thrower. He just kept going. That's what made him such an inspirational captain.

"Wombat went out after the '83 grand final. He hung his boots up like Igor but he went back and got them later of course. People ask me who's the best player I ever played alongside and the answer's Wally Lewis. But the best Manly player? Graham Eadie. There was nothing he couldn't do. He gave us such a great feeling of security knowing he was behind us. Sometimes there'd be breaks made and you'd think, 'He's Harry Hundred-to-One' but, sure enough, he'd get them.

"His secret was he didn't wait for the man with the ball to come to him. He'd go in to them. He'd move in and when the guy looked for support, that's when Wombat would go in for the kill. They'd take their eyes off him and bang! He'd leave blokes a crumpled mess, more often than not a stretcher case. He was just as good in attack. I remember there would be times when he'd be bringing the ball back and you'd think, 'Wombat's good for 10, 20 metres here' and he'd beat the first man, then bump off the second and head off for 40 or 50."

And then there was Thompson. "People used to describe Thommo as a great team man but there was a hell of a lot more to him that. He was like Wally Lewis in that he could completely control a game. He'd tell the rest of us where to run, where the gaps were going to come. He could really read a game. It's true that he did fit into a team well and back up and provide the link, but he had a great step and plenty of pace. He was a terrific individual player in his own right. He was a great character, Thommo. He used to break his nose every week. He'd come up to me after the game and say, 'How's it looking, Fatty? What way am I pointing?' and I'd tell him if it was broken to the left or the right. He loved a drink and a smoke. There were stories that he'd have a smoke at halftime. Well, I never saw it — although I must admit to seeing him stub one out as we were walking down the tunnel once or twice."

With the last of the legends gone, Fulton was left with the task of finding a new captain to replace Thompson for the 1985 season. His choice raised some eyebrows around the club. With new club secretary John Tenison dying suddenly after just one year in office, Doug Daley took up the position. Fulton says he had to do some convincing to have Daley and the committee accept Vautin as captain.

"Fatty wasn't touted by anyone inside or outside the club," Fulton recalled, "but to me he seemed a logical choice. I'd struck a similar situation at Easts when I made Royce Ayliffe captain against the wishes of most people around the place. Royce was a big success and I felt Fatty would be too. Like Royce he was intelligent and well liked by the other players. Nobody could ever accuse him of not having a dig. He always gave his best on the field and even though he'd been around since 1979 he was still only 25. That meant he'd be able to relate with everyone right through the place."

Fulton approached Vautin during a baseball match the club put on as a pre-season get together. Vautin was standing in the outfield drinking a beer when Fulton walked up. "Hey Blue," he said, "what's doing?"

"Not much. How about with you?"

"Oh, I've got a bit of news. It wasn't a hard decision, you're the best man for the job ... you're captain for 1985 and for as long as I'm here and you're doing the job, it's yours."

Fulton provided Vautin with a two-page list of what he expected from a captain. He also asked that Vautin provide input into the running of the team whenever he felt inclined and stressed that his door was always open.

"That's when we started getting closer," Vautin said. "Up to then it had just been coach and player. I always thought he was a good bloke but I never had much to do with him outside football. From then on we got to know each other as people and worked pretty well as a team."

Off-field yes, but on-field Vautin was on his own and developed into an outstanding captain, according to long-time teammate Des Hasler.

"He was inspirational," Hasler said. "He led from the front. We played together for seven years and I always found him great to play with. He was noted for his high work-rate but he read a game very well too. That's what made him such a good captain and what will make him a good coach too.

"As a captain I think he would have been a lot like Alan Thompson. He was level headed, he never panicked behind the line, but if he thought we needed a change of direction he'd let you know. He certainly didn't yell at his players but he got the point across.

"He had this way of doing things. If he felt the side needed a lift he'd get to you on the quiet. He'd say it so only you could hear. Like 'Des we need something from you here, we need something special'. And it would lift you because he'd singled you out as the one who could do it. It gave you confidence to know he had confidence in you."

Fulton said one of Vautin's greatest qualities as a captain was an ability to make all players feel part of the club. "It didn't matter whether they were internationals or in under-23s," Fulton said. "Fatty would give them a bagging. He was merciless. He wasn't like some captains who never talk to the kids, Fatty was at every under-23 match, and a lot of the junior games around the place too. As far as I'm concerned he was captain on-field and captain off-field as well. I don't believe in this club captain business. That's a dead-set wank. Fatty was Manly captain, that's all there was to it, and he had the personality to make it work.

"No-one was safe from his tongue, but the thing is nobody got upset by it. It was just Fatty and it brought everyone together. When he started his newspaper column he used to write things like, 'Jughead Jones was seen on the Corso last week in his singlet five times too small to show off his muscles ...'" and next night at training everyone would be giving Johnny Jones a hard time. Jonesy just copped it sweet ... everyone did. That's why we won three club championships when I was there, two with Fatty as captain. Everyone got along well and enjoyed being together.

"Personally, I just liked the guy. If he had any problems off the field, he used to come to me and I like to think I was a help to him from time to time."

One such time was when Vautin was finding it hard to get a job. Fulton contacted Packer.

"Tell him he can start as an ad rep on *The Manly Daily* on Monday," Packer said. "Usual deal. If he works he can stay. If not, he's out."

That was pretty well how Fulton viewed Vautin's appointment as captain and, as with the sales rep job, it worked.

"I was a bit nervous that first training run," Vautin admitted. "It's a bit of a jump from being one of the boys to being the one calling the shots. While I was the most experienced player in the team at 25 there were still a few blokes who fancied themselves as leaders. I was expecting a bit of ill feeling but there was none there. I came away that night feeling pretty good and it kicked on from there."

Unfortunately the season didn't unfold as well as that first training run would have suggested. "We had a pretty good side with a lot of new names," Vautin said. "We had new guys like Tony Melrose, and Andy Goodway from England and New Zealander James Leuluai. We got to the play-off and could have gone further."

Goodway and Leuluai didn't make the impression that had been expected, although Vautin says Leuluai did make a lasting impression on him personally. "We were down getting ready for training one night and Doug Daley pushed open the door and walked in. He said, 'Paul, I'd like you to meet James Leuluai who is joining us', and James stepped out from behind him. Well, I just burst out laughing. He was a nice bloke but he had the funniest head I've ever seen. I was pissing myself and Doug was getting pretty embarrassed so I pulled myself together. But the blokes behind me had got a look at him and they were laughing by this time too. Good fella, but rough melon. He never really hit his straps with us."

Vautin had his problems too, on the field. He injured a shoulder early in the season and played for 23 weeks with a pain-killing needle. "Every week the doc would come in at exactly the same time and give me a needle in exactly the same spot. I couldn't watch," he said, "it would last exactly 67 minutes and then I'd be in agony. But what could I do?"

When news of the weekly needles got out, the critics had a picnic. Former Manly tough man Rex Mossop attacked Vautin three out of five nights on his nightly TV sports bulletin. "He had a go at me but what did he want me to do?" Vautin said. "I wasn't going to have an operation and miss the season. Everything else was fine. It was an area the size of a 20 cent piece and there was no way I was going to stop playing because of that."

At least he did better than Phil Blake who, after his brilliance at halfback in 1984, had been replaced at the scrumbase by Des Hasler and was playing on the wing. "One day we were playing Balmain at Leichhardt and Phil tackled some guy right on half time and got up clutching his arm," Vautin said.

Blake then committed the cardinal sin of turning his back on the opposition as he went back to position and Balmain made the most of it. A quick play the ball and Tigers winger Russel Gartner was on his way. Blake stuck out a hand as Gartner flashed by but it was too little too late. Balmain try in the corner. As the players trooped into the dressing room at half time, Fulton zeroed in. "You're kidding, Blakey," he shouted, "what the bloody hell do you think you're doing? Never turn your back!"

Blake was still clutching his arm. "I think I've broken my arm," he said.

"I don't give a stuff," growled Fulton. "When you do a tackle get back in position."

Sure enough, Blake's arm was broken. He was out for the year.

"That was just Bozo," Vautin said, "winning was everything. He was one of the most determined blokes you'd ever meet."

It was Paul McCabe's turn to feel Fulton's ire when he came into the dressing room after the semi-final play-off against Penrith later in the season. It was a Tuesday night and Penrith were pumped up for the biggest night in the club's history. They had never made the semis before and their young side spearheaded by the brilliant Greg Alexander had turned the corner towards re-spectability. Up against them Vautin had one of his best games for Manly. At half-time he had pulled off 24 tackles but it was almost a lone hand. TV commentator Ray Warren saw the halftime stats this way: "Well, Vautin is leading his team with 24 tackles and let's see ... oh Noel Cleal four. Gee, that tells a story."

Vautin made the break for Manly's try and at fulltime it was 6-

all. Three minutes into the first 10-minute period of extra time he got the ball 10 metres in from the sideline and 15 metres from goal. 'Why not?' he thought, and kicked the first field goal of his life.

Then Fulton sent out McCabe in jumper number 23. Almost immediately he was penalised for an infringement in the play the ball. Penrith 8-7. Three minutes later, he was penalised for offside. Penrith 10-7. Fulton's words in the dressing room later left anyone within earshot in no two minds about the state of his mood. He was not happy.

The coach partially overcame his disappointment by going shopping. While just missing the choice signature of Mal Meninga, he did manage to sign two less-sought-after players who would go on to have great impact with the club. Ron Gibbs and Cliff Lyons.

Although Gibbs came from Easts as a centre, his crash tackling and complete disregard for self preservation would soon see him in the Manly pack. "He was fearless," said Vautin, "just the type of bloke you love to have in your team. There was a story going around that when he was playing for Easts he was driving back after an Illawarra game with Paul Dunn, David Trewhella and Trevor Gillmeister. Apparently they got a bit bored and started flicking his ear. He said if they did it again he'd pull the car over and beat the shit out of them. One of them did it again and he pulled the car over and beat the shit out of them one by one. Then he put them all back in the car and drove them home. I can believe it. That was Ronny all over."

The other recruit, Lyons, went to Norths when his country coach Greg Hawick took on the job at the Bears. When Norths sacked Hawick midway through the year Lyons marched into the office of club secretary Bob Saunders and told him he wouldn't be sticking around. "They did the wrong thing by Greg," he said. "I couldn't play for them again after that."

Lyons was only with Manly for one minute before Fulton gave him his nickname. During a playing stint at Warrington in England, Fulton picked up the euphemism "napper", meaning "head". When Lyons arrived at Brookvale for his first training run, Fulton took one look at him and burst out: "Hey Cliffy, what about your napper? How bloody big is it?" And so it stuck. Napper Lyons.

While Vautin would have liked to have gone further in the semi-final race, he could still feel some satisfaction with 1985 and look towards 1986 with confidence. He had come through his first year as captain and earned the respect and co-operation of his clubmates. He had represented his country for the fourth year in a row and, with a Kangaroo tour coming, could logically expect to be on it. Wayne Bennett had been appointed Origin coach and Vautin was looking forward to playing a part in the interstate campaign.

Funny how things don't always work out. In the seventh round of the competition, against Penrith at Brookvale, Vautin moved in for a routine tackle and with one sickening jolt, all his plans evaporated. "It was the simplest of tackles," he said. "Royce Simmons was running it up from the 22, I went in to tackle him and as I did he ducked his head and it hit my arm. I thought, 'Shit, that hurt', and it went numb. I didn't know what I'd done. I thought I'd be right in a few minutes."

The Manly trainer ran to Vautin's side. "What's up?" he asked.

"I think I've hit a nerve. It's gone numb. I'll be okay."

Vautin stayed on for another seven minutes, actually pulling off two more tackles using his good arm before Panthers lock Craig Connor ran at him and Vautin tried to grab him with the damaged arm. "When it hit I felt the bones move," Vautin recalled. "I thought, 'Hang on, something's not too good here.' I stuck up my other hand straight away and got off as quick as I could."

Vautin was to miss 16 weeks. For the first eight weeks he was in plaster and couldn't do any exercise at all, but as soon as the cast was removed, he headed for Narrabeen Fitness Camp. "I'd played for Australia for the past four years and I knew they usually stuck by the guys who have done the job in the past," he said. "I thought if I could just get back on the field and show my fitness before the end of the season I'd be okay."

Vautin mapped out a horror stretch for himself around the hills behind Narrabeen, with a 70-metre climb the centrepiece. One day Fulton volunteered to put Vautin through his paces. "He was the worst trainer I've ever seen," Fulton said, "anything over 200 metres he just didn't want to know about. He was lucky that he was one of those blokes who didn't have to do a lot of fitness work on the training paddock to be able to perform on the field, but after that long break he really needed to put the effort in. He wasn't training with the rest of the team because they were so far ahead and I knew I couldn't ask anyone else to train him because he'd talk them out of it. I decided to take him for a session myself."

Even speaking of the day's activities years later can make Vautin break out into a sweat. The two started with a 3km run through the sheer hills above the fitness camp, then moved into a series of six 150-metre sprints and six 120-metre sprints — up the meanest hill Fulton could find. They then ran back down for 45 minutes of gym work and a session on the tackling bags, diving, climbing up and diving again for 15 minutes straight.

"After that I was completely stuffed," Vautin said. "I started heading for the cars with a 'Good session, Boze.'"

Fulton stopped him in his tracks. "Where are you going?" he called. "We're only halfway through. We're going again."

Although Vautin was exhausted, they started off up the hill again. Fulton made a race of it. "Don't let me beat you," he said, and Vautin started putting in the big strides. Then, all of a sudden, he stopped. "What are you doing?" Fulton shouted.

"Gotta be sick," said Vautin, who started throwing up in the bush. Fulton grabbed him and pushed him back onto the track.

"Spew on the run," he barked, and off they went again, Vautin running and vomiting at the same time.

"Say what you will about Fatty as a trainer, but he's determined." Fulton laughed, "He wasn't going to give up. He ran up that hill spewing every inch of the way."

And Vautin is just as full of praise for Fulton. "He wasn't the megaphone type." he said. "If he sent you off for a run he was right there with you. That day he'd given up his own time for the run. There's not too many people who'd do that for you — even if he did nearly kill me."

With just two games left in the season Vautin was rushed back into first grade. "There just wasn't any time for anything else," he said, "I had to show I was okay."

The team made the preliminary semi-final against Balmain but again lost in the worst possible way. Leading 14-2 after 20 minutes they capitulated after Cliff Lyons was sent off and lost 29-22.

Vautin was placed in the 1986 Kangaroo train-on squad but on grand final night, for the second time in his career, he was shattered when left out of the touring party. It was to be exactly a year before he wiped off some of the disappointment — but not before surviving the greatest slap in the face of his career.

CHAPTER 9

A Premiership Fairytale

The phone call came from Doug Daley early on a Monday morning.

"Paul," he said, "we've got something to discuss. Be in my office at 10."

The meeting would have been a complete surprise if not for a conversation with Fulton the previous day. "We've got a problem," the coach had said. "They're going to take the captaincy off you. They want to give it to Crusher."

Vautin was shocked. Over the past two years, 1985 and '86, he had led the club with pride and distinction. They had not won a premiership, or even figured strongly in the semi-finals, but Vautin had never taken a backward step on the field and had worked hard to build team harmony off it. He believed he had filled the criteria which Fulton had set down in that two-page letter when he was given the job. The prospect of captaining Manly in what promised to be a successful and enjoyable season had been one of the few bright spots in an otherwise depressing summer. Desperately unlucky to have missed out of the Kangaroo tour, he had watched the games on television with mixed feelings. He was glad to see the team doing well but heartbroken not to be with them.

"I watched every game," he said. "I had to tell myself that's life and think about getting ready for the club season. The Manly guys were going well, which looked good for the club. I remember seeing Crusher break his arm. I really felt for him."

And then, just when he was putting the selection disappointment behind him, this latest bombshell. When he could speak, he asked Fulton for his views on the matter. "It's out of my hands," he said.

When Vautin walked into Daley's office Fulton was already sitting in front of the desk. Vautin took the seat beside him and Daley started reading from a piece of paper in front of him. "Paul Vautin," he read, "we the committee feel that Noel Cleal should be rewarded for his excellent form on the Kangaroo tour and accordingly we have decided to appoint him captain for the 1987 season."

Vautin spoke up. "Doug," he said, "I've done nothing wrong. I'm proud to be captain of this club and I think I've done a good job. Surely just because someone has made a Kangaroo tour you can't make him captain. It doesn't make sense."

"The decision is final," Daley said. "With Noel out with a broken arm, the committee has decided you can remain captain until he returns. We could have given it to Des Hasler, but we have decided to stick with you for the time being." Daley then asked if Fulton had anything to add. He didn't. "I threw in a few 'You're kiddin's' and told him I didn't deserve to be sacked," Vautin recalled. "Then he said we didn't have anything more to discuss and I walked out.

"I remember when I was walking down the stairs from his office it sort of struck me, 'Why didn't Bozo say anything?' If I'd had a captain who was being sacked I think I would have had something to say about it. I couldn't believe the whole thing. I was totally despondent, really pissed off."

Half an hour after he got home, Vautin's phone rang. It was Fulton. "Mate," he said, "you handled that well, you stuck to your guns. My hands were tied, there was no point me saying anything, they'd made up their minds. But that's what committees are for, to make decisions and we can't always agree with them. I'd been on the end of a few bad ones myself. All you can do is get on with things. There's no point in getting upset with everyone."

Vautin didn't get upset with everyone, just one person — Cleal. At the first training run after the decision had been announced, Vautin walked up to Cleal, shook his hand and promised to give him his support. In actual fact, that wasn't how it turned out. "I was dirty on him," he said. "I blamed him for what had happened and I shouldn't have. It probably had nothing to do with him, he was just the one who I focussed everything on. I thought there was a conspiracy to take the job off me and I thought Crusher was at the centre of it."

The problem between the pair was the worst-kept secret in

Sydney football. For months the club was split as players and officials took sides. The popular knockabout Vautin who had led the team for two years in one corner and the quietly-spoken giant Cleal who had never asked for the job in the other.

"He didn't have any support from the players," Vautin said. "It split the joint down the middle. As far as Crusher and I were concerned, nothing was said. We still got along okay on the outside. I wouldn't call it a feud. Things were just a bit strained but we were always civil to each other. A cold war I suppose. I had nothing against the bloke personally, I just thought he was the one behind it all. I was probably wrong but that was how I felt at the time."

But if anyone was expecting Vautin to drop his bundle, they were soon very much disappointed. Although seething inside, in public he kept up appearances. He described himself to the team as "Stanley Stand-In." Within a few days he was answering to the name Stanley.

And once the season started, his form was outstanding. "It just seemed to lift me," he said, "I felt I only had the job for a while and I wanted to prove them all wrong. I probably started the season better than I ever had."

The first game of what would prove Vautin's most rewarding season in club football was against St George and he was thrown into the front row against the world's No.1 prop Craig Young. Despite playing out of position against such an opponent, it was generally accepted that Vautin took the points on the day and Manly managed a 4-all draw. It carried on from there, with Vautin eventually being judged the club's most consistent first grader for the year.

But always, through those early days, there was the spectre of Cleal's return. It came in the eighth round. After a match in reserve grade, it was decided Cleal would be used as a replacement in the match against Eastern Suburbs. Vautin decided he would give a performance to remember. "I put everything into having a good game," he said. "I figured it was going to be my last game as Manly captain and I wanted it to be one to remember. I wanted to make it hard for them to finally take it off me."

He succeeded. In front of a packed Brookvale Oval Vautin put in one of his best performances. In the second half, he took the ball, dummied, beat a few tacklers with sheer determination and scored.

Soon afterwards, he saw Cleal coming to the sideline. "I thought, 'This is it'," Vautin recalled. "He ran on and I walked over and said, 'It's all yours' but he waved me away. He said to keep going for the match. He'd take over next week. It was funny, just having him on the field spurred me on even more. I'd have to say I played like a madman or something. I was throwing myself in everywhere."

Late in the game Vautin ran onto another pass, spotted a gap and put through a grubber into the in-goal. There was a blur of maroon and charging onto the ball for the try came ... Noel Cleal. "I thought, 'This is lovely'" said Vautin. "I'm supposed to be keeping him away from the captaincy, and here I am setting him up for the winning try."

The next week Fulton announced the team and called Vautin and Cleal into a room. "Crusher," he said, "at this stage the side is going so well that I'm going to leave Fatty captain."

"Good as gold," said Cleal, "not a worry."

Cleal might have been agreeable, but the committee was not so magnanimous. "The mail I got later was that Bozo got called up before the committee to explain what was going on," Vautin said. "They'd made a decision and he was ignoring it. It was making them look bad. I heard he told them he didn't want to disrupt what had become a happy camp. They said they'd run with him for the time being, but if anything went wrong, I was out."

Until he left the club nearly three years later, Vautin was never again to be challenged for the job. And, just as importantly, Vautin and Cleal ended their "cold war" as the season progressed.

That match against Easts marked the start of an unprecedented 12-match winning streak for the Sea Eagles who developed into the most feared outfit in the competition. They had power in the forwards, proven class in the backs and, under Fulton, they were disciplined enough not to give away too many penalties. Not that they were angels, but when the team was on the wrong side of a penalty count, Fulton tried every trick he knew of to square things up.

"When we were down in the penalties Bozo used to send a runner on to tell me to speak to the ref," Vautin said. "The runner would come on and say, 'Bozo said to tell the ref the penalty count is 10-1 against us.' I'd say, 'Is it?' and he'd say, 'No, but the ref won't know that.' Bozo always reckoned that if you told the ref the count was one-sided he'd get it in his head and try to even things up before the end of the game because it wouldn't look good on his report to be seen caning one side. I'd always give it a go. I mean what was the ref going to say, 'Get stuffed'? Usually they'd just say, 'I don't care what the count is, Fatty, just get your team onside and you won't get into trouble', but Bozo reckoned it was always worth a try."

One time it didn't work was when Bill Harrigan was in charge of Manly's away game against Cronulla. The runner told Vautin the count was 12-4 against in the second half. Vautin went up to Harrigan. "Hey Bill, the penalty count is 12-4 against us. Are Manly really playing that badly?" Harrigan's answer was brief and to the point. "Yes."

With Manly leading 13-12 with minutes left, Harrigan sent halfback Des Hasler to the sin bin for repeated scrum-feed in-fringements. Vautin was instructed by Fulton, via the runner, to advise Harrigan an official complaint would be lodged after the game. If Harrigan was perturbed by the prospect, he hid it well. "Good as gold, Fatty," he said, "play on."

Cronulla won the match and as Vautin and the Manly players filed past Fulton in the tunnel, they heard him say the fateful words to the assembled press: "I hope he (Harrigan) gets hit by a cement truck on the way home." Harrigan wasn't hit by a truck, but Fulton was hit by a $1000 fine. Did he pay it out of his own pocket? "I doubt it," says Vautin.

The loss, and the fine, were minor aberrations in the 1987 season for what went on to be recognised as one of the great club sides of the modern era. It was a team of outstanding players performing at their absolute peak, largely due to the successful combination of Fulton and Vautin. "They worked very well to-gether," Manly centre Michael O'Connor said. "Fulton only had a few close confidantes, people who he would confer with about selections and that sort of thing. Fatty was one of his main men. They genuinely liked each other and made a good team. When I came over from rugby union in 1983 Fatty was someone who had always stood out for some reason. Maybe it was the red hair, but, whatever, I always had respect for him as a player. We'd gone away to New Zealand with the Australian side in 1985 but that wasn't a happy tour and I never really got to know him. When I came to

Manly in '87, I obviously came to know him a lot better and he impressed me not just as a player, but as a captain as well."

Fulton says Vautin's captaincy during 1987 cannot be undervalued. "When I think back on that side the contribution of Fatty was enormous, his input was superb," Fulton said. "The relationship between the captain and the other players is very important, but the relationship between the captain and the coach is just as important. Whether it's club football or representative stuff, it doesn't matter, the coach and the captain have to get along. Find a team where there's a problem between the captain and the coach and you'll have a losing team. There wasn't any problem between Fatty and me. We got along exceptionally well and that filtered back through the side. I think every member of that team enjoyed their football that year. Whether it was training or playing or just being around each other, they wanted to get there. They were having fun, and that's half the battle."

The element of fun within the Manly camp that year was no accident. It was as much part of the routine as any training run, and the players threw themselves into it. "We worked hard at training, but we enjoyed ourselves as well," Vautin said. "Once a fortnight we had a social get-together. We might go out for a meal or into Kerry Packer's private gym for a workout and then on to a Chinese restaurant.

"One night we went to the gym and out to a restaurant at Neutral Bay. We had a little mini-bus and a driver to cart us around so there were a fair few beers over dinner and in the bus. When we left the restaurant we were driving back down the peninsula and we had a Nude Doug Daley Competition. Blokes would have to get their gear off and stand in the aisle doing an impersonation of Doug. Mick O'Connor won it easily. He was standing there in the nude going, 'Gentlemen, as executive director of the Manly Warringah Rugby League Club it is my duty to inform you ...'

"There was no malice in it. Doug's son Phil was in the bus and he was laughing along. Everyone liked Doug in those days. We were winning and he was really looking after us, he'd do anything for us to keep things running along smoothly. He just had this very official way of talking which we used to take off. We used to do Doug Daley impersonations to his face. He thought it was funny."

O'Connor remembers the club going to any lengths to keep the players happy. "Nothing was too much trouble," he said. "They were very generous. Any problems you had, any money worries, they'd just fix it. There was no fringe benefits tax in those days and they really looked after us. It was different to St George, my old club. There you were more on your own. At Manly they looked after all the little things so everyone was happy. They used to put on social nights so the wives and girlfriends felt part of everything too. It was a very happy team, a very good social scene."

The closeness of the team off the field transferred onto the field as well. Daley and Fulton had recruited well in the lead-up to 1987. Manly had the best personnel in the competition — although it was nothing to what they could have had.

At the end of 1986, two days after Manly had lost to Balmain in the preliminary semi, a strange-looking character of eastern European appearance was seen loitering at Sydney Airport. Dressed in dark glasses and an overcoat, he was lucky not to be pulled in for questioning. It was Max Krilich, waiting for Wally Lewis and Gene Miles.

By then two of the most sought-after footballers in the world, Lewis and Miles were keen to join Manly and club supporter Kerry Packer was just as keen to have them. As when Packer had brought Bob Fulton to Eastern Suburbs, money was no object. When Lewis shared a beer with Vautin at his home later that night, Packer, Fulton and Lewis were all certain he and Miles would be playing alongside Vautin in the coming season.

A few days later Lewis rang Vautin to tell him the bad news. Wily Queensland Rugby League boss Ron McAuliffe had snookered them. Under the terms of their QRL contracts, Lewis and Miles were tied to Queensland. The contracts stated that as long as the QRL could meet any rival contract lodged with the NSWRL, the players would stay in Queensland. The package offered by Manly and Packer far outstripped anything the QRL could offer, but McAuliffe found a loophole. The contract lodged with the NSWRL only included the Manly portion of the package. Packer's involvement was a private deal between him and the player. McAuliffe matched the Manly money and Lewis and Miles stayed put.

Manly had also missed out on gaining the services of Steve Mortimer from Canterbury and Brisbane Souths sensation Mal Meninga. It took a concerted effort from Canterbury chief Peter

Moore to convince Mortimer to stay a Bulldog but Manly came closer to signing Meninga.

"I thought we had him," Vautin said. "He came down to Sydney at the end of 1985 and Bozo, Doug Daley, me and Mal and all our wives went out to dinner. The next day I drove him all around the area, right up to Palm Beach and he seemed to fall in love with the place. Bozo and I were very confident he was coming and wherever he went it looked like Gary Belcher was going too."

So what went wrong? That's the question Vautin put to Meninga on the 1989 Australian tour of New Zealand. "Mate, I was keen to come but I hadn't quite made up my mind," he said. "Then one day we were playing a game at Lang Park and I'd had a few beers after the match and got home about midnight and just after I'd got to sleep the phone rang. It was this official from Manly. He asked me what I was going to do. I said, 'Fair go, it's after midnight and I've just got home, couldn't we talk about this tomorrow?' but he said I was jerking them around and he had to know right then and there. I told him to get stuffed and hung up the phone. That was it, I never heard from them again."

But while Manly missed out on five of the top players in the game, they did manage to snare a few others who would go on to make mighty contributions to the club. Cliff Lyons and Ron Gibbs were already settled in, but it was the signings of Michael O'Connor, Darrell Williams and Kevin Ward which were to provide the winning edge.

"No-one knew anything about Williams," Vautin said. "I think Fulton heard about him and snapped him up. He was a mystery to us, he just lobbed, but what a great buy he turned out to be.

"Mick O'Connor was the real big one. We were all very excited about him coming. He'd played superbly on the Kangaroo tour and we knew he was going to make a real difference to the side. Doug Daley did all the negotiating on that one and 'Snoz' turned out to be one of the best buys the club ever made."

O'Connor had nearly come to the club at the beginning of the 1985 season but had been convinced to spend two more years with St George. By the time he finally came to Manly he was a seasoned international and one of the biggest names in the game. Manly was one of several clubs clamouring for his signature.

"I could have got more money elsewhere but Manly's style of

play was very attractive to me," he said. "Fulton was known as a backs coach and Manly used to score a lot of tries out wide and attack from anywhere on the field. In the end that was what won me over. From day one they struck me as a much more professional outfit. There were more internationals and the whole place was a lot more high-profile."

And then there was Kevin Ward. Manly were heavily into negotiations with English star Lee Crooks when Fulton came into the picture. "Forget Crooks," he said, "if we're going to get a Pom, get Kevin Ward."

The Castleford prop provided the firepower that wins grand finals. Alongside Phil Daley, who was producing the form which would win him a Test jumper the following year, Ward was an inspiration. "Bozo called him 'Pommy' at the first training session and that's what he was from then on," Vautin said. "What a hard man. I remember once we were playing Wests at Brookvale and we were behind 25-22 with about 30 seconds left on the clock and 20 metres out from their line. I thought, 'What'll we do here?' The obvious thing was to punch up one or two and then put up the bomb. The first bloke running on the ball was Pommy, he went on a 15-metre run, bashing and barging all the way, then, with three blokes hanging off him off-loaded to Dave Ronson who scored without a hand being laid on him. That was the element of power and aggression he added to the team."

But while the Manly players had no problems relating to Ward on the field, off-field it was a different story. His accent was so thick they literally couldn't understand what he was saying. Michael O'Connor attempted to remedy the problem. "When someone won the club best and fairest award for a match they had to get up and make a speech at the club," Vautin recalled. "Kevin would be up there going, "Arrr oooh ee arrr," and Snoz would stand behind him. After a while Snoz would go, 'Hang on, hang on' and Kev would stop and Snoz would say, 'What he said is, I'm very happy to win this wonderful award ... okay Kev, carry on', and he'd keep going for a bit longer and Snoz would jump in again and translate."

With Ward and Daley providing the power, Ron Gibbs gave Manly another element, what Fulton describes as the "blitz". "He was the player that every top side has to have," Fulton said. "He was the one the opposition players were looking over their shoulders for, the one they liked to know where he was. Penrith had Mark Geyer the year they won their first premiership, we had Ronnie."

Gibbs was known as the wildman of the competition. A centre with Easts, he turned into a ferocious back rower with Manly, his tackling feared by every opponent in the game. "He was absolutely fearless," Vautin said. "You talk about someone putting their body on the line, that was Ron. He had that quality you can't attain yourself no matter how hard you work at it. It's in-built, something you're born with. He just used to throw himself at blokes. I really don't think we would have won the competition without him.

"He was a good bloke, too. There wasn't a night he wouldn't arrive at training without a pile of posters for us all to sign. You didn't ask, but you knew they were for some kids' home or orphanage or something like that. He loved kids, he was always trying to help them. Dead-set every time you saw him he'd have something for you to sign. We'd go, 'Fair go, Ron, not again' and he'd just laugh and say, 'Sign 'em or I'll knock youse all out' and we'd sign them because when Ronnie said he was going to knock someone out, he usually did."

Clever hooker Mal Cochrane, a future Rothmans Medal winner, made up the pack along with Vautin and Cleal. All were at the peak of their careers and all complemented each other's play.

"If one player had a weakness other players would make up for it," Vautin said. "Noel Cleal wasn't the best defender but he made up for it by being one of the most dangerous runners in the game. If that meant the rest of us had to do a bit more tackling, that was fine as long as we kept that balance. Bozo used to say to us, 'Crusher isn't there to tackle, he's there to score tries and make breaks.' We knew it, we accepted it, so there was no problem. Sometimes Bozo used to bump up Crusher's tackle count. He'll probably deny it but I saw him do it. He'd be walking up the tunnel with the stats guy and ask how many tackles Crusher had made. If it was too low he'd tell him to put a few more after his name. It was no big deal to me. Some blokes got the shits but I knew what Crusher's job was and as long as he did it, I was happy."

In the backs the class of Hasler, Lyons, O'Connor, Shearer and Williams was backed up by Manly's honest wingers Stu "The Bug" Davis and young David Ronson.

"The Bug was a very underrated winger," Vautin said. "He'd always beat at least two blokes every time he had the ball. We used to say, 'Come on Bug, give them a chance, stand front on.' He was that skinny we reckoned you couldn't see him if he stood side on."

Ask Vautin to name the outstanding player of the side, though, and he'll probably say Hasler.

"Des was a schoolteacher and he just happened to be teaching one of Bozo's kids," Vautin said, "they got to talking and Des said he wasn't too happy at Penrith. The rest, as they say, is history. I'd have to say Des was my favourite player for years. He just did so much work, was so fit. He'd do anything for the team. He was the type of bloke who could get you out of a hole by never giving up – – just the type of player I've always admired. Winning the competition was a team effort but if things ever looked like going off the rails it was a bloke like Des who could get you going again."

As the side gelled and they strung together 12 wins on the trot, their confidence soared. "We knew we weren't invincible but we knew it would take a great side to beat us," Vautin said. In August at Henson Park Eastern Suburbs proved to be that side, although Vautin wasn't too upset by the loss.

"It had got to the stage were I was almost hoping we'd lose," he said. "I wanted to get it out of our system. We sure did that. Crusher took it up early in the match and Tony Rampling and David Trewhella absolutely belted him. That set the tone for the day. They bashed us, they battered us and they beat the pants off us. At one stage they were winning 20-nil. We came back to 26-16 but they had it over us all day. In retrospect it was probably the best thing that could have happened to us. It brought us back to earth and showed what could happen if we let up. We knew we were the only ones who could beat us. We were too good, we had every position covered, but we had to keep our minds on the job."

One thing that could have upset the team was the news that Ron Gibbs had signed for the Gold Coast and would not be at Brookvale the next year. There were calls that he should be barred from playing with the side and one spectator raised the famous sign: "Give Back Randall's Jumper." If it was worrying the club's supporters, it had no effect on the team.

"Our view was good luck to him," said Vautin. "We're all professionals and Ron had done what was best for himself and his family. The money was something like $73,000 a year for three years. That was great money, especially since he'd never played any rep stuff. I remember at training I went up and congratulated him. That was a great deal, we all thought, 'well done'."

As a sign of solidarity the Manly players stood around Gibbs and all shook his hand prior to the kick-off against Canterbury and any doubts that "Rambo Ron" would give his all in his remaining weeks were assuaged in the match against Souths. With the "Give Back Randall's Jumper" sign waving provocatively at Redfern Oval, Gibbs kicked ahead, raced through and caught the ball on the end of a spectacular dive for a try. The next week a new sign was erected at Brookvale: "Gibbs for PM."

Manly won the minor premiership in a canter and headed to the Sydney Cricket Ground for the major semi against Fulton's old club Eastern Suburbs. It was to be a test of steel for Manly. Ward had been forced to return to Castleford and Phil Daley was making his return after breaking his jaw in a State of Origin match months earlier.

His place in the side had been taken by Mark Pocock who had proven a worthy replacement. "Poky was one of those blokes who love a stoush," Vautin said. "He was forever walking into places and getting belted. I think he had one of those heads that blokes just love to punch. Not that it worried him, he used to give as good as he got. A mate of mine once told me he was sitting on the hill at Brookvale one day and heard two blokes talking. The game had been going about three minutes and one bloke asked the other if Pocock had thrown a punch. He said no. 'Been to the sin-bin yet?' 'Nope.' 'Oh well, won't be long,' said the other bloke. Sure enough, five seconds later Poky belted someone and got sent to the bin. That was the kind of bloke he was."

With Ward back in England, Pocock and Daley were front rowers for one of the hardest semi-finals on record. The first time Daley took the ball up he was hit by three Easts defenders, hard and high. When his jaw remained intact, his confidence rose.

"That was the best game Milton played for us all year," Vautin said. "With Ward gone we needed someone to take them on, and he did the job. It was a tough game. A few years later when I went to Easts blokes like Hugh McGahan, Trevor Gillmeister and David

Trewhella told me it was the toughest game they'd ever played in. I knew what they meant."

Early in the first half Vautin and Cliff Lyons both went in to tackle Easts fullback Garry Wurth. Vautin's head hit Lyons' elbow and down he went. "I felt the warm wet stuff coming out and I knew I had a head cut but I didn't know how serious it was," he said. "When there was a break in play the trainer came running on and had a look."

Trainer Peter Byrne took one look and quickly looked away. "Shit," he said, "you've got to come off."

"Why?" asked Vautin, "it's only a cut."

"No, it's more than that, come to the sideline."

The rule in those days was that players had 10 minutes in which they could be replaced in the head-bin. Vautin jogged to the sideline where he and Byrne were met by doctor Alwyn Keighran. As was customary, Dr Keighran tried to pull the wound together with a staple gun. Byrne looked on in horror.

"You're kiddin' doc," he said. "You wouldn't do it to him would you? Not the staple gun, not the staple gun."

Vautin was wondering what the fuss was about. "Come on," he said, "hurry up."

When Keighran couldn't pull the wound together he grabbed Vautin by the jumper and the two men ran into the dressing room, assisted by another Manly trainer, Brian Hollis. Vautin lay down on a rubbing bench as Keighran started putting in stitches. He'd got to eight as Hollis counted down the 10 minutes.

"45, 44, 43 ..."

"Hurry up doc ..."

"Hang on, just one more ..."

"33, 32, 31 ..."

"Come on ..."

"That's it ..."

Vautin jumped off the bench ... and fell down. Only Hollis catching him stopped him knocking himself out cold on the dressing room floor. "It was one of the gutsiest things I've ever seen," Hollis said. "He'd lost a lot of blood but he still got back out there."

Vautin went back on to play his part and win man of the match. Des Hasler describes the performance as "a mighty captain's knock" and the hard fought 10-6 win which earned Manly a two-week rest as Easts fought it out with Canberra the following Sunday.

"We had about eight blokes make it to training the next week," Vautin said. "I remember saying to Bozo, if this is how we feel, imagine how Easts must be."

"You're right," said Fulton, "Canberra will kill them on Sunday. That's who we'll be playing."

And that's exactly what happened, although there was a slight doubt that Vautin would make it. The next week his eye was closed and the gash became infected. As Dr Keighran cleaned the wound he off-handedly told Vautin just how bad the cut had been.

"I didn't tell you at the time," he said, "but it really was quite bad. When you lay down the whole side of your head opened up and I could see the eye socket, right down to the bone." Vautin didn't continue the conversation.

"People said we'd had our grand final against Easts," he said. "And that's pretty spot on. That was as hard a game as you could play and whoever won that was going to win the comp. Easts were tipped to beat Canberra but they were never a chance. They were absolutely bashed by us. Canberra made the grand final, but to be perfectly honest, I really didn't consider them a threat at any time."

The public had two main talking points as the game approached. There was the fairy tale of Canberra's first grand final and the perception of Bob Fulton's "monkey". The monkey on Fulton's back was reference to him coaching two sides to grand finals, only to come way empty-handed each time. There was no shortage of people hoping it would happen again. Fulton played down the spectre of a third defeat in the lead-up to the game but the players had it foremost in their minds.

"People outside the Manly club didn't want Fulton to have success but I wanted to win it for him because I thought he deserved it," Vautin said. "He was the best coach around and at that stage we were pretty close mates. I was working with him at that time and we saw each other every day. Most of the time we just sat around talking football, but we spent a lot of time together. To win for him was very important to me and I reiterated it to the players every time we got together. To blokes like me and Crusher it meant even more. We were survivors from '83, we really wanted to do it for Bozo."

Manly had a low-key build-up to the match, which suited Vautin. "All this hype around grand finals is too much," he said. "It gets to the stage where you're reading 'Phil Daley had three shits yesterday'. It's boring, especially that year. We always thought we were unbeatable, all we had to do was play to our ability."

The team got a boost with the return of Ward from England three days before the match. "He lobbed at training and it was like nothing had changed," Vautin said. "We still couldn't understand what he was saying."

In the back office Manly management decided to honour their captain by flying his parents down from Brisbane for the game. Leila rang George at work. "Do you want to go to the grand final?" she asked.

After sitting through two losing deciders, he was sticking to his word. Feeling himself to be a Jonah, he had refused to take holidays for the trip down south. "If you think I'm taking time off to drive down there and watch them lose again, forget it," he snapped.

When Leila explained the trip would be courtesy of the Manly Warringah Rugby League club he changed his mind. The Vautins flew down first class and stayed at a hotel near the beach. "We felt like the king and queen of rugby league," said Leila.

The Manly players drove themselves to the match, saw their families settled into seats and wandered into the dressing room.

"There was no big deal," said Vautin. "No bus or big psych-up. We just went about the job like we had every week. When we'd been there in '83 there had been plenty of nerves but there was nothing like that this time. It was more an air of excitement and anticipation. We expected to play well and we just wanted to get on with it. The game itself was probably a bit of an anti-climax. We had it won by half time. Cliffy just ran riot, and Kevin Ward was unstoppable. He was belting them out of the way."

Fulton gives Ward the ultimate compliment. "If I was picking an all-time great Manly side I'd have Ward in the front row along with John O'Neill," he said. "That's how highly I rate him. The way he played that day ... it was the hottest day ever and there he was with his lily-white skin. He got straight off the plane and had a blinder. That was a sensational performance from him."

It was also a pretty good performance by the coach, who used the head-bin rule to maximum effect in the energy-sapping heat. Twice

Gibbs was replaced, and Cleal once, by game-breaking halfback Paul Shaw. Pocock was given a run nine minutes from fulltime when Manly had the game safely sewn up.

When the fulltime hooter sounded, the feeling for Vautin was not of elation, but relief. Finally, after all those years, all those near-misses, he had done it. Jubilation would come later. The Manly players hugged each other and shook hands. Daley, Shearer and Cochrane hoisted Vautin on their shoulders.

"I don't go for that but I let them do it long enough for the photos then made them put me down," Vautin recalled. And then there was a familiar voice at his shoulder.

"Fatty, Fatty ... mate, how do you feel?"

It was Wally Lewis, the almost-Sea Eagle, moonlighting as a television reporter. He had thrown off his headphones and run onto the field to congratulate his old friend. "That meant a lot to me," Vautin said. "I was experiencing something that he could have been experiencing if things had been a little different. He must have been hurting, but he was the first to congratulate me."

Vautin accepted the trophy from Prime Minister Bob Hawke as Ken Arthurson looked on proudly. For Vautin, holding the trophy aloft and looking down at his team-mates, thinking how far they had come together, was a moment he'll never forget. The ultimate in his career. He stepped to the microphone and made a speech which would be repeated often over the next few days. "Well," he said, "it was a fairy tale for Canberra but it looks like someone tore out the last page."

Photos of the players surrounding the Winfield Cup trophy were taken in their hundreds. One now looks down from Vautin's office wall. The giant colour shot is of Vautin, Fulton and Cleal flanking the historic Giltinan Shield. Their smiles tell the story: any bitterness about the goings on nine months earlier is long forgotten. Three copies of the photo were ordered and framed by Fulton. He presented one each to Vautin and Cleal, the third sits on a wall in his home.

"I just thought they deserved them," Fulton said. "They'd been with me a long time. I know how much it meant to me to win my first premiership."

The Manly players went to their families, then did a slow lap of the Sydney Cricket Ground, the last premiers ever to do so before the move to the Sydney Football Stadium next door. They savoured the feeling, soaked up the adulation of their fans and returned to the dressing rooms where the champagne corks were popping. Ron Gibbs picked up the largest bottle he could find and started shaking it.

"It was a howitzer," Vautin recalled, "and everyone's yelling and cheering as he pulled out the cork and whoosker — all the booze flew out of this thing and poured over Bob Hawke. Not a drop went on anyone else, but it was all over him. In his hair, dripping off his eyebrows, rolling down his nose, all over his suit. It's like time stood still. Nobody moved, we were all just staring at him, and then Doug Daley and John Quayle have got their hankies out and they're racing over there mopping it all up."

Daley was the first to regain the power of speech. "Mr Hawke," he said, "on behalf of the Manly Warringah Rugby League Club, may I assure you we will meet the full cost of dry cleaning ..." Hawke waved them off with a laugh and retreated to the safety of the Canberra dressing room.

Upstairs, George and Leila stood quietly out of the rush with other Manly supporters, Leila still wearing the maroon rosette she had been given by Ken Arthurson. A spectator spied the rosette and ventured: "You must be very happy."

A Manly official jumped in. "Happy? This lady happens to be the mother of the Manly captain."

"And he reached over and gave me a big kiss," she says, her fingers absent-mindedly brushing the rosette which still sits on the opening page of a scrapbook back home at Everton Park.

As the ruckus died down in the dressing room, the players started filing out and driving back to Manly. The Vautins dropped their two children at home and returned to the club. Supporters danced on the footpath as they drove up. As Vautin stepped from the car he was spotted and the word spread. "Fatty's here, it's Fatty." Soon he was surrounded and picked up, then handed across heads into the club. The last sight Kim had of her husband was a shock of red hair disappearing through a doorway.

"That was the most scared I've ever been in my life," he said. "Now I know how those rock stars must feel. Everyone was off their trees, anything could have happened."

Across the room Vautin could see Ron Gibbs being similarly

man-handled. "Put me down," Gibbs was shouting. "Put me down or I'll knock youse all out."

The players and their partners finally retreated to a private bar where drinks, post mortems and congratulations continued all night. By the time the last player left, Vautin was well and truly home, but not asleep. It had been an exhausting but invigorating day. He was in bed around 1.30am but after a few hours of staring at the ceiling he got up and watched the replay of the game. He watched Lyons and Ward jab away at the tenacious Canberra and O'Connor finally deliver the knockout blow. He saw the scenes of jubilation immediately after fulltime. He saw himself being congratulated by Hawke and Arko and heard his crack about ripping out the last page of the fairytale.

And he heard himself thanking his teammates, their opponents, the referee, the sponsors, the Prime Minister and the League. In fact he heard himself mention just about everyone in the ground ... except Fulton.

"I just stared at the screen waiting," he said. "I couldn't believe it. I thanked people I didn't even know. It was a mental block."

The next morning before meeting the rest of the team at a local restaurant, Vautin rang the coach. "Bozo," he said, "I'm sorry ..."

"Don't worry about it Blue," he said, but Vautin was not convinced.

"I'll never forgive myself for that," he said, "and in a funny way I doubt Bozo ever will either."

Later, when Wally Lewis reiterated his question, "How did it feel", Vautin would tell him that holding the premiership trophy aloft for Manly was his greatest moment in rugby league.

"He told me that to do that for your club, after working for all those years, was the ultimate," Lewis said. "I asked him if it was better than playing State of Origin and he thought for a while and said, 'Yes'. That really stuck with me because for something to mean more than State of Origin to Fatty ... well, that just shows how much he loved that club."

CHAPTER

It's Great To Be A Queenslander

Five minutes into the first State of Origin match of 1984, Paul Vautin knew something was wrong. His tongue felt five times its normal size, he was dehydrated and couldn't swallow. His heart pounded crazily and the sounds of the huge Lang Park crowd seemed to come and go in frantic waves, like a giant stereo on the blink.

He was drugged.

The first time he took the ball up, only seconds into the match, it spilled through his hands like soap. And now this; he couldn't breath, couldn't seem to get on top of his emotions. He felt like his performance was okay, his mind told him to get stuck into anything in blue, but this thirst, his tongue like a huge rock filling his mouth, choking him. What was wrong, what could it be?

And then it dawned on him: "Oh God, those pills, those bloody white pills."

He thought back to the dressing room. Five minutes before kick off, one of his teammates pulled him aside. "Fatty," he said, "how are you feeling?"

"Great, I'm ready to go."

His teammate unclenched a hand and offered two small white pills.

"Here," he said, "take these."

"What are they?" asked Vautin who even today cannot believe his own naivety.

"Don't worry mate," he said, "they're great. They're good for ya."

And so he took them, and here he was, less than half an hour later, slap-bang in the middle of the biggest match of the year. Dying.

Somehow he made it to halftime and while his teammates regathered their wits for the second stanza, Vautin drank glass after glass of water. It did the trick. He made it through the match and played his part.

At fulltime he grabbed the player who had slipped him the pills. "Mate," he said, "what the hell were those things you gave me?"

"Ephedrine."

Vautin recoiled in shock. "Well, that was bloody stupid," he said, as much about himself as the supplier. "Don't ever do that again. Not to me, not to anyone."

Looking back on the incident today, Vautin can offer no excuse other than to say he was naive. "It was five minutes before the match," he said, "I was all hyped up and I thought it was just glucose or something. It just never crossed my mind that it was drugs. I've got say it was the only time I ever saw drugs in a Queensland dressing room and my impression was it was the first time the other bloke had ever tried it too.

"But one thing I can say is that it proved to me what a load of crap all this talk is about drugs and uppers improving your perform-ance. It did nothing for me except make me feel like I was going to die.

"It showed me that nobody needs drugs to make them perform better on a football field. Especially in State of Origin. Anyone in their right mind would get enough of a rush from just being out there."

Certainly that was the case with Vautin. Indeed, July 8, 1980, was a night that would change his life. One of those occasions the scriptwriters call "a pivotal moment".

When Arthur Beetson led the Queensland State of Origin side out onto Lang Park in front of 30,000 delirious supporters, Vautin was at home in Harbord, watching on television. As an expatriate Maroon living in the dreaded south he had been isolated from the euphoria surrounding the return of Sydney-based players such as Beetson, Rod Reddy and Johnny Lang to play against NSW. He, like most people south of the border — including commentator Rex Mossop — thought the game was a one-off, an exhibition. Column-ist Ron Casey was adamant that club teammates would go easy on each other despite playing for their home states.

Beetson's much chronicled punch to the head of Parramatta

teammate Mick Cronin changed all that. As Mossop so succinctly put it: "Gee, they seem to be taking this pretty seriously." The Maroons' rampaging battleship Chris Close ran riot, the Brisbane newspapers heralded "The Night We Beat The Blues" and broadcaster Kev Kelly screamed, "It's great to be a Queenslander." From that moment on, Vautin was hooked, for if Wally Lewis was the undisputed king of State of Origin football, before too long Vautin would become the prince in exile. Queensland team manager Dick "Tosser" Turner, who locked horns with George Vautin as a Redcliffe forward of the mid '50s, prefers to describe Vautin as Wally's "lieutenant".

A self-made millionaire who shuns the limelight but has become every bit as much a part of the Queensland Origin success story as Lewis, Beetson, Mal Meninga, Wayne Bennett or Vautin, Turner almost turned down QRL boss Ron McAuliffe when asked to take over the management duties in 1982. He readily admits: "It would have been the worst mistake of my life." Tosser (a boyhood nickname the reason for which he says is not for publication) lives for the team and its core members, who he refers to as "my boys".

And none more so than Vautin.

Turner's office, in one of two buildings he owns in a Brisbane outer suburb, is stacked with memorabilia of his days with the side. Team photos abound but, more than coincidentally, of all the players who have represented the Maroons only three rate a framed individual photograph: Wally Lewis, Mal Meninga and Vautin.

"I believe they were the main characters of the era," Turner said. "When Mal first came to the team he was no way the dominant personality that Wally and Fatty were. That came later for Mal. Now he is comfortable with the leader's role, but in the early days Lewis and Vautin were the two whose personalities melded the team into the force it became. Perhaps it was just as well there were only the two of them. Any more and the right blend wouldn't have been there.

"Paul had the sense of humour to keep things easy-going and loose but at the same time the intensity was just below the surface. He could handle any situation on or off the field. His bravery was an inspiration and his pride at playing for Queensland was tremendous. I would never say that one player was prouder than any other to play for the team but to me Paul epitomised that pride."

Wayne Bennett, who coached the side from 1986-88, accepts the suggestion that Vautin may have felt he had something to prove to Queensland's supporters. "He left Brisbane very young," he said. "He was never really established as a star player. It's probably fair comment to say he wanted to show the people who knew him as a kid that he'd kicked on."

Turner puts the same thoughts into different words. "Having gone to Sydney at 18 Fatty thought the opportunity to play for Queensland had passed him by. When he got his chance he was honoured and I think he felt he had to pay back the state for giving him the opportunity."

That opportunity came in 1982 in the first of the three-match State of Origin series. Vautin had watched the first match with an almost detached interest. Like the rest of the viewers in NSW he saw it as an oddity. "It was like 'Gee, they're doing alright, they might just win this'," he said. "When they did I was happy for them but it wasn't until the next year that I really started hoping I'd get in the side. By the time the third year came around and it was going to a full series, there was a hell of a lot of interest. I was dead set keen to get a run."

The call came at home one night from Ken Arthurson, telling Vautin he was in the side to play at Lang Park. George and Leila had just driven down to Sydney for a long-planned visit. Paul paid for them to fly straight back with him for the game.

Arthur Beetson, hero of the first match, was now coach, Wally Lewis captain, and the laid-back but highly effective pre-match routine was already in place. Vautin and his teammates Paul McCabe and Bruce Walker in Queensland's all-Manly backrow had never experienced anything quite like it. Frank Stanton would have pulled his red hair out at the thought of it but there was no doubting it had brought results for the first two years — and was still working just as well when Vautin played his last Origin game seven years later.

Wally Lewis remembered the routine this way: "The first night was a big drink and the second night ... well, that was a big drink too."

The reunion of the team was an annual ritual that all looked forward to like 10-year-olds waiting for Christmas. The Sydney-based players would arrive en masse on the Thursday night. Turner, Lewis and just about everyone else in the squad would be there to greet them.

The scene resembled a family get-together or — perhaps more fitting — out-of-town hitmen getting picked up by the mob.

Sometimes the team would split up and jump into cabs; once the QRL hired limousines to deliver them to the Travelodge and when they couldn't avoid it, all were driven back by Lewis in the 20-seat mini-bus hired for the duration of the camp.

"There have been a lot of jokes about Wally driving that bus," said Vautin. "But the truth is he's a good driver — he had to be, because we came very, very close a couple of times. I honestly feared for my life. Everyone reckoned it was a big laugh driving down the main street of Brisbane with the window washers pointed outwards squirting people, and sometimes it was funny seeing how close we could come to telegraph poles or if we could get some little old lady to jump so her hat fell off, but there were dead set times when there was nothing to laugh about. I could see the headlines: "QLD Team — Dead."

Vautin's initial Origin match was not a happy experience. He remembers it as the worst game he played for his state, with nerves beforehand bringing on the first and only migraine headache of his life. The hours before the match were spent lying on his old bed at Everton Park, Leila applying cold compresses.

Brisbane TV commentator Mick Veivers would say midway through the match: "I hate to say it, but Paul Vautin is not playing very well." It was a fact. Vautin could not get into the match, won 20-16 by NSW, and it must have been a close call as to whether he or Walker would be the one dropped for the second game of the series, also at Lang Park. The answer was not long coming. The Manly teammates stood together at the Lang Park bar bemoaning their poor games and speculating whether they would be around for the rematch, when a Queensland selector walked towards them. They both stood watching, willing him to head towards the other one. Happily for Vautin, not so for his friend, it was Walker who was pulled aside and told he was out.

Vautin, enjoying the reprieve, was determined to make amends for his poor showing. He threw himself into the preparation and was looking forward to the match when, only hours before kick-off,

Beetson called him into his hotel room. "I know you'll be upset, but I'm putting you on the bench," he said. "I want to start with Rod Morris."

"I was devastated," Vautin recalled. "The first thing I did was ring Dad and break the news but he said not to worry about it. He said just to make sure if I got a chance, to do my best and give it everything I had."

That chance came with only 15 minutes left on the clock and Queensland leading by a point. Vautin was sent on and 90 seconds later ran on to a Rohan Hancock pass to score the try which sealed the match 11-7.

The Maroons wrapped up the series in Sydney the next week when Phil Sigsworth and winger Philip Duke botched a pass in the Blues' in-goal. Lewis dived on it for the winning try. The Queenslanders couldn't believe their luck and Sigsworth was entertaining his Manly team-mates with impressions of the interchange between him and Duke years later.

Vautin had been part of a historic victory and even got his name on the scoresheet but over the next few years his contribution to the team would prove to be much more than could be recorded by cold statistics.

"Having him in the side was always a huge bonus," said Lewis, "he was just so keen, so happy to be there. We'd be warming up at training and all of a sudden he'd get this big grin on his face and say, 'Arr, it's great to be a Queenslander, isn't it? It's great to be home.' That rubbed off on everyone and as far as I was concerned, it made my job a lot easier. A captain doesn't have to do a hell of a lot if his team is happy."

And there was the added advantage that unlike many of his teammates in the early years, Vautin played with and against the NSW players week in, week out. As the older hands like Reddy and Morris drifted out of the side, a new nucleus of young locals such as Neibling, Conescu and Tessman took their place. Vautin's first-hand knowledge of the NSW players proved invaluable in helping them settle in.

"I'd always wanted to go to Sydney but the timing was never right," Lewis said, "so I was always asking Fatty what it was like and the new blokes in the side would ask too. He used to say, 'Mate, it's no different. They train a bit harder and of course they've got two things that are bigger than anything you blokes have got." Of course we'd ask what they were and he'd say, 'Bigger pay cheques and bigger egos'."

When Wayne Bennett prepared to take over the side in 1986, he travelled to Sydney to talk with the NSW-based players. The coach, who had never featured the redhead in his pre-match talks a decade earlier, was now well aware of his importance to the Queensland side.

"It was very flattering really," said Vautin. "He asked me my opinion about certain players and the way we should go about things. He really let me know how big a part he saw me playing in the whole thing. Then I went and broke my bloody arm and couldn't play."

Vautin was out of the series but Bennett still wanted him aboard. He arranged for the QRL to appoint him assistant coach.

"When I got together with him in Sydney I was more than impressed," said Bennett. "And when he busted his arm I still wanted him involved because he was so widely respected by the players. He'd been there a number of times, I hadn't. I valued his opinion.

"The first game was in Brisbane and about 20 minutes before kick-off he and I went down to the dressing room. There was a lot of hype going on, guys walking around thumping their chests and saying what they were going to do. I thought it was a bit over the top and I looked over at Fatty to see if he agreed. He said. 'Gee Coach, these blokes are really ready to play.' From my own experience I thought they were more likely to lose, but he was the expert so I went along with him.

"We went upstairs and NSW were 14-nil before we even switched on. I turned to him and said, 'Hey Fatty, I'd hate to see these blokes if they *weren't* ready to play'. He said, 'Bit over the top, you reckon, Coach?'

"From then on we cut out the bullshit. We lost a few more games, but we lost without any of the bullshit."

Vautin might not have been on the field for that series, but he still found himself in the thick of the action. When Brisbane reporter Steve Ricketts rang the team hotel and asked Vautin for his opinion of the two sides the answer was candid. "I think if it gets right down to it NSW won't have the team spirit needed to win," he said.

As is always the case come Origin time, any spark can start a bushfire. The comments were picked up by the Sydney press and Vautin was portrayed as saying the Blues players had no heart. TV commentator Jack Gibson said on air that Vautin had: "A battle-ship mouth and a rowboat brain."

Vautin was incensed by the comment and instigated legal action. He was going for damages but his legal advisers pressed for a public apology. He got neither. The payback was to come when Gibson took over the NSW team in 1989.

"I was desperate to beat them," Vautin said of that series. "I couldn't wait to get out there. That was the time Jack insisted on having complete say on selections. We absolutely thrashed them three-nil. That was when I realised Jack Gibson wasn't the be-all and end-all when it comes to coaching."

But that series was still three years off. When Vautin made his ill-fated comments to Steve Ricketts, Queensland were very much underdogs and Bennett was to go through an uncomfortable learning curve as Maroons coach. The process started that night at Lang Park, with both Bennett and Vautin the students. From then on, out went the hype and Vautin's main contribution was his ability to help the other players keep perspective.

"His value off the field was absolutely enormous," Bennett said. "He gave us balance. He never took himself too seriously and he never took the stuff written in the papers too seriously. He understood the fickleness of it all and kept everyone's feet on the ground."

Not only did the Queenslanders learn to discount what was written in the newspapers, they used it to their advantage. The Sydney papers were a must in Maroon training camps and each afternoon the players would sit around reading the pre-match hype-fest out loud.

"It says here the bloke you're marking is going to be the greatest player since Dally Messenger," one would read to another.

"The bookies have got NSW 3-to-1-on and *The Mirror* reckons this is the biggest pack ever to wear a blue jumper."

"They've worked out how to shut down Wally."

And each statement would be met by derogatory shouts or laughter.

Years later, when Vautin had retired from the game and was working in the media, he found himself seated next to one of Sydney's most respected newspaper league writers. "Mate," he said, "I know you were only doing your job but that crap you used to write ... we loved it. The QRL should give you a medal."

Lewis said if any of the players was in danger of believing his own publicity, Vautin was quick to set him straight. "One year we're out for the big drink on the first night and this new bloke who's come up from Sydney starts telling some story about himself which is just way over the top. He's saying how he's run around this bloke and belted that bloke and it's getting further and further from the truth every second. Fatty is standing alongside me listening when he gives me this look like, 'What is this crap?'

"He grabs the bloke by the arm and says, 'Now listen mate, I'm not having a go at you here, I reckon you're a good bloke, but that is bullshit. I mean, do you really expect us to believe this stuff. Come on, we've been around a bit and that is just a load of porkys. Now it's not a bad story, so how about you go back to the beginning and start again only this time, leave all the crap out, okay?'

"That's just how he was, he called a spade a spade and he didn't mean anything by it. With anyone else it could have developed into a fight, but with Fatty the bloke just copped it, cut out the bullshit and settled into the team well."

If Vautin liked his teammates to keep the bull to a minimum, he liked to keep the on-field job nice and to the point too. "One time we're sitting there before a game talking about our defensive pattern," Lewis recalled. "It was, 'You go here and take this bloke in this zone and you slide over here and cover this section' and all of a sudden Fatty pipes up, 'Stuff this, let's just tackle 'em. If they've got the ball, belt them. That's all there is to it.' And he was right. He could break it all down and the blokes who'd never played in Sydney realised they didn't have to do anything fancy, they just had to do their jobs.

"People like me and Fatty used to go out to Lang Park when we were kids and watch NSW give Queensland a hiding year after year. Some of the younger blokes in the side felt the same way too. They'd seen the NSW players on TV and read about them in the papers and thought they were superstars. Fatty knew they were just like us."

Vautin remembers the bad times well. "When I was a kid if Queensland got a draw we thought it was a win," he said, "I remember one time "Bunny" Pearce from Redcliffe kicked two goals and we drew 4-all. We were that happy you'd have reckoned we'd won 45-nil. Because of that we grew up thinking there was something special about anyone who played in Sydney. It was only through playing with them and against them every week that I knew there wasn't. When players like Reddy and McCabe came into the early Origin sides it lifted the guys like Close and Meninga to their standard. When State of Origin is being talked about Chris Close doesn't get as big a wrap as he deserves. You only had to look in his eyes to see the way he felt about playing. He was a huge influence on the Queensland-based players."

Bennett once asked Vautin to prepare a dossier on the NSW players as part of the team's preparation. As he had as a kid, he sat down at his parents' dining table with his exercise book and scribbled down his thoughts. Bennett had the notes typed up and read them to the team.

"Okay, fellas," he called out, "here's Fatty's assessment of the NSW team. Fullback: Can't play. Left winger: Pussycat, can't play. Right winger: Prettyboy, can't play ..."

After five damning reports Bennett looked up. "Fatty," he asked, "can any of these blokes play?"

Vautin thought for a split second. "Nup."

Bennett screwed up the piece of paper and threw it on the floor. "Okay," he said, "that's it then. Team talk over."

It wasn't that Vautin didn't have any respect for any of the NSW players, more that he believed the Queensland spirit was enough to overcome any individual brilliance. Plus he believed some of the New South Welshmen were overrated.

Lewis remembers one other time when Vautin prepared a dossier on the Blues. "One bloke in question was a very respected player, very hard and tough," he said. "Fatty's description was: 'Dead set can't play. Big sheila, hates getting his hair out of place.' The room just broke up. We thought, 'Doesn't this bloke take anything seriously?'"

Vautin still believes his rating system was correct. "Some of the blokes used to believe what they read about these guys," he said.

"They used to think Steve Folkes was hard. I didn't think we should be too worried about him. Crusher Cleal was another one. We respected his attacking ability and knew we had to look out for him when he got involved, but a lot of our attack revolved around him. He wasn't noted for his defence so we'd look out for him to drift out on the blind and try to run at him.

"Wayne Pearce was a fit bloke who tried hard but I felt he was lacking a bit in natural ability. He made up for it with strength and determination though. We were pretty fierce rivals. If ever I saw him running at me I'd make sure I put a little extra in, and he'd do the same to me. I never used to talk on the field but with Wayne I'd make an exception. If he got me with a big hit I'd say, 'Good tackle, Junior.' There was always something a bit special about playing against him.

"I used to enjoy playing against "Blocker" Roach. He'd always be mouthing off at me: 'Run this way, you red-headed bastard, I'll smash you' so I'd run at him and he would smash me, but we'd have a few laughs after the match. He was the original tough man, Blocker, he always got them going forward, but we had a plan to shut him down. He used to make a lot of ground in club football because people would go high on him. The big legs used to keep pumping and he'd usually drag a few tacklers along with him. In State of Origin we always went low on him. Round the legs and down he went.

Roach remembers the battles well.

"Yeah, I used to tell him to run towards me so I could belt him," he laughed. "Course I did. That's what it was all about in those games and he was a tough bastard. He was a great support player, you'd think a movement had broken down and he'd charge up from nowhere and keep the thing alive. That was one part of his game – – and the defence of course, but I always respected his guts. He wasn't the biggest player in the world but he was never afraid to run the ball up. He reminded me a lot of Wayne Pearce in that respect, all heart. Geez, didn't they turn it on when they played each other. That's why Manly-Balmain games were so good in those days. They always saved something extra.

"He was a great competitor in every game he played but Origin was really his go. He exemplified what that Queensland spirit was all about. I see the games now and I wonder if they're the same without blokes like Wally and Gene Miles and Vautin. I wonder if the hatred is still there."

Certainly the Queenslanders never seemed worried about who the Blues put up against Lewis.

"The five-eighth we never used to have to worry about," Vautin said. They'd be bringing them out every year to do a job on Wally and he'd outplay them time after time. Brett Kenny, Terry Lamb, Allan Thompson, Steve Ella, Cliffy Lyons ... they were all going to be the one. The Sydney papers would be going on about it every year and in the end it just got boring. Wally never said anything about it, but he loved it. He absolutely loved it.

"But, saying that, Brett Kenny was always the class player of their team. If they didn't have him they wouldn't have gone as well as they did. And of course there was Sterling. Brilliant. Wherever he was the point of attack was so we paid special attention to him. He was such a good player. When he got the ball we'd be shouting: 'Sterling, watch the left foot step, left foot step, watch it, watch it' and you would. You'd watch him step right past you."

The respect was mutual. Sterling has always had a high opinion of Vautin as a player.

"I always thought he was a super player at club level," Sterling said. "At Manly it always seemed to get down to him or Des Hasler to make the crucial plays. If there was a break or half-break on they were the ones who stopped it and that got back to sniffing out problems, reading the play. Fatty's contribution over 80 minutes was very good and he had a lot to do with success Manly had when he was there.

"I think he was probably under-rated by plenty of people — except the selectors and his teammates, particularly at Origin level.

"When people are talking about Origin football the likes of Lewis, Miles and Meninga get plenty of wraps but one thing I have found is that when they talk about Origin football, the name Vautin invariably comes up. I think that says a lot."

Garry Jack was another the Queenslanders "spotted."

"Garry Jack was always dangerous running the ball back or coming into the line, we always had to watch him, and Pricey always played it hard, but I felt Steve Mortimer was the closest thing that they had to our type of player.

"You could tell how much it meant to him to beat us. The year he was captain and they won the series, you only had to see the way he collapsed after fulltime and threw his hands up in the air. That was how we felt every time we won. The whole match he never shut up. We'd hear him yelling at them, pushing them on and when their intensity was dropping he'd take it from dummy half himself and fly into us again. He played a great series that year. It was almost like he'd learnt the secret of what it was all about. I could never understand why they didn't give him a chance as coach."

Mortimer said he borrowed from the Queenslanders' intensity to steer NSW to that first series win. "Coming from the country it meant a hell of a lot to me to play for New South Wales," he said, "but it didn't mean as much to some other people. There was no humbleness in the team. Everyone thought they were big stars and all we had to do was show up. They were going one out. For a while there I was doing what everyone else was doing: trying to get through the game without getting hurt. It might be a big club round the next Sunday, I could be up against Sterling or something, so all I did was try to finish the game in one piece.

"When I became captain by default I took a leaf out of the Queenslanders' book. I could see how much it meant to them to play for their state, I knew how much it meant to me. It was a case of getting everyone else in the NSW team to feel the same way and get us all pulling together. And that's what happened."

Vautin's assessment of his own teammates was a lot less critical than the way he saw the Blues, but often just as inciteful, Bennett recalled. "In 1987 Mark Murray was out after injuring his eye and Alfie Langer came into the side," he said. "The opinion was that Alf wasn't anywhere near as tough as "Muzza" had been. We had a team meeting before the game and I was telling them the options I'd worked out. We could put Alf on the blind behind the forwards or in the second line, back between the winger and fullback; all these different ways to give him protection. Alfie's sitting there with his head down listening and Fatty jumps up. 'Hang on coach,' he says, 'he's a Queenslander. He'll do the job. Put him in the line where he belongs.' I asked Alf the question and he said, 'I can do it', and that was it, no more discussion. We put Alfie in the front line and he's never looked back.

"That was how it was with Fatty, his opinion was always no

matter who NSW put up against us, we were a team of Queenslanders and we'd be better."

Bennett-coached Queensland teams lost the first four times he prepared them, before a nine-match winning streak which continued into the second Beetson era. Bennett gives a lot of the credit for the change in fortunes to Vautin. "In the second game of the 1987 series we were playing in the wet at the SCG and they were starting to get on top late in the first half," he recalled. "It was 6-nil to NSW and we were really starting to lose our way. Then Fatty took the ball about 22 metres out and launched into them. He only ran about 10 metres but he belted a couple of them out of the way and took a couple more with him. He didn't score a try and he made a lot of longer runs than that in his career but none more important. It lifted every member of the side. I was sitting 50 metres away in the stand and it inspired me. I get goosebumps when I think about it."

Commentator Darrell Eastlake, calling the match for Channel 9, saw it this way on the night: "Geez, they've got a fair bit to do the way they're playing tonight. That's the 22 line you can see. Queensland using short passes. Some pretty wild passes coming back from Gene Miles as little Langer is caught ..."

Langer, tackled by replacement Paul Langmack, gets to his feet and plays the ball, with NSW hooker Royce Simmons at second marker. His Maroon opposite Greg Conescu moves into dummy half as Eastlake continues the call.

"He's just a jockey sized man, a tiny little man but he showed plenty of courage in Brisbane as ..."

Langer plays the slippery ball and Conescu heaves it out to Vautin, running hard and straight back into the ruck. Simmons, coming from Vautin's right is first man to him. Langmack comes across one pace behind, and Wayne Pearce and Brett Kenny move up in a line on Vautin's left. It should be a straightforward tackle for Simmons. Pearce moves up quickly and Vautin runs straight past him.

Eastlake raises his voice a notch. "Vautin makes a busting run ... look at Vautin ..."

Simmons goes high, expecting the Queenslander to take the tackle. Vautin hits him with his shoulder and the NSW hooker slides down his body. Vautin's legs are pumping high as Langmack arrives. He dives low but Vautin steps out of the tackle and continues upfield.

"Will ya look at the determination on Vautin's face ..."

Pearce, realising his mistake, tries to turn but slips on the wet surface. It is left to five-eighth Kenny to prop, turn towards Vautin and grab him around the shoulders. The two men continue for a few more metres before Kenny's weight and his own momentum force Vautin off balance and onto the ground.

"What a run, that's taken it to just 12 metres out. Queensland is in with a chance now as Gene Miles raids away ..."

Vautin's run takes exactly five seconds and advances the ball just 10 metres but Bennett earnestly believes it changed the course of Origin history. Six minutes later, after Queensland come close to scoring three times, Dale Shearer moves into dummy half behind Alf Langer on the Maroons' line. Diving low he pushes through the tackles of Jack, Les Davidson and Michael O'Connor. Queensland go in at half time only two points behind at 6-4.

During the break Jack Gibson sums up the situation this way: "Queensland have got to risk defeat now more than NSW because they've got to win this game. If they don't the series is out the winda ..."

As he was speaking, the Queensland side was standing in their dressing room, pumped up, ready to get back on the field. "I've never seen a team so eager to get back onto the field for the second half in my life," said Bennett.

Queensland come back to win the match 12-6. They won't be beaten again for three years.

"He had that ability to know when the team needed a lift," said Turner, "and he was one of the bravest players ever to play for the state. When we were down on one knee and all but out this rotten dumpy little red-headed thing would take it up and take it up again and then take it up once more. I lost count of the number of times it happened. I'd be sitting there in the stand thinking, 'Take it up, Paul' and through he'd come again. It was like mental telepathy."

The emotion Turner exudes when speaking of Vautin and the rest of "his boys" gives a hint of the force behind Queensland's Origin success. Vautin is asked time and time again what it was that drove them to beat star-studded NSW outfits when the experts had all but written them off. He still isn't sure of the real answer.

"I've never been able to put it into words," he said. "It might sound corny but I think in a way it was the love we had for each other. We were so close that there wasn't anything we wouldn't do for each other.

"In all those years, you know I never heard one Queenslander bag another one on the field no matter how badly things were going, but on the other side they were always going off at each other. Benny Elias was notorious for it — nothing was ever his fault — and Blocker would have a bit to say, usually at Benny.

"That was the difference. It was like Queensland against a bloke from Canterbury and two blokes from Balmain and a bloke from Parramatta. When the pressure was on they used to fall apart. We used to thrive on it. They'd start mouthing off and we knew we had them. Once we heard that we'd think, 'You beauty'. They'd start unravelling in front of our eyes.

"There's some people give me a lot of credit for contributing to the spirit in the side but I was just part of a team. Everyone played their part. Right from the start blokes set the mood. Choppy Close would be so excited he was almost frothing at the mouth before the game. That match in 1984 when he lost his jumper in the fight I was standing about a metre away. I remember thinking he looked like a big out-of-control walrus.

"It just carried on from there. Colin Scott: for a bloke who couldn't see he was great. He was blind as a bat but he was safe and solid. There was a lot of pressure on the fullback in those games and Scotty never let us down. Kerry Boustead was another. If there was a better winger going around at that time I didn't see him. Miles and Meninga in the centres, what a partnership.

"Then you had blokes like Wally Fullerton Smith. Talk about wanting to get out and play. Three days before the game he'd be saying, 'Fatty, we're gonna belt these blokes'. There wasn't a lot to him but he never shirked the hard stuff.

"And Mark Murray. I always used to say he was the type of bloke I'd like to have next to me in the trenches. At lock I'd be up in the defensive line and I'd look to the left and there'd be a prop there and I'd know we were covered there and then I'd look to the right and there would be Muppet and I'd think, 'Well, we're covered here.' He was one of the best front-on defenders I ever saw.

" 'Turtle' Conescu wasn't one of those hookers who'll never make a 30 or 40 metre break, but he'd make you seven or eight every time and keep the momentum going. And he was tough.

"Dave Brown, Gilly, Neibling, Dowling, everyone played his part. When Shearer came into the side he added the pace. We weren't the quickest side up until then but Rowdy added another dimension. He could turn nothing into something, he was that fast. There were no headline grabbers in the team, no-one wanted to take the limelight. We just wanted to beat NSW. You'd look around the dressing room and the sheer determination was on everyone's face. Nobody wanted to give those blue bastards anything. We wanted to beat them and we wanted to hurt them. It wasn't a game, it was war.

"There was never any ranting or raving. All the talk was positive. We just used to draw from each other's strength. It's hard to describe, but it was there in that room before every match. A feeling, a spirit."

Lewis believes a lot of Queensland's spirit came from the traditional laid-back build up. "We'd get together on the Thursday and have a big blowout and another one the next night and not really start thinking about football until the Sunday night. I always had the feeling they got together and started getting all serious from the first minute. It was like it was this real serious pressure game. Not for us. It was fun. When we got together it was handshakes all around and welcome back. Now let's get out and have a big night."

Vautin was not always a big participant in the early "blowouts". In fact, he dreaded them. "We'd all be putting on our good gear and Fatty would still be in his shorts and thongs," Lewis recalled. "I'd ask him what was going on and he'd say he wasn't coming. I'd have to drag him along kicking and screaming. He's the worst drinker you ever saw. Six pots and he's gone and the next morning he's so crook you feel like you should get a rifle and put the poor bastard out of his misery. Once you got him out to the pub you'd have to keep your eye on him. He was notorious for saying he was going to have a leak and sneaking back to the hotel."

Lewis and Gene Miles did manage to nail the reluctant drinker one night. After Beetson had been reappointed coach in 1989, the players chose Sheilas nightclub at North Sydney for their Thursday night get-together. It was a big night all around. Big Artie led the way through the crowd, plonked himself down in a corner and got a game of cards going while the rest of the squad got on with some serious team bonding. Mal Meninga took his mission so seriously that when it came time to leave at 2am he was so relaxed he walked straight into a slow moving car and flew over the bonnet. The driver was just getting out to investigate when he saw an angry Sam Backo and Gene Miles walking towards him from the darkness. He jumped back in, locked the doors and disappeared into the night.

Vautin missed all that action. He was back at Rushcutters Bay Travelodge, watching the ceiling go round and round. "Wally and Geno kept buying me beers all night, which I thought was very generous of them," Vautin said. "But after a while I starting feeling right out of it. About 1am I staggered outside and had a big up and under, poured myself into a cab and went back to the hotel. When I got out I had another big hurl on the pavement and someone had to help me up to my room. The next morning about 7 there's a knock on the door and I hear, 'Wally here, mate, just seeing how you are.' I said, 'Wally, what was in those bloody drinks last night?' 'Just beer,' he says, 'oh ... and double vodkas.' Apparently they were all in on it.

"I've never felt so crook in my life but I got them back. Artie used to take us for a team walk before breakfast. When we walked out the front door, there's my up and under from the night before still sitting there. Artie growls, 'Who owns this?' I put up my hand. 'Me, Arthur' and as we filed past I could hear all the 'hup hup hups' as everyone came out in sympathy. Served them right."

Another time Wally took the points when he left Vautin with a classic "Kenny Couldabeen'. "Some bloke who used to play with Wally in the juniors comes up and says, 'Hey Wally, remember me?'" Vautin recalled. "Wally shakes the guy's hand and says, 'You remember Fatty, don't you?' and walks off. I'm left standing there and in the background Wally is having a great time while I'm listening to this bloke going on about how he could have been as good as Wally if only he hadn't hurt his knee or his shoulder or something. He's saying, 'Fatty, Fatty, where did it all go wrong?' Finally I had to say, 'How the hell would I know where it went wrong, you goose. I've never clapped eyes on you before.'

"Spare me. I'm a patient sort of bloke but one thing I cannot stand is drunken bores. I shouldn't give the people who support the team a hard time — they're what it's all about — but blokes who get in your ear about how good they used to be or how they'd play the game if they were still around really get to me."

Lewis remembers Vautin had a unique way of dealing with the "Kennys". "He had this word, 'arbity'. Some old drunk would come up and start going on and Fatty would look straight ahead and go 'arbity'. The bloke would keep talking and Fatty would be going 'arbity, arbity, arbity' until finally he got the message and walked off. He didn't suffer fools gladly."

Bennett doesn't remember Vautin being even that diplomatic. "Usually he'd just say, 'Yeah mate, you'd know, you've done it all, yeah, sure ...' People were always coming up to the boys and telling them how to play. Fatty used to sort them out. He could say some shocking things to people. One time we were at some bar and he said something to this girl as she walked past and she just reeled off and belted him in the mouth. He went down like a sack of potatoes. When he got up he just said, 'Righto, that's it, I'm going home' and walked out. He really shouldn't have had a drink. He'd be as silly as a wheel."

The bingeing wasn't really an enjoyable part of the Origin experience for Vautin but he battled on manfully, doing what he felt was his duty for the team. What he really enjoyed, other than beating NSW, was the camaraderie, the highjinks that pervaded the camp up until match day.

"It was like we all went back to kindergarten for the week," he said. "Someone would spend three bucks on a water pistol and squirt everyone, then for the next four hours every toyshop in Brisbane would be scoured to find the biggest, most elaborate Super Sopper money could buy. The first bloke would buy a little gun, the last one would come back with a cannon."

The water battles raged throughout the rooms, in the hallways, in the lifts, wherever the players went, and in it up to their eyeballs were the officials and Turner. "That was part of the spirit of the whole thing," Vautin said. "Tosser wasn't like some sort of head-master in charge of the naughty little boys. He wanted to be in everything. He just loved it all. We used to go to this place down the coast to drive the go-karts and Tosser would be the first one in line. He was just such a great manager. No problem was too big or too small. His job was to make sure all we had to do was relax and get ready for the game. He didn't want any hassles to get in the way. You could go up to him on the afternoon of the game and say 'hey Tosser, my aunty is going to be at the gate at five o'clock and she wants 18 tickets' and he'd say 'alright Fatty, I'll take care of it, you just go and get something to eat and have a sleep', and you would because you knew it would be done.

"Same with the coaches. Whether it was Artie or Wayne, no-one ever went crook at anyone for having a beer or feeling sick at training. If someone had an up and under there would be laughs all round and most likely it would start a chain reaction. We were all like little kids."

Beetson's big-match build-up was highly successful, but not one you'd find in the coaching manuals. "To all of us Artie was Mr State of Origin," Vautin said. "He'd been the first captain and led the way. Then as coach he did everything right. He was one of the fellas, he enjoyed the wins and took the losses to heart as much as any of the players.

"As a coach he was okay on tactics and things like that but his main thing was motivation. He'd stand in the dressing room before a match, all 25 stone of him, and start talking about Queensland — how much it meant to him to be a Queenslander, how proud he was to be involved with us. I've dead set seen his bottom lip quivering. That would really get to us. We'd be thinking, 'How much does Arthur want to win? We've got to win for him.'

"In 1984 they took the Australian coaching job off him before the series. It was like, 'Look what these bastards have done to Arthur, we've got to beat them.' We won the series in the mud in Sydney and we all walked off absolutely filthy. Arthur had this beautiful long coat on, it would have cost a fortune. By the time we'd all hugged him it was ruined. He probably had to throw it out, but it wouldn't have worried him, it meant that much that we'd won."

In the dressing room before a match Beetson was without peer. On the training paddock ... well. "We'd be training for a while and Arthur would yell out 'that'll do, I'm gettin' hungry' so we'd pack off and head for lunch," Vautin said. "He wasn't a real disciplinarian. I remember one morning Muppet Murray arrived blind. He looked like he hadn't been to bed. He was dropping the ball and falling over. We were all laughing about it but some other coaches probably would have dropped him from the side. Not Arthur, he put him on the wing to run it off.

"He was very approachable. In 1989 Jack Gibson took over the Blues. Arthur was in awe of Jack and for the first few days of the camp he seemed really concerned about what Gibson was going to do. He'd be telling us that Gibson might be pulling such and such a ploy and that Jack liked to run such-and-such a move. We had some young blokes in the side, people like Alfie who hadn't been around too long and I felt they might be starting to worry. It was like, 'If Arthur's worried about this bloke, what hope have we got?' I spoke to Wally and he felt the same way, so we went and saw Arthur in his room. We said, 'Arthur, it seems to us you're putting too much emphasis on Gibson. He's not going to be on the field. You're as good a coach as him and besides, you've got the better team.'

"Some coaches might have told us to mind our own business. Arthur just said, 'You're right' and for the rest of that camp he never mentioned Gibson's name again. We thrashed them three-nil."

The openness of the camp made for closeness and team sprit — so did the practical jokes. One of the big gee-ups was impersonating journalists and "interviewing" teammates. "Wally used to do a very good Ray Chesterton," Vautin said. "He got me a beauty once. The phone would ring and it would be: 'Oh hello, Paul, Ray Chesterton from the Sydney *Daily Telegraph* here.'

"'Yeah Ray, how are you.'

"'Fine thank you. Paul, I was just doing my preview of the match and I must say you have been in really tremendous form.'

"'Well, thanks Ray, I suppose I am doing okay.'

"'Okay? Oh no Paul, I think you've been doing much better than just okay. You've been absolutely tremendous. Brilliant. By far the best player in the series ...'

"And he'd go on and on until finally you'd agree with him and give yourself a big wrap, then you'd hear this roar of laughter come through the phone and Wally would have about six blokes listening in."

Other times players were rung by "reporters" asking them to get into their team uniform for a photograph outside the hotel. When they walked out of the lift resplendent in slacks, shirt, tie and blazer, their teammates would be waiting, dressed in shorts and T-shirts.

Little wonder then that when Brisbane's Andrew Gee was rung by a legitimate Sydney reporter on the eve of his state debut he refused to answer any questions until the reporter had furnished such information as his home address, postcode, phone number and date of birth.

The practical jokes were all part of the team bonding and more often than not Lewis was at the forefront. His antics at the wheel of the team bus became legendary. "One of his favourites was telling us to close the windows so he could put the air conditioning on," Vautin said. "We'd all close them and be driving along and after a while someone would say, 'Geez, it's hot in here.' Blokes like Sam Backo would have their tongues hanging out. Then we'd look up the front and Wally's shoulders would be going up and down and he'd be giggling away. He'd have put the heater on full bore.

"Another one was when Artie was coach. He'd always be the last one into the minibus and Wally would wait until he just got on and everyone was getting into their seats and he'd roar off. The blokes down the back would hear "whoaa" and look up to see 25 stone of Artie rolling down the aisle towards them. Anyone in the way would be absolutely flattened. Artie would get back on his feet and just be getting his balance and Wally would stick his foot on the brakes and he'd go flying back up the aisle again. Everyone would be diving out of the way. Someone like Alfie could get killed."

For building up the team spirit, such tomfoolery would be every bit as important as any tackle drill or backline move. It was all part of what the Sydney papers started calling "Factor X". That indefinable something that Queensland teams seemed to have which lifted them when the chips were down. The spirit was no accident, nothing was left to chance by the team management. Something as innocuous as choosing roommates was given great thought by Turner and the team coaches.

Lewis and Miles would always room together. Mates since childhood, they would share quarters for club, state and country in hotels around the world until Lewis's sacking as Brisbane club captain and subsequent replacement by Miles ended their close friendship. Other partnershps were equally successful.

"We used to put a lot of thought into it and worked out different pairings for different reasons," Turner said. "Sometimes some humour went into it. When Paul Hauff came into the side we put him in with Alfie Langer. It was a pretty incongruous sight. Little Alfie and the giant Queensland cop who needed to get a specially long bed put in the room. It just appealed to our sense of the ridiculous.

"Fatty always roomed with Trevor Gillmeister. When Gilly came into the side he didn't know much about a lot of the other players and he hadn't had much experience of representative football. By that time Paul was a veteran but Gilly was very much like Fatty had been when he first came into the team. He was a strong-tackling forward, a hard worker and he played in Sydney. We thought it would be a good move to put them together and it proved one of the most successful pairings we ever made.

"Fatty helped Gilly settle in and they became the closest of mates on and off the field. The only problem I ever had with them was on the afternoon of a match. We had a tradition that before the match the players would stay in their rooms and order whatever they wanted on room service rather than coming down to the dining room for lunch. Then they'd lie around and relax and try to have a sleep or just think about the game. That quiet time was an important part of our big-match preparation.

"One year Fatty and Gilly ordered up a feast on room service and put a big bet on some horse. Everyone was trying to sleep or meditate and the floor of the hotel was deadly quiet when this almighty scream went up. It was Gilly and Fatty riding their horse in as they listened on the radio. You could have heard it in Sydney as they came down the straight. I had to chip 'em a bit on that one."

The pair became best mates despite the fact that Vautin played for Manly and "The Axe" Gillmeister for Easts. One year they were scheduled to play against each other the weekend after an Origin match. In an incident which Vautin refuses to confirm, Bennett remembers going to their room in the lead-up to the Lang Park game. "I walked in and they were lying there watching Humphrey Bear — which was Fatty's favourite program, and he was saying to Gilly something like, 'Then we call Pinetrees and Crusher will come down the blind'" he said. "He was telling Gilly about one of the Manly moves so that he could give Crusher Cleal a tickle on the weekend.

"That's how he was. It was only early in the series and Gilly would be coming up against Crusher for Queensland again in a couple of weeks. Fatty wanted to give him something to think about. If you were from Queensland he'd back you over a New South Welshman any day."

That is one theory. Another could be that the tip-off was because Vautin and Cleal weren't the closest of friends following Manly's decision to replace Vautin with Cleal as captain in 1987.

It was almost too fitting then that at the height of their cold war *Rugby League Week* chose them as the pair to be photographed in US civil war outfits for the cover of the magazine's special 1987 LA State of Origin issue. The icy glares on their faces as Crusher wore the grey of the south and Fatty the Yankee blue were not faked, said Neil Cadigan, then NSW editor of the magazine.

"They weren't talking to each other. It was one of *Rugby League Week's* all-time famous covers, but there was a lot going on behind the scenes."

Vautin made no secret of his disappointment at missing out on the 1986 Kangaroo tour, his place going to Steve Folkes in controversial circumstances. When Folkes faced up to Vautin in the Origin series the following year it was The Axe who put the Canterbury forward out of the play with a brutal tackle. As Folkes was carried from the field the laconic Jack Gibson remarked: "Folkes'll be wishin' he was four or five yards faster. Gillmeister's mugged him. That was a back alley job, that one."

The tackle was par for the course in Origin football which had quickly developed into the hardest, fastest and best rugby league in the world. "Mate Against Mate, State Against State" the advertising copywriters called it, and they were never more right than in 1983.

As one of several Queensland players in the Manly side, Vautin was used to representing his state against clubmates. The games were always hard, but he made a point of offering his hand to Manly's NSW players after the match. Only once was he refused.

Vautin will always remember the first match of the 1983 series as his best for Queensland but it will be recalled by most football watchers for something else — Les Boyd's elbow smashing the jaw of Darryl Brohman. The Penrith prop was playing the game of his life when Boyd ended his evening — and his dream of playing for his country.

"They were picking a Test team to play New Zealand that night and I was pretty happy with the way I'd been going," Brohman said, "then *that* happened. Dave Brown came on to replace me and when they named the Australian side he was in it. You don't have to be Einstein to figure out I was a pretty good chance."

Vautin was right behind Brohman when the incident happened. "He was taking it up and we were all following up behind him," he recalled. "It was never going to be anything but what happened. I don't know what Boyd was thinking about, whether he wanted to maim him or just put him out of the game or what. It was the worst thing you could ever see."

Vautin had a shot at Boyd over the incident a few minutes later. Boyd went at him and their Manly teammate Dave Brown clipped Boyd across the side of the head. "From then on Les chased me all over the field," Vautin said. "I could hear him every time I had the ball. 'You little red-headed prick ...' He got me once or twice too, and I got him."

Wally Lewis, seeing the ongoing altercation, couldn't help smiling. "Every time Boydy took the ball up everybody piled on him and without fail the last ones off him would be Fatty, Dave Brown and John Ribot — all Manly blokes," he said. "I couldn't help thinking how much fun Manly training was going to be that week."

After the match, Vautin walked into the NSW dressing room and shook hands with his Manly teammates Max Krilich and Alan Thompson. He then walked up to Boyd, who looked away. "I walked out thinking, 'Gee, I don't think Les likes me any more'," Vautin said. "I thought, 'This is going to be great!' We were the Manly secondrowers at the time. We spent half our lives with our arms around each other."

Any concerns were assuaged when Boyd walked up to Vautin at the next Manly training with a "well-played, Fatty" but Vautin's fears about the pair teaming up again proved academic. Boyd was cited and suspended for 12 months over the tackle. Brohman took out a civil complaint which was settled out of court for an undisclosed sum.

The way the Manly players combined against one of their own that night was an example of the deep pride that players on both sides felt in Origin clashes. It was that kind of spirit which made the series such a success. Club loyalties were forgotten for the duration of the matches, although Vautin says sometimes friendships would surface even in the heat of battle.

"For the third match in 1983 they had a heap of dropouts," he said, "They had blokes like Paul Field and Lindsay Johnston and Stan Jurd. At one stage we were winning 33-nil." Late in the first half Vautin felled Max Krilich with a low tackle and the Manly captain's head hit the ground hard. After having attention, he climbed to his feet groggily to play the ball, Vautin at first marker. "How ya going, Thrower?" Vautin asked.

"How am I going?" replied the still-dazed Krilich. "I'll tell ya how I'm going. Get me outta here. How did I get myself into this mess?"

When things were going bad there was no more mournful sight than Max Krilich. His pitiful cry that night doubled Vautin over in laughter, for as Tosser Turner will vouch, there were few better winners than Fatty. "All us Queenslanders are like that," he says, "great winners and shocking losers, but Fatty was one of the best winners I've ever seen. He wrote our victory song for us and would lead the singing. It wasn't a very complicated song. It only had five words. 'The Blues Can't Play, The Blues Can't Play, The Blues Can't Bloody Play'."

It was all part of the experience of State of Origin for Vautin. Once he had become an integral part of the team, he was like a kid with a new toy. For him the series was the embodiment of everything he'd dreamed off when he left Brisbane to try his luck in Sydney. He had gone down south and become a success, yes, but what was the fun in that if he couldn't share it with the people who mattered most to him? Where was the satisfaction in becoming the type of footballer he'd always wanted to be if he was playing 1000 kilometres away?

State of Origin gave him the chance to return home and be a hero. To show that he had never really turned his back on Queensland, that, sure, he was living down there, taking their money and dancing to their tune, but when it came down to it, he was as proud a Queenslander as anyone alive.

It also gave the two sides of his personality the only legitimate chance to live in harmony that they would ever have. He could be Fatty without any risk of a rap over the knuckles, lead the water pistol fights and send everyone scurrying out of the dining room in horror at his table manners, but at the same time he was applauded for it — he was doing it for Queensland. Yet when he needed to be serious, when he needed to be Paul and speak sincerely of his love of home and state, no-one laughed or teased. Emotion was every bit as important as water pistols in the Queensland camp.

And there was another thing. For the first time he could share his success as a footballer with his parents, to whom he always remained close. When he first started making good money in Sydney Paul tried to buy his father a new car. He was advised to put his money in the bank. He felt frustrated. He wanted to show them how well he had done, show his father he'd become the type of player he'd always wanted him to be. Wanted to share in their pride ... and then along came State of Origin, the biggest, fastest, hardest, most spectacular games of the year, and for George, Leila and Paul, they became an annual ritual.

Paul would visit his parents' home several times in the week leading up to the Brisbane matches to eat his mother's cooking and discuss the match with his father. Leila still keeps Paul's first Origin jumper in a plastic bag, washed and meticulously folded, like it was the family jewels.

They never missed a match. The Vautins would sit in the stand with the Lewises — although George wasn't great company. He never said a word during the games and, to be honest, never really watched the match. "I only used to watch Paul," he said. "I'd keep my eye on him the whole game, watch where he was standing, see if he was in position. I'd really only see the game when I went home and watched the replay."

And Paul was always there with him. As he had in his days at West Mitchy and Wests, Vautin would go home straight after the game, have a shower and a cup of tea before watching the replay and returning to the hotel with his parents for the after-match festivities.

"I've never been one to have a beer straight away after a game," he said, "particularly after State of Origin matches. I'd be too keyed up. I needed to relax and besides, the celebrations usually went on pretty late. I didn't have much trouble catching up."

As he speaks of the Origin days, Vautin's eyes shine and the words can't come quick enough. It was, quite simply, the best time of his life. Seven years, 22 matches, 15 wins.

When it ended, it ended probably the only way it could. As Wayne Bennett put it, "They had to drag him out feet first, there was no way he was going to walk away from it."

In 1990, with Lewis out with a torn hamstring, Vautin was handed the captaincy for the second time. The first, in 1988, had been one of the proudest nights of Vautin's life. Peter Jackson had taken the King's spot at five-eighth, Vautin became only the third Queensland captain in Origin history. The occasion almost proved too much for him, as Bennett recalls.

"I never had to say much to Fatty," he said. "He'd come up to me and say, 'How am I going, coach?' or tell me himself. He'd say, 'I have to lift it a bit' and he'd be right. He was that type of player. Even his warm-ups were legendary. Everyone would be putting themselves through some hard stretches and Fatty would put one foot over the other, try to touch his toes once or twice, get about halfway down, then give up. I'd say, 'Is that it?' and he'd say, 'I'm ready, let's get into them'. You learned not to argue.

"But on that night in '88 he was trying to do too much. He was telling everyone else what to do, not doing it himself. He came off the field thinking he was going okay but I had to set him straight for the first and only time. I told him to forget about the 'C' next to his name and get on with his own game. Everyone else would follow his lead."

And so it proved. Vautin led by example and the Maroons came home to win 26-18.

The second stint at captaincy was not so successful. With Queensland behind despite two try-saving tackles by the captain, age finally overpowered pride. Coach Beetson sent out word that Vautin was replaced, with 20 minutes left to play. It was the harshest blow imaginable for the player whose life had been Origin football for the past eight years.

The replacement and subsequent sacking from the team created a furore in Queensland. Newspaper articles, talkback radio programmes and public opinion raged over what had happened to one of the state's favourite sons.

For the only time in his association with the team, Tosser Turner broke ranks. "I didn't agree with what had happened and I let Arthur know it," he said. "I didn't say it then, we had a series to play, but as soon as the third game was played I told Arthur what I thought. That boy deserved more than that and I'm still not convinced that he couldn't have turned things around.

"I'm not saying we would have won the game, but I am saying that from what I knew about that player and what was inside him, if we were to win, we needed to have him there."

Unlike some, Paul Vautin does not have to close his eyes to conjure his greatest memories. They are all there on video tape, every game he ever played for the State — except the last, which he has never been able to watch — all in chronological order and some notated with special comments on the box. "Oh What A Night!" "Make Mine a XXXX Mate!" "You Little Beauty!"

One tape takes pride of place. In 1988, when Bennett left the team, he had Channel 9 put together a special compilation of highlights of his time at the helm and presented it to each of the players. The tape starts with a shot of Vautin putting in his mouthguard readying for battle. There is superimposed footage of World War I diggers climbing out of the trenches, and a stirring soundtrack liberally sprinkled with words and phrases such as "love in my heart", "hand in hand", "let the world around fall apart, maybe we can make it if we're heart to heart."

Some might call it sentimental or jingoistic, but those people weren't in the dressing room the night Vautin and Meninga couldn't continue, when Langer and Lindner were lying on stretchers with broken bones and Wally Lewis outsprinted the latest pretender to his throne to score the winning try. The same night Beetson and Turner wept like babies in their pride.

They weren't there the night Queensland went in at halftime only two points up. The coach had his say, the captain had his say and then they turned to the vice-captain. "Anything to add Fatty?"

"Yeah," he said, "if they don't score we win."

And that was exactly what happened. The Blues didn't score, the Maroons won. That was the night they christened the "Queenslander" call. The call suggested by Gary Belcher one afternoon at training. The call to lift them when things were at their lowest. They screamed it that night until they were hoarse.

The tape is playing. Vautin is tansfixed. "I can't watch it without getting chills down my back," he said, "and the words, the words say it all."

He mouths along as the chorus blasts out: "and we can build this dream forever, stand this tall forever. Nothin's gonna stop us now ..."

That tape is just one of a roomful of memories Vautin calls his office, opening out onto the pool at his Cromer home. There are programmes, newspaper cuttings, signed footballs and framed photographs hung on the walls.

But one picture stands alone. On the desk, where he sees it every day.

It was taken after an Origin match at the Sydney Cricket Ground. It is 1987, a wet night, and Queensland have won 12-6. The stands are slowly emptying and Vautin is walking off the field alone. It's one of those pictures which photographers snap almost absentmindedly, perhaps the last shot on the reel. For some reason, this photographer is not with the pack, they are all back in centrefield. You can see them over Vautin's shoulder. At least a dozen of them, crowded in a semi circle, lit by the arc lights of the television cameras. In the centre of the circle stands the King, holding court, while his loyal lieutenant trudges off home for a cup of tea.

His jersey is steaming in the mist, heavy with sweat and dirt. His hair is matted and there is a slight trail of blood from one eye. And the look is one of such such unbridled happiness, such satisfaction and pride at a job well done, that you can't help smiling.

Paul Vautin says he can't put into words what it was that drove that team, what made them the best at what they did for so long.

He doesn't have to. It's written all over his face.

CHAPTER 11

Wally And Wayne

A bonus of the Origin experience for Vautin was the opportunity to renew links with Wally Lewis and Wayne Bennett. Vautin and Lewis had played together in the under-age representative matches of the mid to late '70s and were keen rivals for their respective club sides. Lewis and his Valleys teammates dubbed Vautin the "shithouse with the red roof". To the West Mitchy boys the man who would be King was simply: "the long-haired lout."

In the early rep games they vied for the same lock position, Lewis invariably winning out, and as teammates they got along well. For up to 12 matches a year they wore the same jumper and shared a few laughs but Vautin says they were never close friends. "We got along well but because we played for different clubs we didn't see enough of each other to be real mates," Vautin said. "He was always a good player, very quick and strong and even then, playing lock, he had a very good kicking game. In those days we didn't pass much, we just used to get the ball and see what we could do and he had enough toe to do plenty."

One of the last matches Vautin and Lewis played together was when they came up against a particularly fierce Townsville touring outfit including future Maroons Gene Miles, Greg Dowling and Colin Scott. The game degenerated into a brawl and Vautin and Lewis found themselves fighting side to side. "The last punch I ever threw," says Vautin.

After those few years in the juniors, their paths didn't cross again until Vautin was called into the Origin squad — but they had followed each others' careers with interest. Lewis because he had always wondered how he would go in Sydney and saw Vautin as a yardstick, and Vautin because it seemed every time he picked up a Queensland newspaper it had the name Wally Lewis plastered all over it.

"Not going to Sydney was probably the best thing Wally ever did," he said. "He suddenly became the focal point of all the press up there. You couldn't read about Queensland rugby league without reading about Wally Lewis. My only thought was 'geez, he must have improved a bit.'"

When Vautin came into the Queensland side, he was to see just how much Lewis had indeed improved. "I'd seen him play in the '80 and '81 games on TV but it wasn't until I came into the side that I realised just how good he really was. He amazed me with the things he could do. Even when I was on the field with him sometimes I'd just have to stand there shaking my head.

"All the stuff the Brisbane papers had been saying was spot on. When I'd last seen him he was this long-haired lock with pace and good cover defence but by the time I started playing for Queensland he was a five-eighth who could completely control a game. He had that time, the time to do things that everyone says is the mark of a good player. Well he had more time than anyone I ever saw. And he was so strong. It took two or three players to bring him down every time he ran. I was always telling him to run more because I thought he never really realised just how strong he was."

But Lewis didn't have to run himself to make the metres. He could make them with his kicking game or the adroit passes to set up his supports. And the key to that was his ability to read the play.

"I saw him do it time and time again," Vautin said. "You'd be coming back into the ruck and he'd say, 'Hang on — stay there, Fatty, and I'll put you through this hole'. You'd look and you'd think 'what hole?' but sure enough, he'd get the ball, take a pace or two and the next thing you knew you'd have the ball in your hand and there would be something on. He did that to everyone in the team at some stage. He could see things that no-one else could see. That's what made him such a great captain.

"I remember the second game at Lang Park in 1988 we got a penalty about 25 metres out. Normally a captain would kick the ball out, have the forwards hit it up and then swing it out the backline. Not Wally. He ran up, took a quick tap, ran straight to the blind, drew three and popped an overhead pass to Tony Currie who scored in the corner,

"Another time, the third game in '88 in Sydney, the Blues really stuck it to us for once. We were behind 18-6 at one stage, then right on halftime Wally got us back into it.

"I remember looking at the clock and there were only 20 seconds left. The obvious thing was to put up a bomb — there just wasn't any time for anything else. Then Wally ran up to dummy half. 15 seconds, 10 seconds, he took the ball, drew three in again, turned his back and slipped a pass to Sam Backo who scored.

"In both those cases I don't think there would have been another player alive who would have taken that option, or been able to make it work. He was just the best player I ever saw. Simple as that."

Vautin was one of millions in awe of Lewis's skill as a player but the Origin years gave him much more than just a ringside seat to watch the King in action. It gave him the chance to do what very few can boast. He became his friend.

From the first day Vautin arrived back in Brisbane to join the squad, Lewis made him welcome, reminding him of the under-18 days, teasing him about the night at the Cross or the barracker at the SCG. Vautin admits Lewis wasn't always an easy man to get to know, but now counts him one of his closest friends and confidants.

"There were times in the early days when you didn't know where you stood with him," he said. "There were times he would like to stay aloof but you have to realise the pressure the guy was under. South of the border he was hated, up there he was God. He couldn't afford to fail."

But once the two established common ground, their friendship progressed. It was a bond based on a shared obsession with beating NSW and fired by the camaraderie of the Maroon squad.

In all sporting teams there is a definite pecking order. All Black rugby winger John Kirwan admits he never felt he had really made it until he was allowed to sit up the back of the team bus. Wally of course went further: he drove the bus, but other than that the Queensland team was amazingly egalitarian. Wally was King, there was no doubting that, but newcomers were quickly made welcome — and there lies part of the team's success.

"There were a few of us," Vautin said, "blokes like Meninga, Miles, Mark Murray, Colin Scott, Wally and myself, who kept getting picked year after year. We formed a sort of nucleus of the side and one of our main priorities was to make everyone else fit in as easily as possible."

The process involved the much talked about Big Drink, and an open door policy. Any player wanting to discuss any aspect of the game — or anything else — had easy access to the senior players and coaches.

And there were also the practical jokes and stunts which footballers the world over would recognise as part of the fun. Others might write them off as childish, crude and, at times, downright disgusting.

When a Wally Lewis Roast was held to launch the King's testimonial year in 1989, Vautin was part of the entertainment. Held at the Sydney Football Stadium and sponsored by Power Brewing, the breakfast function was an up-market event attended by notables in the fields of sport, entertainment and politics.

Roasters included Wayne Pearce, Johnny Raper and Greg Hartley but as a roast it made a pretty good breakfast. The hardest punch of the morning was thrown by compere Billy J. Smith who told the crowd that Lewis had spent an hour combing his hair before the function "then forgot to bring it along". Other than that, despite the opportunity that most New South Welshmen would have savoured — a free crack at Wally — nobody could think of anything nasty to say. Rather than a roast, it resembled a meeting of the Sydney branch of the Wally Lewis Fan Club.

And then his mate Fatty stepped up to the microphone.

In what must go down as one of the most fearless displays of his career, Fatty told the tale of Wally's initiation routine for newcomers to the Queensland team. "He'll go into their hotel room after breakfast and tell them to get down to the bus for training," Vautin told an appreciative audience which included NSW Premier Nick Greiner, league bosses, heads of industry and social and sports writers, "then he'll stay in there after they've gone and drop a monster Henry the Third in the dunny. Then he'll turn off the air-conditioning, stick a 'Do Not Disturb' sign on the door and leave it baking there all morning. By the time they come back after training the wallpaper will be peeling off ..."

It went over like the proverbial lead balloon, although Lewis can see the funny side. "That's Fatty for you," he said, "everyone else was saying all these nice things about me but he didn't give a bugger who was there. He'd been told to roast me, so he roasted me."

And besides, what others might see as being in questionable

taste at best, Lewis and Vautin laugh off as "gee-ups".

"He's always going on about how much money I've got," Lewis said, "He keeps asking me how many millions I'm worth and I tell him, 'Look Fatty, I've got just the same as you." One time he came up for Christmas and I took him around to see the new house we were building. It was just at lock up stage, nothing was connected. Fatty walks in and says 'strewth, how much is this worth? A million, two million?' Then he goes off counting all the bedrooms and bathrooms.

"We're just about to go, but I have to talk to the builder because he's taking a few weeks off over Christmas, so Fatty wanders off and says he wants another look around.

"A couple of weeks later I go back with another mate and the place has been locked up for two weeks. We walk in and straight away this smell hits us. Finally I notice one of the toilet seats is down. I opened it up and the first thing I said was, 'Bloody Fatty!'

"When I rang him that night he started laughing straight off. The only thing he could say was, 'Yeah, well if you didn't have so much dough you'd only have one dunny like everyone else and it wouldn't have taken you so long to find it.'"

To an outsider, the thought of someone taking such liberties with the King is almost inconceivable, but Vautin says the Lewis he knows is someone who loves a laugh — even at his own expense.

Vautin likes to remind Lewis of the time a photographer came into the dressing room after an Origin match to take a shot of the two of them. As he approached Lewis picked up a huge ice bag and placed it on the part of his body which he claims was injured — his little finger. Vautin made sure he got a copy of the photo and has it framed on his wall.

For his part, Lewis is quick to show visitors a picture he took of Vautin during an Australian tour of New Zealand, sporting what he describes as "the scungiest most ridiculous red beard you've ever seen." Somewhere along the way, the two developed a special greeting. They would click their heels together Colonel Klink style, half bow, stick out their arms to shake hands, then bend down and shake each others' feet.

"I don't know where it came from, it might have been The Three Stooges or The Marx Brothers or something," Lewis said. "It's just habit now."

When Lewis and Vautin prepared to play against each other in Wally's debut match in the Winfield Cup, the handshake was part of the agenda. The match was Brisbane versus Manly at Lang Park. The interest was phenomenal and in the days leading up to kick-off the Lewis phone would ring regularly. "Watch out for the Manly lock," the voice on the other end would say. "He's a pretty tough fella. He's gonna belt you."

And then the line would go dead, so Lewis would ring Vautin back. "Watcha doing?" he'd ask.

"Nothing much," would come the answer, "just preparing for some footy game on Sunday."

"Yeah? Who ya playing?"

"No-one much. New team from Brisbane. Bunch of pansies ..."

The match was the biggest thing to hit Brisbane since the '74 floods. Anyone arriving from overseas in the week leading up to the game must have thought everyone had gone mad. No-one spoke about anything else. It was as if the future of every Queenslander depended on the Wayne Bennett-coached Broncos beating the reigning premiers. The Manly players, in their naivety, thought they were travelling to Lang Park to play a game of football.

Back home at Everton Park, George Vautin knew better. "I could see how important it was to everyone up here," he said. "I rang Paul and said not to underestimate them. They were building up to it like it was an Origin match."

Part of the festivities included a ceremonial toss of the coin by the captains in centrefield. Lewis suggested that instead of the traditional handshake after the toss, they should pull the Three Stooges stunt. "It'll bring the house down," he said. Vautin agreed.

The huge crowd which watched the match at Lang Park and around the country on television would have wondered about the animated exchange between the two captains. Perhaps they were talking about the atmosphere or, as old friends, wishing each other luck. Perhaps they were offering the time honoured disclaimer: "No mates on the field, okay?"

Not quite. The discussion went like this:

"Come on Fatty, let's do it. Shake."

"No. Just shake my hand, willya."

"No way. Come on, you said you were going to do it, now do it."

"No, Bozo will see."

A day he'll never forget: against Wellington on the 1989 tour of New Zealand Vautin played five-eighth and took over Wally Lewis' jumper. He also won man of the match!

177

Left: At training, if not exactly training ... with Wally Lewis on the New Zealand tour, 1989.

Above: The man Vautin rates the "best manager ever" — Dick "Tosser" Turner.

Above: The euphoria of a State of Origin victory has never been better captured than in this 1989 shot as Peter Jackson embraces Vautin (foreground) with Alfie Langer and Wally Lewis moving in to the scrum.

178

Left: Vautin, State of Origin forward, Sydney Cricket Ground 1984 ... and a muddy 14-2 win to Queensland.

Below left: Fatty (with ball) prepares to bid "howdy" to a welcoming committee in the shape of Blocker Roach, Lang Park, 1985.

Below: Wally Lewis rocks the Blues' Tony Rampling in 1982. Vautin is ready to add the extras.

This photo says a lot about Vautin's perception of himself in football's scheme of things. It was snapped at the end of the rain-soaked SCG Origin match in 1987. Vautin quietly leaves the field while in the background photographers and media people crowd Queensland captain Wally Lewis.

Right: Noel Cleal and Paul Vautin pose for RLW's famous "Civil War" cover of 1987. Vautin remains adamant that there was no major problem between himself and "Crusher".

Below: The winning Maroons outfit of 1987. Back row (l to r), Colin Scott, Gary Belcher, Peter Jackson, Gary Smith, Martin Bella. Middle row: Bob Bateman (co-manager), Trevor Gillmeister, Greg Conescu, Ian French, Tony Currie, Paul Vautin, Ken Rach (trainer). Front row: Gene Miles, Dale Shearer, Dick "Tosser" Turner (co-manager), Wally Lewis, Wayne Bennett (coach), Greg Dowling, Allan Langer.

Left: Jack Gibson — a prickly relationship between he and Vautin.
Below: Doug Daley. As Manly boss he and Vautin were seen to be in head to head conflict in 1989

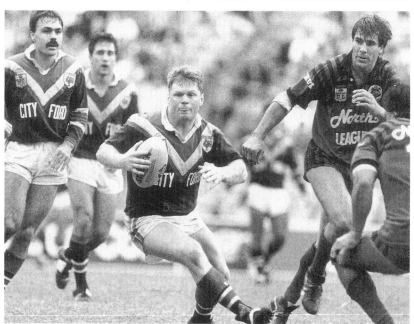

Above: Fatty the Rooster carting the ball up against Norths at the SFS. Players in the background are (l to r) Kurt Sherlock, Jeff Orford and Norths' Pat Jarvis.

182

Below: Mark Murray — a former Maroon teammate. But the relationship cooled in 1990-91 between Murray the coach and Vautin the player. Right: Vautin on the charge for Easts.

Above: Saying the last goodbye. A solitary fan offers a handshake as Vautin enters the race at the Sydney Football Stadium after playing his last game for Easts (against Penrith) in 1991.

Coach Terry Fearnley.

Above: The Australian touring team to New Zealand, 1985. Back row (l to r): Wally Fullerton Smith, Steve Roach, Peter Tunks, Peter Wynn, John Ribot, Paul Vautin. Middle row: Larry Britton (trainer), Des Hasler, Garry Jack, Mal Meninga, Greg Dowling, Noel Cleal, Chris Close, Michael O'Connor, Greg Conescu, Terry Fearnley (coach). Front row: John Garrahy (manager), Ben Elias, John Ferguson, Wally Lewis, David Barnhill (co-manager), Wayne Pearce, Mark Murray, Steve Ella, Dr Bill Monaghan.

Above left: Vautin crunches Kevin Iro in a 1989 Test. Above right: Vautin got 15 minutes of action against Papua New Guinea in 1988.

184

Below: Vautin and Hugh Waddell swap jumpers after the Third Test of 1988.

Right: Fatty is down for the count, after an accidental knock from the Kiwis' Brendon Tuuta in the Second Test in 1989. Brian Hollis attempts to return him to the vertical.

Above: Celebrations after the 22-14 win the the Third Test of '89 against the Kiwis, at Auckland's Mt Smart Stadium.

185

Below: Golf or guffaws? Vautin and "Rowdy" Shearer got together on the New Zealand tour of 1989. Right: Anyone for (jumbo) tennis? Fatty was a fraction short of Wimbledon class at a charity day at White City.

Bottom: The horse was called "Brookvale Oval". With unerring aim it managed to stand on Fatty's foot when Bob Fulton (left) and Vautin posed with the nag for a publicity shot.

Above: Vautin and Lewis, 1988. Queensland's training was generally fun.

Above right: Vautin, Gary Belcher (centre) and Peter Jackson after the win over Wellington (New Zealand) in 1989.

Right: Vautin (left) and coach Bob Fulton shape up for a 1987 grand-final victory barbecue.

Below: Vautin and Ian "Magilla" Thomson with pet pooch Luca, in 1980.

*Above: Fatty and Simon O'Donnell hammer
and tongs in a typical Friday sporting
debate on Ray Martin's "Midday Show".*

*Above: People misunderstand
Wayne Bennett (pictured) says
Paul, who has had closer
glimpses of the coach's warmth,
and wit.*

*Left: Vautin with his parents
George and Leila in 1982.*

The making of the 1991 Lowes' catalogue, highlighted by a photo session at North Sydney Oval, was little short of riotous. Above: Fatty, flanked by Rod Wishart (left) and Peter Sterling, clearly wins the "silly faces" prize. In front (l to r) are Kevin Walters, Steve Roach and Michael O'Connor. Below left: The gear looks great as Mick O'Connor (left) and Fatty pose. Fatty's expression, however, prevents too much seriousness. Below right: Ear plugs all round as Darrell "HUGE!" Eastlake (right) steps into the act with ironman Craig Riddington and Fatty.

189

Above: Australia Day, January 26, 1985, Newport, Sydney. "The happiest day of my life," said Paul of his marriage to Kim.

Left: Ken Arthurson, a strong and positive influence on Paul Vautin's life since the day he signed him for Manly.

Left: Vautin with Kylie (left) and Nikki after the semi-final against Easts in 1987.

Above: Son Matthew was there for Paul's last match in 1991.

Above: A happy Vautin scrum in the kitchen. Kylie (left) and Nikki in front with mum and dad, Paul and Kim.

The Vautin clan at home — Paul with Matthew (2), Kylie (10) and Nikki (6) in front, and Kim.

"You gutless wonder. You've shit yourself haven't you!"

"No. I just don't ..."

"Admit it Fatty. You've shit yourself."

"Yeah, okay. I admit it, now just shake hands okay?"

They shook hands and went back to the dressing rooms. One-nil to Lewis.

Worse was to come. The Broncos were on fire, Lewis played probably his greatest game for the club and the premiers were decimated. In the second half, Vautin came close to scoring, but was pulled down only centimetres from the line by ... Wally Lewis.

And if that wasn't bad enough ... "I felt sorry for the poor bugger but I couldn't help myself," said Lewis of what was to come next. "We were close to our line and I thought if I could get his mind off the game for a second I might be able to get the ball."

As they got their feet Lewis started talking.

"Sorry Fatty," he said, "you nearly got there."

"Yeah, thanks a lot. Couldn't you have missed just this once ...?"

Just as the distracted Vautin placed the ball on the ground Lewis's foot struck out. He raked the ball back and fell on it. As Lewis played the ball back and it was safely run out of the danger zone, Vautin fell into step beside him. "You bastard," he moaned, "why did you have to do that to me! Bozo is going to think I let you talk me into it."

"Don't worry," laughed Lewis, "you're the only one going okay, You'll still be in first grade next week." Two-nil.

In the return match later in the season it was Vautin who took the points. Sort of.

Only minutes into the match Lewis had the ball and caught Manly forward Glenn Ryan in the throat with his elbow when he came in for the tackle. Referee Greg McCallum immediately blew his whistle as Vautin raced over. "Geez Greg," he shouted to the ref in an attempt to gee-up Lewis, "did you see that? That's got to be worth 10 minutes in the sin bin for sure."

McCallum went one better. "Lewis," he said, pointing to the dressing room, "you're off!"

It was line-ball as to whose jaw dropped further, Vautin's or Lewis's. Vautin stood there stunned as Lewis walked past. "Yeah, thanks Fatty," he snarled, "terrific."

"It was probably the worst thing that could have happened,"

Vautin said. "They lifted themselves with 12 men and beat us again."

Onfield they might have been on opposite sides, off-field they were very much there to provide support when needed. At the end of 1989, when Vautin was dumped by Manly, it was Lewis who offered a helping hand. Maroons team-mate Peter Jackson, then playing for the Broncos and working for a leading Brisbane radio station, started a "Bring Back Fatty" campaign. As the dollars poured in from Vautin supporters, Lewis rang with the good news. "Looks like you'll be coming back up here," he said excitedly, "the money's really rolling in."

"No, mate," said Vautin, "there's no way there'll be enough to pay the transfer fee. I don't know what'll happen."

Vautin later found out that Lewis then went to Broncos chief executive John Ribot with an offer. With two years of his contract still to run, he told Ribot to take $5000 from each year and put the $10,000 towards signing Vautin.

The offer wasn't enough to sway Broncos management who never really supported the idea of Vautin joining them, but it was further proof to Vautin of Lewis's friendship. Throughout the trauma surrounding Vautin's sacking he was in constant contact with Lewis.

Unbeknown to either, Vautin would soon be offering similar support to Lewis. John Ribot would later say that Vautin "leaked" news of Lewis's sacking from the Broncos captaincy to the Sydney media at Wally's request. This is not true.

When Wayne Bennett told Lewis of his removal from the captaincy, it was agreed to make a joint announcement after Wally had returned from a family holiday to the US. Broncos management believed the fact that a Sydney newspaper broke news of the sacking and quoted an un-named "teammate" while Lewis was out of the country was just too convenient, but in fact the initial "leak" came not from Vautin, but from within the Broncos hierarchy.

A Queensland friend of a Sydney sportswriter was at a Brisbane nightspot late one night when he went to the bar to order some drinks. While waiting to be served, he recognised a Broncos director holding court nearby. In a voice which could be easily heard above the music, the director was telling his drinking partners that the club was out to "get Lewis". "We're going to take the captaincy off him," he said, "and if he doesn't start behaving then we're going to get rid of him altogether."

At that stage there was not the slightest hint of problems between Lewis and club management outside the club. The mere thought that King Wally was anything but the Broncos' favourite son would be decried as heresy. But yet, there was something about the way the director spoke that hinted there was more to it than a few too many Bundy and Cokes.

The next day the eavesdropper rang a friend of his who worked in an honorary capacity with the Broncos. In the course of the conversation he dropped it in. "Hey," he said, "that's pretty amazing about Wally getting stripped of the captaincy ..."

There was silence for a few seconds before the reply: "How did you hear about that? It's supposed to be a secret."

The next call was to his friend in the Sydney media. "Listen," he said "... I know you won't believe this but ..."

The next week it appeared in a column in the *Sunday Telegraph*, even though the reporter himself didn't believe it to be true. The four-paragraph story, mentioning a "loose-lipped Broncos heavy" was laughed off by most who read it. A Brisbane *Courier Mail* columnist said the Sydney reporter who had broken the news to "his handful of readers", was, to put it mildly, an idiot.

One person who read the *Courier Mail* article didn't think so. Jim Lewis rang his son in the US to tell him the news was out. Lewis rang Vautin who contacted the Sydney reporter. After speaking for a few minutes about the weather he ventured: "Oh by the way, that thing you had about Wally in your column ..."

"Umm, yeah, I know it's crazy but this bloke I know in Briso ..."

"It's true."

"What!"

And so it was out. Vautin confirmed the story and was indeed the un-named teammate, but only after the leak from deep inside the Broncos organisation. The next Sunday, after the second story appeared in Sydney, Ribot opened his door to a gaggle of excited reporters and admitted that yes, Lewis was through as captain and the first step to removing him from the club altogether had been taken.

In the next few days, Vautin was to be Lewis's conduit with home. Away in the US, he was cut off from the goings on in Sydney and Brisbane. Vautin was in constant contact.

"When I was sacked from the captaincy it was the worst thing that had ever happened to me," Lewis said. "Apart from my immediate family, I only told three people and Fatty was one of them."

Vautin recalls it as a hard time for more than one reason. For a start there was the hurt that his friend was going through — hurt that he of all people knew only too well. Next there was the fact that Lewis and his family were slapbang in the middle of the San Francisco earthquakes. "I'm godfather to Wally's son Mitchell and our families are very close," he said. "You can't help being worried at a time like that. Wally's wife Jacqui finally got through to us on the phone and said, 'Hey Paul, listen to this.' She held up the phone and I could actually hear the building rocking and everything shaking. It was a very weird time."

And there was another reason for Vautin to feel uneasy about the whole situation. The effect it was having on the relationship between Lewis and Wayne Bennett. Bennett and Lewis are very different but in other ways, very similar. Outwardly, they appear opposites. Bennett is taciturn, quietly spoken to the point of being terse, Lewis a media animal.

Bennett has been known to turn down reporters' requests for interviews with a sharp "no thanks, I don't need the publicity". Lewis makes a point of being available 24 hours a day. There is little doubt each has his own reasons. At present Bennett appears very happy being a football coach, he simply has no reason to seek personal publicity. Lewis on the other hand has learnt to use the media better than anyone else in the game. To an extent he is a product of media hype and is canny enough to see the benefits. He has done well out of football, but plans to keep doing well long after his days in the game are over.

In that respect they are different, but in another they are the same, and bound to clash. One doesn't have to be with either long to realise these are two very powerful men, with equally powerful egos and personalities. Given that, it was almost inevitable that their time together would be brief and eventually stormy. In an atmosphere as close and competitive as club football there can be only one leader. Bennett, with the support of club management, proved to be that man.

It was a situation which still fills Vautin with sadness. "Wally is one of my best mates," he said, "and I'd have to put Wayne in that category too. The fact that there is a problem between them makes things difficult."

Just as Origin football inspired Vautin's friendship with Lewis, so too did it bring him closer to Bennett. From the time Bennett first asked Vautin his views on the upcoming series during that visit to Sydney, Vautin realised this was to be no usual coach-player relationship. "He listened," he said, "he asked my opinion and he listened. That really impressed me. So many coaches these days don't want the opinion of anyone. They think they known everything and everything they know is right. More often than not, that's not the case.

"Right from the start he showed he was willing to put his trust in me and that was pretty touching really. From then on he never let me down. He's got to be one of the most genuine blokes in rugby league — and there aren't that many of them going around. You always know where you stand with him. That's what I like about him, what I like about people in general."

Vautin only played or was assistant coach under Bennett for three seasons — a total of 10 games, but it is obvious he made a huge impression.

"He never held anything back," he said. "If he thought you were going bad, he'd tell you and that is the right thing to do. There's no point telling someone they're going well if they're not. At halftime in 1988 when I was captain for the first time we were struggling. He told me in front of the whole side that I wasn't doing my job.

"Looking back on it, it's probably the only time in my career when the captaincy affected my game. I guess that's an example of the pressure we were all under. But he was right, and in the second half I forgot about being captain and got on with playing my own game. He could have said nothing, tried to be a nice guy and stayed quiet, but what he said was spot on."

In the second half Vautin went back to leading by example and made a decisive run which led to a Peter Jackson try. The Maroons went on to win easily.

Bennett was a strict disciplinarian, but he saw the value of the lighthearted Maroons camp early in the week. He not only tolerated the high spirits, he encouraged them. "My old man told me never to trust a bloke who doesn't drink," Vautin said. "But with Wayne I make an exception. He has his reasons for not drinking — he's told me what they are — and that's fair enough, but for a bloke who doesn't like a drop, the things he let go were unbelievable.

"At the start of every camp he'd say, 'You blokes go out and enjoy yourselves', and we didn't let him down. The next day on the bus he'd be like a little kid wanting to know what went on and who did what. He'd laugh and cackle away. He'd be the one telling us to turn the washers around so we sprayed people and he'd be the one laughing the most — except for the time we squirted this copper.

"But at the same time, he was a very deep thinker. You could go into his room at any time and talk to him about any subject, anything you wanted. Sometimes he'd say, 'Fatty, what are you going to do with your life?' and he'd get you thinking and talking about that too.

"Football-wise I always rated him a good coach. He had a good knowledge of the game and he could come up with some good tactics, but I'd say his main thing was motivation — not that we needed a lot. He knew we hated those bluc bastards and wanted to smash them. All he had to do was keep our minds on the jobs."

"And if someone's mind was wandering, Bennett would be quick to pick up on it. He'd pull me aside and say, 'How do you think Kerrod Walters is going?' for example 'I think his attitude might be a bit off.' And he'd ask me to have a word to him. I'm just using Kerrod as an example. It might have been Sam Backo or Dale Shearer — although you could never tell what Rowdy was thinking. Wayne was always concerned with the player. That was the best thing about him, he knew the players were the most important thing. He believed players make the game, not coaches.

"The best thing he could do for a player was come up after a win and shake your hand and say, 'Thanks, well done.' It felt good. You knew you'd earned it."

It didn't take anyone close to the team long to see that Bennett and Vautin made a perfect team: the no-hype, no-nonsense coach and the no-hype, no-nonsense player. Bennett placed plenty of responsibility Vautin's way and the redhead responded.

If Bennett thought something was wrong, he would tell Vautin and Vautin would take it back to the player concerned. At the same time, if the players were unhappy about something, they'd tell Vautin and he would go to the coach.

"Fatty was the perfect link." said Bennett. "The blokes looked at him as a leader. He showed you don't have to be a big head to be a big man. He had an ability to inspire by what he did rather than what he said. His policy was he was going to do the job, no matter what it took. No matter how many tackles he had to make, he'd make them, no matter how many times he'd have to take the ball up, he'd do it, and if you gave him the ball, he'd make the most of the opportunities.

"He just loved playing. He knew a lot about the game — I'd call him football smart — but he never made it complicated, just gritted his teeth and said 'follow me.'

"He feared no-one, but it was all in himself. He never threw a punch, there wasn't a dirty bone in his body, but the harder the game got, the tougher Fatty got. He wouldn't back down to anyone.

"It's been said that NSW haven't had the success that Queensland have had because they never had the same team spirit. Well, that's right, because they never had a Paul Vautin."

There was one time though, that even Vautin's spirit took a battering and for the only time in his years with the team Bennett lost his cool. It was 1987 and the Origin match in Los Angeles. "We didn't have our minds on the job and Wayne knew we were in trouble right from the start," Vautin admitted. "It was late in the year and we'd already won the series and a lot of the guys were thinking about club football.

"Wally had a bad leg, he could hardly walk, but Wally being Wally, he had to be there. He was what State of Origin was all about and this was supposed to be a promotional game.

"We used to train in the mornings and have the afternoons off to look around and it would be like, 'What'll we do today? Want to go to Long Beach or Disneyland or check out the Queen Mary?' and off we'd all go.

"I found out later that when we were all off having a good time Wayne would go to the library at the university and read all these books on coaching and philosophy and stuff written by Vince Lombardi and people like that. Even then he was thinking of the future, trying to improve his knowledge of the game."

While Bennett was trying to improve his coaching, the Blues

were out to win back some lost pride. Their preparation was a lot more serious than that of their Queensland counterparts — even to the point of an alcohol ban on the flight over. "They went okay, we were not okay," said Vautin, whose game turned out to be a less-than-enjoyable experience.

"Brian Niebling went off after about three minutes and I had to go to prop. I was up against David Boyle and every scrum he'd headbutt me, belt me, do anything he could to me.

"It was okay for him. He had a head which would frighten Freddie Kreuger, but I had to think about my looks."

Finally Vautin tried to initiate some peace talk. "Fair go Dave," he said, "we're in Disneyland mate, remember? We're here for a good time, aren't we?"

The reply suggested worse was yet to come. "You're kiddin' Fatty," Boyle growled, "I'm really gonna give it to ya ..."

If Vautin thought halftime was a respite in which Bennett might reshuffle the team, he was soon wishing he'd stayed on the field. Bennett, who had watched the match from the sideline with growing disgust, tried the only approach which might shock his players back into action. The first person he zeroed in on was Vautin's roomy, Trevor Gillmeister. "Trevor, Trevor, " he barked, "you're kiddin', aren't you? The way you're going you might as well be back in Australia ... knitting." Gillmeister was not impressed.

"I didn't think Gilly was going too bad," Vautin said, "and he really got the shits. I looked over at him and sort of shrugged, which was the wrong thing to do because Wayne started in on me."

"Fatty," he said, "you're not going much better."

Vautin thought it best not to ask for a move back to the second row and took his chances with Boyle.

"That was the only time I ever saw Wayne really angry," he said. "It was the only genuine upping he ever gave us. You could tell he was very disappointed, but we all considered that game a real Mickey Mouse job. The Blues reckoned they'd levelled the series, but that was bullshit. The worst thing about it was that we'd let Wayne down.

"Geez we had a bloody great time, though!"

The "upping" proved just a minor hiccup in an otherwise close relationship. "I value his friendship," said Bennett who was one of the first to contact Vautin when he was dropped after being replaced as Queensland captain in the first match of 1990.

"I have to say I thought he was very poorly done by," he said, "he went from captain to nothing in one game. I thought if he was good enough to be captain, surely he was good enough to hang around one more week.

"A coach has got to make some tough decisions sometimes and I know how tough that one must have been, but I felt if they only picked him for what he'd done in the past, then they shouldn't have picked him in the first place."

Bennett offered condolences, but no sympathy. "I wouldn't give him the sympathy vote," he said. "I wouldn't insult him. I just told him hard luck, thanked him for what he'd done in the past and told him to get on with things."

It is that kind of straight talking on which the Bennett-Vautin friendship is based, which is probably why the split between the coach and Lewis has been so hard for Vautin to accept. "It's pretty obvious that they are going to say certain things to me and I just have to keep my mouth shut," Vautin said.

"Wally might say Bennett this or Bennett that and if I'm with Wayne and Wally's name comes up I just shut up and keep right out of it. Obviously there is a problem between them but I just have to tell myself it's got nothing to do with me. I'm not going to achieve anything by trying to fix it.

"These things happen and it is very sad to me. They are both good people and I just hope they can sort it out between them."

In the meantime, Vautin maintains close association with both men and is available if either needs him.

Never was that more the case than when the Lewis family was rocked with the news that their daughter Jamie-Lee was profoundly deaf. Since the diagnosis on the eve of the third State of Origin match in 1991, Wally and his family have coped magnificently well. They have become an inspiration to other families in similar situations and if it could ever be said that something good could come from tragedy, this is the perfect example.

But back in the dark days surrounding the diagnosis, Lewis was finding it hard to see the positives. As he had when he felt lowest in the past, he rang Vautin. "It was like something happening to one of your own," said Vautin, but Lewis says Vautin was more help than he'll ever truly appreciate.

"It was the worst time of my life," Lewis said. "Then I rang Fatty to tell him. He was just stunned and I don't know why, whether it was shock or something, but all he could think about was this birthday present he'd just sent up for Jamie-Lee."

Although he is talking about the darkest moment of his life, Lewis is laughing. "I told him Jamie-Lee was deaf and he said, 'That's terrible', and I was telling him how they thought they might be able to do this or that and he says, 'No, I'm talking about this present I sent her. I looked everywhere and bought her this musical instrument. I just sent it yesterday. Geez I'm sorry mate. That'll be stuff-all use to her. Send it back and I'll get her something else.'"

Tears of laughter are filling Lewis's eyes. "I got off the phone and told Jacqui. We hadn't had much to laugh about over the past few days, but we just couldn't help ourselves."

And there wasn't much laughter over the next few days either. Every night Lewis and Vautin would talk, Lewis pouring out his fears and, as so normal in such a case, the injustice of it all, the unfairness. Finally Vautin had heard enough. "Listen," he told his friend, "that's enough of that. You're not the one who's deaf, Jamie-Lee is. Now stop talking about yourself and start thinking about how you can help her."

"I don't think he was necessarily right," said Lewis. "I don't think we were just thinking about ourselves, but the words he said were spot on.

"I got off the phone and I remember sitting down and saying to Jacqui, 'You know, it sure does help, talking to Fatty.'"

He didn't know it, but he'd actually been talking to Paul.

CHAPTER

The Green And Gold Dream

As Vautin walked from the tarmac into the terminal at Brisbane Airport, on July 1, 1982, his parents were waiting. Together, they excitedly walked to the luggage carousel. "Which one is yours?" George asked as the bags slid by.

"There, that's it," Vautin all but shouted, "look, the green one. The one with the emblem on the side."

Together they stood and watched as the green and gold bag with the Australian badge slowly moved past. It almost disappeared back into the baggage room, they were so transfixed. It took radio commentator Frank Hyde to bring them back to reality. Moving up to the family group, he shook Vautin by the hand. "Well done," he said, "and not before time."

Only hours earlier Vautin had been sitting in a room at Manly Leagues Club along with his club teammates, watching a video as part of their regular Thursday night meeting. Coach Ray Ritchie was pointing out areas he wanted improved for the game against Parramatta in three days' time. Suddenly a phone in the office next door rang. Ritchie answered it.

Five minutes later he was back. "Fatty," he said, "that's Arko on the phone."

"What? For me?"

Vautin walked next door and picked up the phone. "Fatty, Arko here champ. I've got some good news," Arthurson said. "Ray Price has pulled out of Saturday night's Test against New Zealand. You're in. I can't tell you how proud I am Paul."

When a stunned Vautin walked back into the team meeting, Ritchie had already broken the news. A huge roar went up and 15 hands reached out to shake his. "It was what I'd dreamed about all my life," Vautin said, "every kid does. All you ever want to do is play for your country, and here it was, it was going to happen against the Kiwis at Lang Park. I can't describe how it felt. I was bursting with pride and excitement. It was unlike anything I'd ever felt. I'd been a guy who had got the chance to play for Queensland and fallen in love with it, but this was something else. To represent your country, and to run out knowing you were the best going around, that took a lot of beating."

The Australian team was in camp in Brisbane under coach Frank Stanton. Stanton had been reduced to tears of laughter once before when Vautin had made a late entrance to a team meeting. This time he got in first. Vautin went straight from the airport to Langlands Park for the Friday morning training run. As he jumped out of George's car, Stanton's voice echoed across the ground. "Come on," he yelled, "you're bloody late again."

Vautin's face broke into a big grin as Stanton walked towards him. "Well done, you red-headed bastard," the coach said.

With Price having left camp and gone straight back to Sydney for medical attention, Vautin took his place rooming with halfback Steve Mortimer. The two had never met before but Mortimer seemed an ideal roommate. "I'd never said more than 10 words to the guy in four years playing against him, but he was great," Vautin said. "I had a lot of respect for him as a player and he proved to be just as good a bloke. He really made me feel comfortable, tried to help me settle in and forget any nerves.

"I thought I was lucky to get him as a roommate, but later that night I realised I couldn't have done worse if I'd tried."

Vautin's account of that night made hilarious reading in the book *Fatty And Chook: Laughing at League*, co-written with John Raper. As he wrote: "After lying staring at the ceiling until about 1.30 in the morning I was finally swept into a deep sleep by a combination of nerves, excitement and tiredness only to be woken after an hour or so by a terrifying noise. I was convinced that a jumbo jet was about to crash land in my 10th-storey room. No, it couldn't be a jumbo, I thought. Maybe it was Freddy Krueger stalking around the room wielding three chainsaws. No such luck. It was worse, far worse. Turvey was snoring and it was snoring like you've never heard.

"The thing about Turvey is that he's got this huge hooter. I can report that the sound issuing from the impressive bugle was definitely king-sized. Having only known Turvey for a few hours I felt as though I wasn't entitled to wake him so I did the best I could and smothered myself with pillows. It didn't work. Nothing would have.

"At one stage, about 4am, the snoring stopped. It was so quiet that I started to worry about him. I stuck my noggin up and took a peep. What had happened was that Turvey's snoring was so strong that he'd nearly sucked the curtains off the wall and they were stuck in his hooter. It took all my strength to pull them out and save his life."

Needless to say, Vautin didn't have the best of nights. Even Mortimer showed concern when he saw him the next morning. "Geez, Fatty," he said, "you look terrible. Few nerves?"

That was the least of it, but Vautin still felt fired up and ready to go for his first Test and threw himself into the match from the kick-off. It was to be a baptism of fire into international rugby league.

The Kiwis had a very tough side, with such rugged campaigners as Mark Broadhurst, Mark Graham and the Tamati cousins, Kevin and Howie. They proved as hard as any team Vautin had ever struck. "Early in the match we got a penalty and Rohan Hancock charged onto the tap," Vautin recalled. "He was really moving and Kevin Tamati absolutely smashed him. I've never seen anyone hit that hard in my life. My jaw dropped so fast I got grass burns on my chin.

"Hancock was lying there in Disneyland and the ref came over, looked down at him and put both arms straight up in the air. I thought he was either signalling time off for injury, or more likely he could have been signalling a six. That's how hard he hit him.

"I remember thinking, 'Jeeesus, this is gonna be tough.'"

Vautin was to have his own run-in with the fearsome Kevin Tamati a few minutes later. The Kiwi forward was attacking and Vautin felled him in a ball and all tackle. As they got to their feet Vautin slipped his hand under the ball and flicked it loose. The ref missed the Aussie hand and signalled a scrum.

"Tamati was not happy," Vautin remembered. "There was a bit of push and shove and I did something I very rarely did — I threw a punch. The reason I never threw many punches was that I wasn't very good at it, but this one was a beaut. I really gave it everything and it landed right on the side of his head. Nothing. He didn't even blink.

"I heard this little voice in my head say, 'Uh oh' but this was my first Test, I was really fired up and I thought, 'I'm going to go on with this, he might smash me all over Lang Park, but I'm going to give it everything I've got.' So I was shaping up and he looked at me with these eyes. I can still see them. They were cold and black and they said, 'You're dead.'"

Tamati cocked a fist and was about to let fly when Aussie prop Craig "Albert" Young stepped in and started wrestling the big Kiwi. Vautin was not impressed. "Come on Albert," he shouted, "let him go. I'll kill the bastard."

As the referee restored order, Young pulled Vautin out of the firing line. "Fatty," the big policeman said, "piss off! He's the ex-heavyweight boxing champion of New Zealand."

Vautin copped the tip. "Yeah, righto Albert," he said, "whatever you reckon ... and thanks."

Australia won the match by virtue of a late try to replacement forward John Muggleton which probably cost Vautin his spot for the Second Test. Price came back into the side and Muggleton stayed reserve. Vautin had his taste of playing for his country and loved it. Coach Stanton hinted it would not be his last experience at that level. After the match he gave Vautin a: "Well done, that's the first of many."

He was right, although the next Australian jumper wouldn't come until after the '82 Kangaroo Tour, the first of two Kangaroo selections which would haunt Vautin throughout his career.

"Paul must be the unluckiest player never to have gone on a Kangaroo tour," says Bob Fulton. "Every time a tour came along he was the bloke who missed out. If they had been picking the sides virtually any other time he would have been the first bloke chosen, but, for certain reasons, he was always the one left behind."

For that first tour Vautin had only just made the Australian team but yet for that, he was still the only member of the side which played New Zealand at Lang Park that night not to make the tour. In 1986, he had only played three games after 16 weeks on the sideline with a broken arm, but there were many who felt he would go away.

One was selector Hugh Kelly who admits there was heated debate over Vautin. "I can't say who anyone else voted for, but just let me say that when Paul Vautin's name came up I wanted him on that plane. I felt he had proven his fitness and he should have been on that tour. He bloody well deserved to be on it. It was a close vote, it had to be close. You hear talk about deals being made in the selection rooms, you know, like you can take that Queenslander so long as we get this New South Welshman, but that's rubbish, it's a myth. Maybe in the old days, but I can assure you that no deals were ever done in my day. All I know is that I came out of that meeting very upset because Paul was my choice and I'll always believe he would have been the better choice. As it was, a player of doubtful fitness went away and only played a handful of games. He was a good player, but I felt Vautin was better."

Outwardly Vautin remains philosophical about missing out on the tours but according to friends such as John Gibbs and Wally Lewis, it is something he will never get over. "I spoke to him about it before the '86 tour and he didn't want to jinx himself but he knew he had to be a good chance," Lewis said. "I thought he was a lot better bet than that. When he missed out I was dumbfounded. I thought he was a certainty. Every time he had been picked for Australia he'd played terrifically. Just on what he'd done in the past he deserved to be there. He didn't let on, but he was very disappointed. It really broke him up."

There is no doubt missing the tours left scars but Vautin has replaced the initial feelings of hurt with a rather callous view of the entire Kangaroo selection process. Throughout his career Vautin's way of dealing with disappointment is to tackle it front-on and push ahead harder. His reaction to questions about having to stay at home and watch the Kangaroo matches on television is no exception. "There's a lot of Kangaroos who never wore the green and gold in Australia," he says. "Getting on a Kangaroo tour is all about luck. Playing a Test isn't about luck, it's about being the best player in your position in the country.

"You've only got to look at some of the blokes who've been away on Kangaroo tours and see what else they've done. Some of them wouldn't get to play a Test if their lives depended on it.

"Of course it hurt at the time. I never felt anything but pride playing for Australia and I always approached the Kangaroo selections knowing that the selectors usually stuck by people who had done the job for them in the past.

"But that's life, good luck to the guys who went. Their luck was in at the time, mine wasn't. Nothing you can do about it."

But while he never got to travel with the Kangaroos, Vautin did play in 13 Tests for his country, some of them ranked as amongst the best and hardest of the modern era. "Some of those games we played against the Kiwis were as tough as any I've ever played," he said. "They were very hard men around that time and they loved to play against us. The Second Test in 1983 was like being on the Russian Front in World War II. I've never experienced anything like that in my life."

That match, at Lang Park, followed the series opener in New Zealand where the Artie Beetson-coached Aussies featured an almost all-Manly pack of Dave Brown, Geoff Gerard, Max Krilich, Paul McCabe and Vautin. Odd man out was Wally Fullerton Smith who was man of the match with a mighty performance in the 16-4 win.

The Australians got home thanks to a spectacular 90-metre try by Eric Grothe but next time around they were not so lucky. Primed by coach Graham Lowe, the Kiwi tough guys ran out determined to take charge and take charge they did.

"It was like being on a headhunters' island," said Vautin. "They bashed us out of the game. There were head highs, late tackles, the lot. The ref lost all control. It was war."

Kiwi Kurt Sorensen ran amok and Max Krilich suffered the neck injury which would eventually end his career. Colin Scott's hard-earned debut turned into a nightmare. He would never play for Australia again and the game also ended Beetson's tenure as national coach.

The following year Stanton was back in charge as Great Britain toured in yet another fierce series. The Poms were short on condition but big on tactics to upset the Australians' momentum. Vautin was left out of the First Test side and watched on television as the locals won the war but lost the battle. "I remember watching Turtle Conescu take the ball up and some Pommy (David Hobbs) belted him with an elbow," Vautin said. "Turtle came to a shuddering halt and you could see his tooth flying across the screen from one side to the other."

Two weeks later in Brisbane Vautin was the one to cop the elbow. "They called me into the side as reserve which I was pleased about," he recalled. "Then Pricey pulled out again and I went into the second row. It was a bloody tough game. The Poms had improved a hell of a lot from the first game but their defence was lacking a bit and we ran in a couple of soft tries. If they'd concentrated on football instead of trying to bash us they might have gone alright.

"There was a lot of rubbish going on, head highs and all that. Wally took a real late shot from their second rower Chris Burton but we were never in any danger of losing."

If there was a danger, it was of getting hurt, and Vautin was the one unlucky enough to be in the wrong place at the wrong time. With three minutes left Great Britain replacement forward Mick Adams took up the ball. As Vautin came in for a smothering tackle Adams lifted his elbow and connected flush on Vautin's cheekbone. "I went down stunned," he said. "As Adams got up to play the ball I felt around my face, you know how you do when you get hurt. I was feeling for blood and there wasn't any but when I pushed on my cheek my middle finger just disappeared into this big hole. There dead set wouldn't have been more than a minute left in the game by then. I couldn't believe it."

Vautin was helped from the field as the fulltime signal was given. Sitting in the stand, his mother was distraught. With Paul going to Sydney so young, George and Leila only saw him play rarely — and never had they seen him leave the field injured. George went downstairs to the dressing room, telling Leila he would see what had happened. When he hadn't returned almost half an hour later it got too much for her. She tried to get into the dressing room herself, only to be turned back by an over-officious security guard.

Enter Wally Lewis's mum. "How is he?" Mrs Lewis asked. "I don't know," said Leila, who then burst into tears, "they won't let me in."

Wally Lewis isn't the only member of his family who knows how to turn defence into attack. Taking Leila by the hand June Lewis stormed up to the dressing room door and launched into the hapless guard with a venom. If the Poms had shown her determination they would have won by 20. Within seconds Leila was beside her son as the team doctor diagnosed a compound fracture of the cheekbone.

"Don't worry," said commentator Rex Mossop, putting an arm around Leila. "That's a tough boy you've got there."

He had to be. When George and Leila took Paul to the airport for the return to Sydney later that night, he was besieged by reporters. At one stage he had to push his way into the men's room to be sick. The cameras and microphones were still waiting when he returned.

The selectors complimented Vautin by choosing him for the return Test but he was never a hope of playing. The broken cheekbone would put him on the sidelines for eight weeks. It also ended his playing association with Frank Stanton.

Stanton remains unsure of whether Vautin ever fulfilled his potential for Australia. "It's hard to say," he said. "I think he had potential as a running forward, but that wasn't the role he was used to playing with Manly. I would have liked to have had more opportunity to work with him in that area because it was obvious he loved playing representative football. Some players don't take to it at all. They might be going great guns at club level but then when they take that step up they can't handle it, they can't settle into the different program. Not Vautin. The way he adapted to State of Origin football meant he was always going to fit into an Australian side. He thrived on rep football. I would have liked to have coached him more."

The feeling is mutual. "That was one of the disappointing aspects of breaking my cheekbone," Vautin said. "I always liked playing under Frank but it seemed I never got to do it enough. I'd enjoyed the time I'd had with the team that week. We all got along well and Frank was a terrific coach. He was a hard man, very big on discipline, but if you did your job you'd get the plaudits."

Those words are a far cry from Vautin's description of his next stint in the Australian team. "The worst three weeks of my life," he says, "the worst three weeks of everyone's life."

The period was the 1985 tour of New Zealand under the coaching of Terry Fearnley, probably the most divisive time in the modern history of Australian rugby league. It is a period which has been written about, spoken about and argued about long and hard. In his book *King Wally*, author Adrian McGregor asserted team captain Wally Lewis had been given the cold shoulder by Fearnley throughout the tour. The clear inference since hotly denied by the New South Welshmen, was that the coach favoured NSW vice captain Wayne Pearce and that Fearnley and Pearce picked the sides on tour.

The decision by Fearnley and his co-selectors, David Barnhill and John Garrahy, to drop four Queenslanders from the final Test team created a furore north of the border. QRL boss Ron McAuliffe came out and said what thousands of Queenslanders had been thinking: that the Australian coach was biased towards NSW and the Maroon players had been dropped through spite.

Any discussion about the situation must be taken in context. Here it was, the middle of one of the most hard-fought State of Origin series — with the two games already played having gone to the Blues — and a combined Australian side was being sent on a three-week tour of New Zealand.

Unlike other years where any tour took place *after* the Origin series, the players' mental and physical scars had not had time to heal. The fiercely-competitive Maroons were still smarting over their first ever series loss and most had had little interest in getting pally with their foes before the final match.

And then, if that situation was not inflammatory enough, the ARL put the current NSW coach in charge of the whole tinder box. Factor in the fact that Fearnley had been the mastermind behind a successful strategy to snuff out the effectiveness of Lewis in the Origin series and the coach was in a no-win situation. As NSW captain Steve Mortimer noted: "Terry worked out how Wally played to a pattern, using his centres at certain times, kicking at others. We had it down so pat in the end, that we knew what Wally was going to do almost before he did."

Lewis was not one to take kindly to being out-thought, and here he was, weeks later, being asked to work arm in arm with the man behind his first-ever Origin series loss. It was a recipe for disaster.

Since Fearnley's ill-fated tour, no current State coach has been appointed to the national job. For Terry Fearnley, that obvious rule was one year too late in coming. Who knows, perhaps it could have worked if another person had been in charge. Perhaps a Bob Fulton, Arthur Beetson or Phil Gould — a "one of the boys" type-coach could have made it work. Terry Fearnley is not, and never has been, that type of coach.

Vautin claims he had or has nothing personal against Fearnley. He prefaces any comment — as he does often when discussing people he has not seen eye to eye with — with the words: "I've got nothing against the bloke BUT ... in my view he was the worst coach I ever played under. He struggled in New Zealand. He was aloof, a loner," he said.

"He had no hope of pulling that tour together, none at all. He got the Queenslanders offside from day one and by the end even some of the NSW blokes were offside as well. It was a disaster."

For Vautin the tour started badly and then got worse. Ironically, perhaps the best thing the come out of the whole tour for him was when he pulled out of the First Test, which was played in Brisbane a week before the touring party left for New Zealand.

"That was when I was having injections in my shoulder every game," he said. "Finally I just couldn't keep going. The shoulder needed that week's rest without a needle and I had to pull out. I hated doing it because I always considered myself the type of guy who could play with pain. There are some players who can't do it but I always prided myself on being able to get on the field and give it a go. Once I started playing I'd forget about it, but this time it was hopeless.

"It probably turned out to be the highpoint of the tour funnily enough because it meant Crusher Cleal got to play his first Test. I felt pretty happy about that, him being a Manly player."

It was also a first Test jumper for Parramatta's Peter Wynn who was rooming with Vautin. "I'll always remember one thing that happened when he pulled out," Wynn said. "When we got back from training he'd already packed up and returned to Sydney but he'd left a note for me. It said, 'Good luck, Wally, you deserve to be there. Kill 'em.' That's always meant a lot to me. We didn't know each other too well but it had taken me seven years to get in that team, and for him to take the trouble to do that ... well, it made a big impression on me."

Pulling out of the Test didn't affect Vautin's selection in the touring party, although soon after he arrived in New Zealand he might have been forgiven for wishing it had. At the first hotel team manager David Barnhill read out the roommates for the duration of the tour. Vautin was sharing with the hulking Queensland prop Greg Dowling.

As with most hotels, the room was fitted with one single and one double bed. It is customary for roommates to toss a coin for the larger bed, but Dowling walked straight up and piled his bags on top of it. Vautin waited a split second for Dowling to start laughing, signalling a joke. He didn't.

"You taking the double bed then, are you GD?" asked Vautin.

"Yeah."

"Fair enough," thought Vautin, who resigned himself to three weeks in a single bed. He kicked off his shoes, turned on the television and lay back to watch one of his favourite shows.

"What's this shit?" growled Dowling, walking over and changing the channel.

Vautin started sweating. Three weeks of this? Finally he announced he was off for some air and snuck down to Barnhill's room. "Listen Dave," he said, "any chance of a change of roomie?"

"Why, what's the problem?"

"No problem, no problem at all. GD and I get on fine, it's just that I'd prefer someone else, that's all."

Barnhill, the NSW country president, promised he'd take care of it. Vautin was halfway out the door when he turned. "Oh, just one thing, Dave," he said. "Mate, it's a bit delicate, can you make sure you're discreet. Make a few changes so it doesn't look like I've been whingeing?"

"No sweat, Fatty, leave it with me."

A few days later, as the tour bus pulled into a new town Barnhill stood in the aisle and made an announcement. "Fellas," he said, "there's been a few changes in the rooms. Just all hang around the front desk as the hotel manager reads out the names, okay."

"Beauty," though Vautin, "he's done it."

The entire touring party stood in the foyer as the names were read out.

"Fullerton Smith and Murray, room 202 ..."

Wally Fullerton Smith and Mark Murray looked at each other and shrugged. They'd been together at the first hotel.

"Wynn-Ella, room 204 ..." No change there.

And so it went, right through the group, until the last one.

"Vautin-Cleal ... 406, and Mr Dowling? You're on your own."

"One change," said Vautin, "he'd made one bloody change. Good one, Dave. The captain always gets a room on his own, which leaves one spare single room. Crusher had had it first off, now GD was in it. Everybody was looking over at me, they knew what had happened."

And staring the hardest was Dowling, with that same look Vautin had seen back in 1982. The Kevin Tamati look. The one that said, "You're dead."

Dowling never did discuss that incident with Vautin. Pretty soon the Queenslanders had more to worry about. From the first training run in Brisbane where Lewis was late, to the last run in New Zealand, there was an obvious communication breakdown between the Maroon players and the coach. They had come straight from the family atmosphere of the Queensland camp where Wally was the beloved big brother, to the more austere surrounding of an Australian team on tour. Fearnley wasn't big on the Queensland way of business and the Queenslanders weren't big on him.

"It was terrible," Vautin said. "When Wally was late for the first meeting in Brisbane, Fearnley didn't wait to hear his explanation. He just stood there, saying: "Captain not here? Very bad, very bad."

"When we were in New Zealand he used to say stuff like, 'The joint's looking good.' Everything was, 'the joint'. He'd say, 'Captain? Captain? Wally? The joint's looking good, Wal' and Wally would just say, 'Yeah, terrific Terry, looking real great.' Then Fearnley would say, 'Okay, vice-captain, Wayne Pearce, take the boys for warm-up, Junior ..." and off we'd go.

"Okay, fair enough, Junior was way ahead on fitness, that was his go and it wasn't Wally's, but Terry never consulted Wally about it. He never pulled him aside and said, 'Listen Wal, Junior's strength is fitness and I think it would be better for the team if he took the warm-ups, okay?' He never said a thing and that embarrassed Wally and, even more, it embarrassed Junior."

Inevitably, factions formed and the blow up came as sure as night follows day. In the second Test in Auckland, Australia trailed 6-4 with only seconds remaining when Lewis threw a long pass to Garry Jack who put John Ribot over in the corner. Ribot converted his own try on fulltime for a 10-6 win.

"We were bloody happy, bloody relieved," Vautin said. "They were a good side, make no mistake. Very tough, very mobile. We walked off feeling pretty pleased with ourselves. We'd won the series and beaten a very good team to do it."

As the Australians slumped exhausted in the dressing room amid handshakes and congratulations, Fearnley walked into the room. "He went right off," Vautin said. "It was, 'You blokes are kidding! That was the worst performance I have ever seen from an Australian team. You should be disgusted with yourselves ...' "Muppet" Murray looked up and told him to get stuffed and he turned and walked out."

The animosity was now out in the open. Murray had not spared Fearnley with what he said in the dressing room and the factions grew stronger. In the midweek game leading up to the Third Test, Murray and Conescu were given the duty of keeping the match statistics. The two blatantly favoured their Queensland teammates. Tackles to players such as Benny Elias and Des Hasler were credited to Queenslanders. Vautin was marked down for three tackles for every one he made.

The day the final Test team was to be announced, Lewis burst into Vautin's room. "I've just seen Pearce in with Fearnley picking the side," he bellowed, his face red with rage. Vautin was incredulous.

"Mate, that's rubbish, they wouldn't be doing that."

"I *saw* it," said Lewis. "They were in there with a bit of paper in front of them and they were going through the names."

Word spread throughout the camp and when the team was announced Queenslanders Murray, Conescu, Chris Close and Dowling were all dropped. In their place was the NSW quartet of Hasler, Elias, Steve Ella and Peter Tunks. The Queenslanders in the party were incensed.

"We blew up," said Vautin. "Everyone was screaming. Fearnley had always said he'd be up front with us, that if anyone was going to be dropped he'd be told first. He didn't tell anyone what was happening. He just read the names out at the team meeting. You could have cut the tension in the room with a knife."

When word reached Pearce that the Queenslanders believed he had been involved in selecting the team, he approached Vautin. "What's all this about me ...?"

"I don't know," said Vautin. "That's what Wally reckoned."

"Well, it's bullshit," shouted the normally-composed Pearce. "We were talking about fitness levels and fitness routines, that's all."

Vautin waved him off. "It's got nothing to do with me," he said.

Although Vautin was closest to Lewis and among the most influential of the Queenslanders, Pearce was probably talking to the wrong man. He and Vautin had a long and hard-fought rivalry, both believing they were the rightful heir to Ray Price's Test lock spot.

"I always felt that Wayne was a bit of media pet," he said, "if he missed a tackle during a televised game commentators would just gloss over it as though it didn't happen. If he dropped the ball, it wasn't his fault — it must have been covered in grease, oil or had a funnel web on it. The rest of us would cop it left, right and centre for even the slightest error but that was the way it was. He worked for Channel 10 and I suppose they couldn't bag their own bloke.

"As a player Junior wasn't over-endowed with natural ability. He knew that and made up for it in other areas. He was never one to draw three players and pop a miracle pass or throw a 30-metre cut-out to put someone in for a try. He was the man who was there to take the ball up when everyone else was looking for somewhere to lie down. He was the one who would make three tackles in a row then chase in cover defence if he saw a break being made out wide. He was ultra-competitive, as tough as they come and we had many great battles over the years.

"We didn't know each other that well, only played a few Tests together and rarely spoke on the field but there seemed to be something between us which made it an interesting 80 minutes.

"It certainly wasn't hatred, not even dislike. Maybe respect. He was a beauty but there were times when I felt like he was too good to be true. I always felt there were times when he got the nod because of his image, because the League wanted to promote this super-fit, non-drinking, non-smoking clean-living image. As I got to know him over the years I found him to be a terrific bloke and he deserved all the success that came his way but sometimes I got the impression they picked Junior first and then picked everyone else around him."

Certainly comments by League boss John Quayle in 1989 did nothing to change Vautin's view. In describing the success of League's Tina Turner commercials and progressive marketing in the '80s and '90s, Quayle said: "We were looking for a way to bring the women and children back to rugby league. Attendances were down, income was down. We looked around for a way to change our image. Then, on the 1982 Kangaroo Tour, a player came forward who was everything we were looking for. He was super-fit, clean-living, good-looking — and it wasn't a put-on. Everything about him was very real. He was the perfect role model. That player was Wayne Pearce."

Fatty, on the other hand? Well, one of the few times he was ever invited to Quayle's office was to be told that the League didn't appreciate comments he had made in the press suggesting there was nothing wrong with a bit of "biffo" from time to time.

But if anyone was doing Wayne Pearce favours, perhaps they forgot to tell Junior. In 1986 he was ruled out of the Kangaroo tour in highly controversial circumstances after fighting back from a serious knee injury. Then he was dumped from Australia's team for the Centenary Test against Great Britain in 1988, despite being the current NSW captain.

Frank Stanton — who coached both at club as well as national level — believes it was just a case of two good players being on the scene at the same time. "They were both good players, but they were contrasting personalities," he said. "Pearce was super-fit, dedicated, a coach's dream. Unfortunately, in terms of size, Vautin's options at that level were limited. He was best suited to the lock role and so was Pearce. It was just one of those things."

Not that Vautin didn't have his supporters. Queensland team-mate Peter Jackson amongst them.

"I've always thought Fatty was an under-rated player," Jackson said, "the guy captained Manly to a premiership, he played Tests and Origin. That sort of record should speak for itself but some-times I don't think it does. In his younger days in particular he was a devastating runner of the football. He was one of the best tacklers in the game and he could step, make a break and off-load. He was a great reader of the game. You don't get too many forwards with that type of skill any more.

"His problem was he came up in the Wayne Paerce era and not many people would put Fatty in the same class as Pearce. That's crap. Fatty was the better player. He had more skills than Pearce. The only thing he didn't have was the public profile."

The Pearce-Vautin rivalry, as with most top players vying for one position, spilled over every time the two took the field in opposition. Whether for their club sides or in State of Origin, a little extra went into the tackles, a bit more force into the runs when they met. Neither player was ever considered a knuckle man but one of the few times either was known to throw a punch was in a Balmain-Manly game when they admitted giving each other one to go on with.

Pearce would go on to play 18 Tests to Vautin's 13 and although he was to be ruled out of the 1986 Kangaroo Tour in sensational circumstances, he did play superbly on the 1982 tour. Missing a 'Roo trip was one of the great disappointments of Vautin's career but if it could be said he did achieve something Pearce didn't, it was playing in the Centenary Test.

While based on mutual respect, their rivalry was very real, so if Pearce was looking for an ally to help smooth things over on the 1985 tour, he was looking in the wrong place. "He wasn't getting anything out of me," Vautin said.

So much for team harmony. The Australians went out to meet a New Zealand team fired up for the performance of their lives. The enigmatic Olsen Filipaina ran riot. A reserve grader for much of his time with North Sydney, the powerfully built five-eighth saved his greatest performances for his country. Once he pulled on a black and white jumper, Filipaina was possibly the only player in the world to consistently bother Wally Lewis — and never more so than this day.

The Kiwis won 18-nil in a game which Vautin describes as "the most ordinary display by an Australian side I've ever been associated with". There was silence in the dressing room after the match. The Aussies sat, heads down, stunned by the way they had been humiliated. Yet they had won the series.

"We won 2-1 but it was a moral victory to New Zealand," Vautin said. "We'd got out of jail in the Second Test and they annihilated us in the third. We had nothing to be happy about."

The post-mortems began immediately and, in most cases — certainly in Queensland — Fearnley was made the scapegoat even though his teams had won both the State of Origin and Trans-Tasman series.

"You can blame the players all you like, but players have to have something to aim for," Vautin said. "You have to want to do it for someone. Most club sides do it because they like the coach. Queensland sides would do it for the coach and for the players they were playing alongside. On this occasion nobody wanted to do it for anyone.

"After that match, you wouldn't believe it, we had to play another game against Auckland. We won easily but nobody could have cared less. All we wanted to do was get on a plane and get the hell out of there."

And back to the final Origin match.

"We'd lost the series already but nobody mentioned that in the build-up," Vautin said. "There was no talk about getting to 2-1 or winning back lost pride for Queensland or any of that. All we wanted to do was beat NSW to stick it up Terry Fearnley. That's what it was all about, us versus Fearnley. That's why you had that famous scene where Greg Dowling ran over to the Blues' bench after a Queensland try and screamed, 'How do you like the scoreboard now, Fearnley? — stick that up your backside!' Or words to that effect."

Fearnley has never spoken at length over what went on during that tour. He says he has never read *King Wally* and has no desire to. Peter Wynn read the book — and was shocked. "I was really stunned," said Wynn, "I honestly didn't think there was any problem at all. If there was one it was all kept pretty quiet." The book said the Queenslanders called Wynn and Pearce the "Suck Brothers" for their relationship with Fearnley.

"It came as a total surprise to me. I had no problem with Wally at all. On the night before the last game we were both out injured so we went out and had a big night together. I didn't suspect any drama until the book came out. I suppose if there was a problem it was because we'd won the Origin series. It meant a lot to those blokes. They'd been together a long time. They didn't like losing and I guess they had to take it out on someone."

Fearnley refused to go on record for this book, either to speak of the tour or of Vautin, other than to say: "I believe if you don't have anything nice to say, don't say anything. I really couldn't find anything good to say about the bloke. Just say he's a Queenslander, that sums it up."

Fearnley did, however, once write his views on the tour for

Rugby League Week magazine, as a warning to incoming coach Don Furner. He wrote: "The past two Test series have shown Queensland players seldom reproduce on the international arena the enthusiasm they show in State of Origin games.

"The indifferent attitude to training of Queensland captain Wally Lewis when representing Australia — as I experienced last year — also indicates a major problem area for the new national coach.

"Anyone who can't make the effort to arrive on time for team meetings certainly doesn't deserve to play for Australia, let alone be captain. Without self-discipline from the leader and overall team discipline you have the makings of a losing side."

Fearnley said in a subsequent article: "Lewis has a lot to learn about the business of captaincy. Lateness for training occurred on more than one occasion and our versions of early morning training sessions vary by about three hours."

Vautin's final word: "Look, I don't dislike the bloke, I didn't dislike him then. In my opinion he's just not a leader of men and that's what is needed in an Australian coach."

Perhaps, but that is just one opinion — and a Queensland one at that. Vautin has never hidden the fact that he is as biased a Queenslander as was ever born. Hide it? He's proud of it. But for every disparaging opinion he holds of Fearnley, there are others — south of the border — who have only praise.

"Terry laid all the foundations for the success that came to Parramatta," said Peter Sterling. "He had a calm assurance about him and genuiness that I liked. I always felt he was a bloke who wouldn't let you down."

While admitting that the captain and coach should share the blame for the debacle in New Zealand, Wayne Pearce said he had always found Fearnley an excellent coach to work with.

"He was a highly intelligent coach who constructed his framework on discipline," he said. "In the NSW side in 1985 Terry worked hard to build a terrific feeling within the side, a bond which went a long way towards us winning the series. Guys in that NSW team who thoroughly enjoyed Terry's coaching were shocked when things went so wrong in New Zealand."

Steve Mortimer always regretted making himself unavailable

for the tour and thus missing the chance to help Fearnley and Lewis overcome any differences. As Wally's roommate on the 1982 Kangaroo tour, Mortimer had struck up an instant rapport with the Queenslander and as captain of NSW in 1985 he had great admiration for Fearnley.

"Terry is one of those coaches who is meticulous and thorough in his thinking and planning but is not overbearing in his dealings with the players," he said. "He allows them a fair bit of input. He treats them like men and expects a contribution in return."

Obviously two completely contrasting views from opposite sides of the geographical fence. His results proved that Terry Fearnley deserved better than the invidious assignment he was handed in 1985. Nearly all the players involved went on to better things. Fearnley, bitter at the lack of support he received in high places, never coached Australia again.

Don Furner, the genial former Eastern Suburbs and Canberra coach, was given the task of bringing the national team back together. After the disaster of 1985 a Kangaroo tour loomed in '86 and Furner had his work cut out. He succeeded magnificently, with the Kangaroos, led by Lewis, returning undefeated to emulate Max Krilich's team of '82. For Lewis, Furner and the Australian Rugby League, the tour was an unqualified success. For Vautin, it was a case of what might have been. After representing his country every year since 1982, the Manly captain was considered a certainty to tour. It was just a case of staying in one piece. Easier said than done. That tackle against Penrith resulting in a broken arm and 16 weeks recuperation changed any plans he might have had of a European winter.

But he never gave up hope. Even before the plaster came off his arm Vautin was out at Narrabeen Fitness Camp, putting himself through hell. "I've never trained so hard in my life," he said. "I set myself a course which ended in a big run straight up this giant hill and I ran it every day. In the time I'd been away the other blokes had got the jump on me so as I was running up that hill I used to imagine them a few paces in front.

"I'd be pushing myself up that mountain thinking, 'There's Folkes, gotta beat him, gotta get in front of Folkes ...' then it would be back down and I'd go up again only this time it would be Crusher. 'Gotta beat Crusher, gotta beat Crusher ...' I'd go through every forward I could think of, every one who I thought might beat me for that spot."

The torture looked like paying off when Vautin finally made it back on the field with just two weeks remaining in the minor premiership. He played both those matches then ran out for Manly against Balmain in the minor semi. Had Manly won that game and given Vautin more of a chance to prove his fitness, he might have made the trip. As it was, the Sea Eagles set off at a frantic pace, leading the Tigers 12-nil after only 16 minutes. Eleven minutes later it was 12-all and Balmain finally ended Manly's year 29-22. Vautin was named in the Kangaroo train-on squad under conditioner Les Hobbs and remained hopeful right to the end.

"I gave myself the slightest of chances," he said. "They'd either stick by me or they wouldn't. I was sitting by the pool at home listening to the radio when the team came over. It was a balmy night, I remember just sitting there looking at the water. I thought, 'Well, I haven't made a Kangaroo tour and it looks like I never will.' How true that turned out to be."

It was to be nearly two years before Vautin was to make his way back into the national side. He was considered unlucky not to be chosen to play against New Zealand in 1987 but by the time Great Britain arrived for the Centenary Test in 1988 he was back in the green and gold and packing into the second row. The match was notable for two things. It was the first time Vautin had played under coach Don Furner and alongside Peter Sterling.

"I'd always admired Sterling as a player but that was the first time I'd had a chance to see close up just what a total professional he was," Vautin said. "Everything he did he did 100 percent. At training we'd be doing 200s and 400s and he'd be leading every one. He wasn't a guy who was over-endowed with pace but here he was at the front every time. You used to hear stories about him being an easy-going sort of guy who liked a beer and a punt and wouldn't get out of bed until midday but when it came to football he was a complete pro. I was very impressed with the way he went about his work.

"As far as Don Furner was concerned, well, he was from the old school. You wouldn't say he was the greatest coach, but he was a great bloke. He knew how to get everyone onside. He wasn't real big on tactics or anything like that. The first time we got together as a team he stood in the middle and said, 'Okay, fellas, here's what we're going to do: forwards, you start running over there' and he'd sort of push his open hand out in one direction, 'and backs, you follow along over there' and he'd point in the other direction, 'and the gaps will come.' And that was it, that was his game plan. As long as the forwards stuck together and did all the hard work and the backs followed along behind, he reckoned we'd win. And you know something, he was right."

The Australians did win the First Test but it wasn't a particularly impressive performance, brightened only by the successful debuts of Peter Jackson and Sam Backo. Vautin took a while to hit his straps but really started to get into the game midway through the second half. He had made two good runs and was starting to get more involved when reserve forward Steve Folkes trotted on and tapped him on the shoulder.

"Fatty, you're off."

"What?"

Lewis looked over. "What are you talking about?" he snarled at Folkes.

Folkes shrugged.

"Geez," said Lewis, as Vautin left the field, "they're kidding, aren't they?"

Vautin left the field nonplussed but, despite reports to the contrary, not bitter. In fact his memories of that match aren't of anger towards Furner but of respect for one of the enemy. "That was the game I saw first hand what a tough bastard Kevin Ward was," he said. "I knew what a great competitor he was from playing alongside him, but that day I went in to tackle him and it was like running into a bus. He went straight through me. They didn't come much harder than Kev."

The next Test Australia wiped the Poms 34-14 at Lang Park in one of the most impressive displays Vautin had been involved in, but the Third Test was to prove disastrous. Going in having already won the series, the Australians were expected to win easily but Great Britain were too enthusiastic and too committed and ended up winning pulling away 26-12.

"After the game the word went around the dressing room that the selectors had been saying that so and so had played his last Test and so and so had played *his* last Test, so the mail was out that there would be some changes for the team to play Papua New Guinea," Vautin recalled.

The Test against the Kumuls was a promotional game played in Wagga Wagga but the selectors showed they were taking it seriously when they made some significant changes to the team beaten by Great Britain. One of them was Vautin, relegated to the bench as Gavin Miller and Paul Dunn came into the side.

The game lost whatever feeling there might have been when at the official function on the night before the match the Papuans approached the Aussies asking for autographs. "It was a joke," said Vautin. "Here we were supposed to play a Test match the next day and they were coming up and asking for our autographs and wanting to shake our hands and have their photos taken with us. How are you supposed to handle that?"

Manager of the team was Peter "Bullfrog" Moore, the canny Canterbury boss rarely seen without a lit Camel in his mouth. "Bullfrog loved those durries," Vautin said. "He always had a Camel hanging out of his north and south. This night he had to get up and make a speech. He's got up and mumbled on about how great it was to be playing this historic match and wished all the best to 'the arghh, Papua New Guinea, errh, Camels.' We just broke up. He didn't know what we were laughing about but when we told him he had to laugh himself.

"Anyway, so we played the Papua New Guinea Camels the next afternoon and it was dead set freezing. I've never been so cold in my life. I was sitting on the bench with Dessie Hasler and we were absolutely freezing. With about 15 minutes to go we're leading 64-4 and I get the call to go on. Well, I could hardly walk I was that frozen. I go into the defensive line and you wouldn't want to know, this little fella comes running at me and steps me. I've gone down to tackle him and ... nothing. I've locked frozen. He just goes straight past me and scores under the posts."

As the Australians stood behind the line waiting for the conversion, Vautin copped his share of dirty looks. "Hang on," he said, "you're kiddin'. It's minus bloody four, I've been sitting on the bloody bench for an hour. I've got splinters in my arse, what do you expect?"

The team started laughing, but the selectors weren't amused.

Vautin was dropped from the Australian side to play the World XIII and the World Cup final in New Zealand.

"I knew I was stuffed then," he said. "I was 30 years old and they'd obviously put the big red line through my name but I was still keen. There was a three-Test tour of New Zealand coming up and I wanted to be on it. I'd never stopped wanting to play for Australia. I never loved it any less than I had that first time. I wanted to get on that tour ..."

Immediately after the final game of Queensland's three-match whitewash in the 1989 Origin series, the Maroon players, officials and supporters had their traditional celebration party at the Brisbane Travelodge. The atmosphere was going to get even more euphoric when Tosser Turner got up and called for silence. "Ladies and gentlemen," he said, waving a piece of paper in the air, "history has been made. I have here the Australian team to tour New Zealand and for the first time ever, an Australian touring party will go away with a Queensland captain and vice-captain. The side is Wally Lewis captain, Paul Vautin vice-captain ..."

"I didn't hear the rest of the side," Vautin said. "I was just over the moon. To go away as vice-captain under Wally. It was just the most fantastic feeling. We'd come so far together over the years, achieved so much. This was the icing on the cake for me. Just when I thought the game had provided me with the ultimate thrill something else would come along and top it."

Vautin later found that the selectors originally wanted Gene Miles as vice-captain but bowed to some gentle persuasion from other areas. Australian coach Bob Fulton refuses to discuss the situation, other than to say his former club captain proved the perfect back-up to Lewis on tour. "There had been some splits within the team in the past," Fulton said. "Even when I was a player you used to get factions forming on tours but in 1989 it didn't happen and I think Fatty was an important part of that. He, Wally and I got along great and the rest of the team just followed on from that."

For Vautin the role of vice-captain meant a lot more than just having two letters beside his name. He was approached prior to departure and asked if he would handle all media interviews on tour in Wally's place. "I didn't mind," he said. "The press likes to give Wally a rubbishing, especially over there, and I don't mind doing that stuff. At the end I was enjoying it. The management just felt Wally had enough on his plate."

That and the fact that Lewis was sponsored by one beer company and the team by its major competitor.

Then there was the fact that Lewis was hampered by a nagging injury and did not take part in any of the mid-week matches, meaning except for the Tests, Vautin was Australia's on-field captain. The first game on tour was against the New Zealand Prime Minister's XIII and provided an easy win for the Aussies and while Vautin can't recall the score, he'll never forget the occasion.

"When I ran out as captain of Australia, it was exhilarating. Okay, it was just a provincial match, but it didn't matter to me. I was captain of my country and there's no better feeling than that."

But Vautin's pride at leading the team out didn't lessen the pain at halftime when the team doctor ordered him off with a suspected broken hand. It looked like his tour was over after only 40 minutes but x-rays showed no break and, along with winger Michael Hancock, he would be one of only two to play all six matches on tour.

One of the most controversial was the First Test, thanks to the performance of Kiwi forward Brendon Tuuta. Tuuta, who had been labelled the "new Les Boyd" by Sydney reporters, was in the midst of a short-lived career with Western Suburbs. Like Boyd, he was a quiet, polite country boy off-field who turned into a ferocious competitor once the ref blew time-on.

"That Test he was dead-set mad. He went out there keen to get half a dozen Aussie heads to put on the mantelpiece. He was just a wildman from start to finish."

Unlike the Tests in the early '80s when the likes of Tamati and Sorensen were in full swing, Tuuta played a lone hand. The Australians were able to ignore him and concentrate on winning the game, although Vautin found him impossible to ignore completely. "I tackled him before halftime and when he played the ball I was still getting up," he said. "Then he just turned around and bang, he kneed me in the side of the head."

Vautin was stunned and remembers little of the game from then until halftime. He recovered in the dressing room and was playing strongly at fulltime, little thanks to Tuuta.

"I reckon he went a long way towards us winning," he said. "They were all so undisciplined and Tuuta was the worst of them. All we had to do was stick to football. They were concentrating on killing someone and we were concentrating on the game. Eventually we won thanks to a great try to Paul Sironen."

A few days later the Aussies wouldn't be so lucky. Vautin led the team against Auckland at Carlaw Park but says no game plan would have helped them beat the locals that night. "It was cruel," he said. "There is no way we were going to beat them. The ref did us no favours whatsoever. We were down 24-16 with about 13 minutes to go and came back with two tries to level it but with a minute to go he gave them a penalty on the quarter right in front. Thanks for coming."

The referee was Bill Shrimpton, the brother of former New Zealand international ref Ray Shrimpton who had been the bane of many Australian sides over the years. At the function after the game both Shrimptons were standing at the bar having a drink when Fulton walked in. "We were all standing around having a beer and Bozo came straight in and starting saying, 'Where's the ref?'" Vautin recalled. "We pointed him out and he went over and gave him the biggest spray you've ever heard. His brother is standing there and he's shaking and his lips are quivering and finally he says, 'Okay, Fulton, come out the back and I'll take you on.' Bozo just keeps on giving them this spray and then he walks up to us, gives us a smile and says: 'I feel better now, who's shout?' But that's not all. Just for good measure David Trewhella goes over and gives them a bagging too. I'd hate to be in any Australian side refereed by anyone called Shrimpton from now on."

The Australians moved on to Rotorua and prepared for the Second Test on the local golf course. Greg Alexander proved the best golfer but didn't have the same success in the match. Fulton pulled him out of the game at halftime. Vautin had been knocked cold by a Tuuta elbow — this time accidentally — but was lucid enough to think Alexander had been hard done by at the time. "I didn't think he was going too bad, but Bozo thought differently," he said. "And it proved a master stroke. He put on Des Hasler and Des had a blinder. It must have been a hard decision, but that's what you have coaches for."

The Australians wrapped up the series with an 8-nil win and Vautin earned a rare wrap from Jack Gibson who described the way he climbed back from being unconscious again as "courageous".

The performance was a perfect embodiment of the way the Australians had developed into a close-knit, hard-working unit. Fulton gives much of the credit to Lewis and Vautin. Vautin gives it straight back to Fulton. "Bozo just has this way of pulling a team together," he said. "It wouldn't have mattered on that tour if a bloke came from Queensland, NSW, Broome or Norfolk Island. We just stuck together, there was no division. We'd drink together, muck around together. It's now a famous story about how Sam Backo and Blocker Roach used to try to pronounce all the New Zealand place names and one day the bus stopped so we could get something to eat. Sam's standing outside the shop going: 'Hey Block, check this one — Takky, Takky, Takky-awae ..." and Block goes, 'Yeah Sam, try Take Away." There were heaps of stories like that. Everyone just got along."

One story from the earlier tour of 1985 which didn't have a happy ending for the Aussie involved occurred when the team was relaxing in the hotel bar one evening. A local lass took a shine to the boys and one of the players stole a march on his mates, putting in some heavy spade work before disappearing upstairs with her to his room. Half an hour later he was back at the bar, ashen faced and ordering a double scotch. After the second drink he told the tragic tale. Things were going great, he said, when late in the affair — very late — he was made painfully aware that his young lady friend was in fact a man.

Another time Vautin, Lewis, Peter Jackson, Michael O'Connor and Fulton spent an afternoon at a funpark outside Rotorua. Centrepiece of the park is the Luge, a hair-raising ride down a mountainside in a one-man wheeled toboggan. "It was like we were 15-year-olds," Vautin said. "It was the most fun I've ever had sitting down. You'd go up on a ski lift then sit on this little thing and absolutely fly down the mountain. You had a brake which you could put on going around corners but by the end of the day you wouldn't be using it much. Jacko was mad, he never touched the brake once. You'd get around a corner and look back to see if the bloke behind you had got around okay and when you turned around again there'd just be a sheer cliff there and you'd fly off. It was unbelievable."

"Fatty just couldn't win a race on that thing," Fulton said. "He even lost his wallet. It was one of the great bagging sessions."

But if Fulton remembers Vautin as the Eddie the Eagle of the Rotorua luge, Vautin remembers it differently. "Mick O'Connor was an old sheila," he said. "He'd be going down the hill and at every corner, on would go the brake and slowly round he'd go and then the next corner, on would go the brake. One time we were going up on the chairlift and watching him coming down. There was this five-year-old kid coming down behind him and he passed him like he wasn't there. There was the five-year-old driving like Nigel Mansell, and Snoz is going like he's 108. We're screaming out, 'You're kiddin', Snoz' and he wouldn't even look up, he was that scared. It was one of the funniest days."

Seeing O'Connor out-driven by a five year-old might have been one of the funniest sights of the trip for Vautin, but for Fulton and Lewis an even more bizarre experience was just a few days away. It started with a phone call to Vautin's room. "Fatty, Boze here, mate. I've got a problem, how would you like to play five-eighth against Wellington tomorrow night."

"Boze, you know me, I'll do it on me ear."

"Yeah, good. Stop stuffing around, willya, I'm serious. All I want you to do is catch the ball and pass it, maybe a kick here and there okay?"

"Sweet as a nut."

The announcement of Vautin's selection to play in Lewis's Australian jumper was greeted with disbelief and cries of "You're kiddin'" from the other members of the touring party, but nonetheless, Fulton remained firm. On the following night Vautin invited the press photographers into the dressing room before the match to record for posterity the sight on him pulling on the number six. Standing in the background was Lewis, shaking his head with a quizzical grin on his face.

He needn't have worried. Vautin won man of the match from the press, setting up two of his team's three tries. The first was one neither he, Fulton nor Lewis will ever forget. "It came from a grubber kick," Fulton said. "Even as he was kicking it Wally was saying, 'We'll never hear the end of this' and sure enough, as the try was being converted there's Fatty back on the halfway still practising the kick, like he was giving a coaching class or something. Wally and I were pissing ourselves."

It was to be the second-last outing in an Australian jumper for

Vautin and one which has been immortalised by those photographs. He went into the Third Test at Mt Smart having achieved just about everything he could for his country. Vice-captain on tour, captain in provincial matches, 13 Tests for 10 wins. But no tries. Early in the match he thought that was going to change.

Steve Roach made a break in centrefield. Vautin burst onto the Roach pass and into open space. There was 40 metres of clear ground between him and the tryline. He put his head down, the legs were pumping, heart pounding and the thought process went something like this: "Five to go, gonna make it, gonna make it ..." Then a blur of black started coming into view. "Gonna make it, gonna make it ..." the black blur got closer, "Shit, I'm not gonna make it." As Kiwi halfback Gary Freeman grabbed him Vautin passed on to Dale Shearer who scored under the posts. That was his last chance. When the fulltime whistle went the Aussies had completed a whitewash with a 22-14 win over a committed Kiwi side. Vautin's international career was over.

That night he was presented with the award for the best team player on tour. Manager Peter Moore called Vautin over and put an arm around his shoulder. "Fatty, " he said, "I've got to say last year, when you were in the Australian side, I didn't like ya, Matey. This year, after three weeks, I love ya. Anything I can ever do for you, just let me know."

Vautin wasn't to know how soon he'd take Moore up on the offer, but right then it was just a nice end to the most enjoyable tour he'd ever been part of. It was also a fitting end to a successful career in the green and gold.

"It was a good way to go out," he said, "that tour to me was an example of everything that is good about representing your country, being proud to wear the jumper. I would have liked to score that try though. Just one would have done.

CHAPTER 13

Murphy The Mouth

The last words Peter Moore said to Vautin as they left the airport after the New Zealand tour were, "Matey, there'll always be a place for you at Canterbury." The fact that Vautin would seriously discuss the offer within a matter of days was testimony to the way relations between him and club management had deteriorated in the two years since Manly had won the competition.

On grand final day, 1987, Paul Vautin was Manly's favourite son. But by the end of the 1989 season his name was poison in the club committee rooms. If his rise within the club had been meteoric since his arrival from Brisbane, his fall from grace was equally sudden.

But that Monday morning, hours after the grand final win, nobody would have dreamed that Vautin and Manly were not headed for a golden era. As the players and coach downed a breakfast of bacon, eggs and schooners at the swish Le Kiosk restaurant, all talk was of back to back premierships and beyond.

"A few of us like Crusher, Snoz and me were getting into Bozo's ear," Vautin recalled. "He was undecided whether he'd coach again. We had this world club championship match against Wigan in England the next week and at that stage all he'd commit to was that. We were saying, 'Come on Boze, you can't leave us now, we'll win this thing again next year.' We couldn't see anyone beating us."

The team did their best to drink Sydney dry over the next few days before Fulton called a training run on the Friday. After a game of touch football he announced he would coach one more year. The next day, in high spirits, the team left for England and the Wednesday night match against Graham Lowe's champion outfit.

Manly would field its grand final team, except for the injured Noel Cleal and Kevin Ward, now back with Castleford. Ron Gibbs, although headed for the Gold Coast, was part of the line-up.

Gibbs' roommate in the team hotel was young winger David

Ronson, known simply as "Kid". They made an odd couple, the feared hit-man and the fresh-faced youngster. A definite pecking order took about three seconds to develop. It was "Kid, change the channel", "Kid, get us a cuppa."

A poster of Rambo Ronnie in his headgear was plastered around Wigan to promote the match, and Gibbs soon souvenired one and displayed it in his room. One afternoon, a group of six players congregated in the Gibbs-Ronson room for a game of cards. When Gibbs went to the bathroom Michael O'Connor jumped up and drew a pair of glasses on the poster.

When Gibbs returned, O'Connor looked at Ronson. "Kid," he said, "that's not a nice thing to do to your roommate." Gibbs looked up. "What, what did you do, Kid?" He spied the poster. "Kid," he said, standing up and rolling up his sleeves, "you shouldn't have done that, now I'm gonna have to knock youse out."

Ronson went white. "Ronnie," he pleaded, "I didn't do it, I swear I didn't do it."

"Okay," said Gibbs, walking over and locking the door, "I'm gonna count to three and if nobody owns up, I'm gonna have to knock youse all out."

The room froze as Gibbs counted down. Just in time O'Connor got to his feet. "Ronnie," he said, "I admit it, I did it but fair dinkum, I wasn't doing it to have a go at you, I was having a go at the kid."

Gibbs stared into O'Connor's eyes for a second. "Snoz," he said, "I know you'd never do anything like that. You're only protecting the kid. Kid, come over here, I'm gonna have to knock youse out."

Finally the players called Gibbs off with the promise of a new poster, but it was one of the longest few minutes in Dave Ronson's life.

Unfortunately nobody was able to help Gibbs as much a few days later. He was sent off in the match for a doubtful late tackle, and Manly had to play a man short for most of the second half. Wigan won 8-2 in a tryless game.

In that respect the match was a fizzer for the Sydney premiers, but in another way it proved most profitable for some. With English clubs desperate to bolster their ranks with Australian stars, the trip became a smorgasbord for the local club secretaries.

Vautin was sitting on his bed one afternoon when there was a knock at the door. When he opened it there was a man aged about

40 and another some 10 years older. "The old bloke had the thickest glasses I've ever seen in my life," Vautin said. "They came in and the young bloke sat the other one down in a chair and I sat on the bed. The old bloke did the talking."

"Paul," he said, "I'm chairman of the Leigh football cloob and we'd loove to have you join us, lud. How does 10,000 pounds sound?"

Vautin raised his hand and waved. "Excuse me," he said, "I'm over here."

"He was talking to the cupboard the whole time," he recalled. "His minder had to point him in the right direction and even then he kept staring about 10 feet over my head."

Vautin thanked the men for their offer and saw them to the door. Half an hour later there was another knock.

"This time it was Widnes coach Doug Laughton," Vautin said. "He walked in with Dale Shearer. He'd just approached Rowdy to sign up for Widnes and wanted me too. I virtually agreed to terms but in the end they signed Rowdy and brushed me. I never heard any more about it, but that was what was going on all over the hotel. The Pommy coaches and secretaries were wandering up and down the corridors trying to sign anyone they could get their hands on. They thought it was Christmas. In the end about half a dozen blokes got firm offers."

With the Widnes game over, the players flew straight to Hawaii where they were met by their wives who had been flown over by the club. "The club management were very generous," O'Connor said. "They couldn't do enough for us in those days. They didn't have to do that, but they did."

"It was very different then," said Vautin. "Before things turned sour they were always doing things for us. They made about $100,000 by us winning the grand final and they could have pocketed the lot. Instead they spent a fair bit of it taking us all on this trip to Hawaii for a week."

The trip proved particularly eventful for one married couple. When they were at Bobby McGee's nightclub one night the entertainment consisted of a beauty contest. When the wife went to the bathroom the husband was invited to be a judge. The wife returned to find her husband on stage surrounded by beautiful, scantily-dressed women. Not impressed, she picked up an ashtray and hurled it at the stage. It shattered harmlessly on the floor but two bouncers immediately grabbed the woman by the arms and started dragging her outside. Her husband leapt from the stage and got stuck into the bouncers. Both husband and wife were arrested and locked up. If Doug Daley thought bringing the wives on tour would keep the players out of trouble he was wrong. He and club president Gordon Willoughby had to bail the pair out of jail and appear with them in court early the next morning.

Back home things were equally eventful, right from the first game of the 1988 season against Brisbane.

The club had lost Gibbs and would only have Kevin Ward for a few matches but yet did not strengthen playing staff to compensate for the loss. They didn't buy a top class backrower to replace Rambo and the only notable acquisition was former North Sydney prop Don McKinnon.

Big Donnie, the likeable giant with the Chesty Bond looks, had been an institution at North Sydney for years. A big-hearted performer who had made the 1982 Kangaroos, he was noted for his physique and heart rather than outstanding ball skills. In fact, during the early '80s he formed one of the biggest front rows in Sydney rugby league history with the even bigger Steve Mayoh. Mayoh had the skills, McKinnon the heart. In one match when Mayoh was replaced midway through the second half a long-suffering Norths supporter screamed from the North Sydney Oval hill: "Cut off his hands and give them to McKinnon."

McKinnon only played a few top grade games for Manly but made an indelible impression. His debut match against Brisbane gave Vautin the funniest memory of his long career.

It was when Brisbane were given a penalty. Vautin was discussing the point with referee Mick Stone as, unbeknown to him, McKinnon was responding to a call of nature in the background. What McKinnon didn't realise was that he was being captured in living colour by the Channel Ten cameras and beamed into thousands of homes around the country.

"I turned around and there was this Morton Stock staring me straight in the face," Vautin recalled.

"Donnie," he said, "what the hell are you doing?"

"Just having a snakes, Fatty," replied the big policeman.

Even though Manly were currently being thrashed by the competition newcomers, Vautin couldn't help laughing. "I'd seen blokes doing it before," he said. "But they'd just do a sneaky one when no-one was looking. Don did it right in the middle of play, right in front of the referee and right in front of the TV cameras. I couldn't believe it."

Neither could the NSWRL who fined McKinnon $1000.

"Hey Donnie," Vautin shouted the next night at training, "what's that, about a hundred bucks an inch?"

"Something like that, Fatty," came the reply.

The team bounced back from the hammering from the Broncos and McKinnon's wee indiscretion to record some massive wins. They were down 12-6 against a full-strength Parramatta but came back to score an amazing 64-12 victory. As Rex Mossop said, "Even Vautin is running like a Clydesdale", as he scored a try.

The next week it was 44-12 against Newcastle. When a try took the score to 36-12 after O'Connor had left the field injured, Vautin took the conversion from about halfway between the corner post and goal. When the kick went over he gave a "hop, skip and jump", clicking his heels together in the air to the delight of the crowd. A few minutes later Manly scored a length-of-the-field try and Vautin ran up from halfway to take the easy kick — his second, and last, in first grade. Fulton said it was the fastest he had ever seen his captain move.

In three matches the Sea Eagles scored a whopping 152 points and there was talk of another premiership to the classy team but it wasn't to be. The side faltered in the latter rounds and went from third spot to fifth to just sneak into the semi-finals.

"For all that I still thought we were good enough to win it," Vautin said. "We were playing Balmain and they had a midweek play-off against Penrith. I watched the game and didn't think they'd be able to come back a few days later."

Vautin viewed the play-off in lofty company. The boy from Everton Park had come a long way: he was driven to the match by Fulton, who stopped off to pick up Kerry Packer and Tony Greig on the way. After the match they went back to Packer's mansion in the Eastern Suburbs. "It was just spectacular," he said. "Big gates, security, the works. When we got in he really made us feel at home. It was after midnight but he told us anything we wanted, just ask. That was the only time I'd been with him in a social situation like that and I found him a very good bloke. He was very stimulating to be around. He was entertaining us with stories about big game hunting in Africa. It was quite a night."

Unfortunately the weekend didn't pan out as well. Manly were well beaten 19-6 by a Balmain team inspired by English superstar Ellery Hanley. "It wasn't a fitting way for Bozo to go out," Vautin said. "We didn't turn it up but we just never gave ourselves a chance. We were never in it. We sat around in the dressing room afterwards and Fulton thanked us for six great years. He had a tear in his eye. Then he walked out and that was it, exit Bozo."

If Paul Vautin's eventual demise from Manly was a landslide, the departure of Fulton could be seen as the first tiny pebble which started it off. Without his powerful friend and coach in charge at the club, once the rot started it continued unchecked. There were several times during the process when, had Fulton still been there, he would have called a halt, put up his hand and said, "Hang on a minute." The warring parties would have sat down and, more than likely, the issue settled. Vautin would have played out his career with the Sea Eagles, been lauded on his 200th game, perhaps had a testimonial year and on his retirement been granted life membership. But it was not to be and that day at the Sydney Football Stadium after Balmain had ended Manly's 1988 season, Vautin had more pressing things to concentrate on than what may or may not happen in the future. He was on his way to St Helens, England, and one of the greatest experiences of his life.

Midway through the season, Vautin had been contacted by St Helens chairman Joe Pickavance. The famous club, coached by the former English great Alex Murphy, was looking for a quality back rower and wanted him to play the off-season with them. Vautin thought about the offer and turned it down. "At the time I was sales manager for Bozo's company United Systems, and things were going pretty well," he said. "Summer was coming up and life was pretty good at Wheeler Heights. Kim and I had the two girls and Kim wasn't too keen on uprooting and heading off to the cold of England for five months. I turned them down and they signed Mal Meninga and Michael O'Connor. It was a hard decision to make and I wasn't sure if I'd made the right one. After a while I started kicking myself. I really wanted to go. Then I had two strokes of luck: Mal broke his arm, which was bad luck for him, and I lost my job.

"I rang St Helens and told them if they were still looking for someone I was available. At that stage I was desperate, I had no job and not too many prospects. I decided no matter what offer they made, I'd take it."

St Helens came back with an offer of 25,000 pounds, plus match payments, bonuses, accommodation and a car. Vautin jumped at it, a contract came a few days later and he signed. It was a generous offer, although he felt like throwing himself from Alex Murphy's moving car when the St Helens coach later let slip that the club was willing to go to 40,000 pounds for his services.

When Manly's season finished Vautin had six weeks before starting in England and he trained with Manly's reserve grade side, coached by Fulton's successor Alan Thompson. "Thommo's side ended up winning the premiership and I enjoyed training with them," Vautin said. "He'd been a great captain and I was sure he'd make a great first grade coach. He had good ideas and certainly had no problems getting the message across. I thought it would just be a case of him picking up where Fulton left off." But that was still six months away when he, Kim, Kylie and Nikki set off from sunny Sydney in October.

"I was really excited," he said. "I'd only been to England that once when we played Wigan, but I'd seen a lot of English league games on TV. It looked different, less defence-oriented and plenty of attack. I liked what I saw and wanted to do well. I wanted to enjoy myself over there but at the same time I wanted to be a success on the field. You have to set certain goals for yourself and my goal was to play well in England."

But first they had to get there in one piece — something which Vautin says was easier said than done. The co-pilot on the Qantas flight was a neighbour from Sydney and a staunch Manly fan. He invited Vautin into the cockpit as they landed at Manchester. "It was the worst thing I could have done," he said. "I was standing in the background saying, 'You guys want me to go?' and they said to stay but they were shitting blue lights. It was a pea soup fog and they couldn't see a thing. They were really sweating. We were completely on instruments and computers. They were checking everything and re-checking and I was thinking, 'Well, we're Gary Goners here.' The pilot even said, 'It's out of our hands, now.' I was sure we were going to die but we got down safely. I was thinking, 'If only the 300 in the back stalls knew what was going on up here.'"

The Vautins walked through the doors of customs to be met by Alex Murphy who handed over some colouring-in books and pencils to the girls and declared it to be a "beautiful day".

"Kim and I looked out at the drizzle and the clouds and thought if this was beautiful, we'd hate to see a shocker," said Vautin.

They drove to St Helens and straight to the club house for introductions to the club board and some photographs for the local press. Then Pickavance led the way to the Vautins' new home. "It was only five minutes from the ground which was good and it was a nice little three-bedroom semi but the funniest thing was the way they took us to see it," Vautin said. "There was a convoy of five cars. There was us with Alex in one car, three cars full of club directors and another car filled with the secretaries from the club in case there was something we needed done. The neighbours must have thought the Queen was popping in for a visit.

"We all piled out and everyone came in to show us around. It was like, 'Ere you go lud, here's your toilet ...' and 12 people would jam into this little dunny, then we'd wander into the kitchen, 'Kim, 'ere's your kitchen, and ere's your toaster ...' Finally they all left and we had a look around. The first thing Kim noticed was there was no shower. Five months and all we had was a bath. Kim reckoned she'd kill for a shower. Still, my impression was they were all very friendly people, all wanting to help us fit in, and that's how it was for the whole time we were there."

Vautin was a bit apprehensive meeting the other players. He had been told of Wally Lewis's experience at Wakefield Trinity when his teammates refused to shake his hand in protest at the high salary he was receiving. Vautin found no such problem. Aussie Phil Veivers had been with the club for four seasons and the other players seemed glad to have Vautin aboard. They would have to wait to see how he performed. A day after his arrival he was taken to hospital with a stomach bug and ruled out of the first match. Murphy invited him to sit on the sideline with him.

"Alex was a real character," Vautin said. "I really liked him and he was very good to me but he was different to anything I'd ever come across before. That game was my first taste of the Alex Murphy style of coaching. Here the coaches like to sit at the back of the stand. There they prefer to sit on little benches down on the sideline. Well, after 10 minutes Alex nearly had to be stopped from running onto the field to abuse his own players. He was screaming and shouting his tits off if someone dropped the ball. That was his style, motivation through fear. Some responded, some didn't. It didn't particularly worry me, but it sure was different."

Vautin's first match was to be an away game at Hull, a four-hour bus trip from St Helens. "We got in the bus and headed off and after about two hours we pulled up at this roadside cafe. I thought, 'What's on the go here?'"

"What's going on, Alex?" he asked, "piss stop?"

"No lud," came the reply, "lunch."

"Lunch?"

"I couldn't believe it," he said. "It was about one o'clock and we were due to play at three. The people at the diner were expecting us and it was really laid on — eggs, bacon, baked beans, toast, coffee, tea and the boys were really wolfing it down because it was a freebie."

"Not eating, lud?" asked Murphy.

"I ate this morning."

"Ee, you *moost* be hoongry."

Apparently the lunch was a tradition but if that was an eye-opener better was to come. As Vautin climbed into his playing gear with 15 minutes to kick off, Jack the gear steward handed out paper cups.

"Drink lud?" he asked Vautin.

"What is it?"

"Sherry."

Vautin declined. Already on edge, he was concerned his fitness may not hold up. He hadn't played for six weeks and was anxious to make a good impression. He needn't have worried, the match was one of the best he would play for his new club. Early in the game he put Phil Veivers in for a try and later scored possibly the best try of his career. He took the ball from the five-eighth, dummied on the run-around and beat five men himself in a run to the line.

St Helens were impressed. They liked this new boy — and he was just the second stringer. The real superstar, O'Connor, was yet to come.

When O'Connor did arrive, the pressure was on him to perform. When Vautin welcomed his Manly teammate to the club it was with the warning, "I hope you've bought your Superman cape with you."

"He told me they were expecting big things," O'Connor said, "and they were. My wife and I had arrived a day late because we'd stayed an extra day in Rome. I never made it to Thursday night training but apparently a couple of hundred people had turned up just to watch."

"They were expecting him to score three tries and kick 10 goals every time he went on the field," Vautin said. "He'd gone so well on the Kangaroo tour that they were expecting him to be another Big Mal.

"That was the problem. Meninga had been over there in '84 and they were a bit spoiled. He was God to them, revered. No-one could live up to the way he'd gone that year. He was absolutely unstoppable."

O'Connor's first match for the club was in the first round of the John Player Cup against Hull — a match St Helens were expected to win easily. The team was in a lot of trouble before a Vautin pass put O'Connor away on a match-winning 40-metre sprint to the tryline. "I thought we'd done pretty well, but they weren't satisfied," Vautin said. "The ones you have to please over there are the 'speckies' — the spectators — and the talk was that we weren't too good."

The tide turned for Vautin during a John Player trophy match against Wakefield. After 20 minutes Saints were down 18-2 and looking shot birds, then just before halftime Vautin made a break before offloading to a teammate who was tackled on the line. From the play the ball Vautin pushed over from dummy half. From there on St Helens turned the match around, winning 34-18. "Perfect Paul" said the headline in the local paper, and Vautin suddenly found himself hero of the speckies.

"It was a great feeling," he said. "They were right on side. They'd stop me in the street and say hello. I had this car with my name on the side and people used to wave at the traffic lights. It made me feel good because some Aussies have gone over there and come home in disgrace. Pat Jarvis went over there and they hated him. For some reason they just didn't like him. Even today if you mention him they're likely to say: 'Jarvis? That so and so ...' So to win the speckies over and get on well with the players too was very satisfying."

That support was sorely tested though when St Helens travelled to Castleford to play the side coached by Aussie Darryl Van der Velde and spearheaded by Ron Gibbs and Gary Belcher. "As we were driving along in the bus I noticed it was snowing," Vautin recalled. "I'd never seen snow before, I thought it was beautiful. I was really looking forward to playing in it, I could see myself tackling on this nice soft stuff and building snowmen and having snowball fights after the match.

"When we got off the bus the temperature was way below freezing. The dressing room was the size of a toilet and the central heating had broken down. There was 15 of us crowded around a single bar heater trying to get warm. It was too cold to warm up, we sat there huddled together in our tracksuits until it was time to kick off. After three minutes I felt like I was running on stumps. My feet were completely frozen, I dead-set couldn't feel anything below the knee caps. You could say it took us a little while to get going. It was 30-2 against us at half time."

If Vautin thought he had seen Alex Murphy in full cry before, he was soon to find out he hadn't seen nothin'. The coach went berserk in the dressing room, abusing players, telling them they were all on the transfer list and when the hooter went for the second half, he was only getting warmed up. He grabbed referee Robin Whitfield in a headlock and gave him the biggest pay Vautin had ever heard in his life.

"Lookit you, ya fut bastid!" he screamed. "You're a bloody disgrace, you are. You can't keep oop with play — why don't you get out and do some trainin'. Look at your big fut goots hangin' over them shorts. You ought to be ashamed of yourself. You make me sick, you do."

Needless to say, Whitfield didn't do St Helens too many favours in the second half and they were beaten 48-12. It proved a minor hiccup in an otherwise enjoyable stay for Vautin.

"I loved the place, I really did," he said. "Michael and I got to be good mates. We didn't have jobs so we'd play golf together and get out with our families to those beautiful little pubs around the countryside. One time we didn't have a weekend match and Alex gave us the whole week off. Kim and the kids and I drove right up north to Loch Ness and had a look for the monster. Didn't see the bastard but it was a great time."

And when he and the family weren't taking in the sights, Vautin was just as entertained standing back and watching Alex Murphy in action. "It didn't take me long to work out that a lot of the players didn't like him but I thought he was a terrific bloke," he said. "He wasn't much of a coach but he was a funny little fella. Our trainer was Eric Hughes who played for Canterbury at one stage. He was a bit younger, he had a bit of an idea but Alex was something else. For training he used to come into the dressing room with us and off would come the civvies and he'd get into all his playing gear, jockstrap and all, then on would go the tracksuit and he'd be off to talk with the speckies who'd showed up to watch us train. Then he might go up and talk to the directors and back for a cup of tea with the speckies. After about an hour and a half he'd shout out, 'Okay Eric, that'll do,' and he'd head in for a bath with the boys."

That bath was to prove one of the greatest culture shocks of the trip. "The first night Snoz and I lobbed for training we noticed there was just this giant bath and one shower," Vautin said. "About 20 minutes before we stopped training they'd start filling up the bath and then after training everyone would jump in together.

"That first night Mick and I walked in and there they all were, 16 players, plus Alex and there was dirt and mud and sweat and blood and you name it. Me and Snoz are standing there thinking, 'Are these blokes fair dinkum or what?' Alex calls out, 'Come on, luds, nice 'ot bath' but me and Snoz took one look and headed for the shower.

"From then on they called us the Mushroom Twins. Circumcision must have been outlawed in England in the '60s. There'd be blokes in the bath pulling back their foreskins to have a bit of a clean ... it was unbelievable."

Apart from abusing players from the sidelines and at halftime, Murphy wasn't a hands-on coach by Australian standards. His match plan consisted of telling the luds to "take the ball and roon 'ard". But he could take credit for some selection masterstrokes.

Soon after O'Connor arrived Murphy decided he wasn't a centre and moved him to fullback. After a brilliant game by O'Connor in the new position, Murphy wrote in his local newspaper column that his gamble had proved little short of genius. Then came Castleford and the 48-12 loss. O'Connor was quickly moved back to centre and Murphy wrote, "Michael O'Connor came to me a few weeks back and asked if he could play fullback. I agreed, but after last week's game I am now convinced that Michael is not a fullback and I have moved him back to his rightful position of centre ..."

Another time he excitedly told the two Aussies of a genius winger he had signed from the Welsh B rugby union side. "He's brilliant," he said. "I spotted him myself in Cardiff and brought him down. He'll score a lot of tries, this one."

After the first training the winger admitted to Murphy he had a problem.

"What's thut lud?"

"I don't know how to play the ball."

Vautin and O'Connor were asked to stay behind after training to give a demonstration. "This bloke just could not play," Vautin said. "The first week he dropped about three sitters and missed half a dozen tackles. The next week he was worse. Finally I went to Alex and said, "Mate, in the fair dinkum department, what's the story? This bloke can't play."

"I know," said Murphy, "I never wanted him but the directors forced him on me. What can you do?"

The winger disappeared after three weeks and was never heard of again. "Probably digging coal in some mine in Wales," says Vautin.

Not all Murphy's selections proved so disastrous. After the Castleford debacle he called the team captain, Kiwi Shane Cooper, and Vautin into his office and announced Vautin was to take over the top job. It was an honour Vautin took very seriously, and one which proved an immediate success. It also brought some new responsibilities.

"In Australia the big thing is the semis and the grand final. Over there they couldn't give a shit about that, it's the cups," he said. "All they want to do is get to Wembley. There is a lot of prestige involved and the directors offer bonuses for winning the cup ties. A normal winning bonus for a competition match was 175 pounds but for a first-round cup tie they might offer 300 and 400 for a second-round and 500 for a semi-final and so on.

"As captain it was my job to go and tap the chairman before a big cup game and see how much we were going to get. I'd go over and say, 'Hey Joe, what's happening with the bonus this game?' and he'd tell me and I'd report back to the boys. They'd all stand around discussing it, whether it was a good one or bad or what.

"I remember one club round we were playing Leeds. We'd just lost three in a row over Christmas and we were up against it. We're in the dressing room before the match and Joe walks in and says, 'Luds, there's an extra fifty pounds per mun if we can beat Leeds today. Good luck,' and walks out. Well, there's absolute pandemonium. Our second rower Roy Haggerty jumps up and he's dead-set screaming, 'Fifty quid luds, fifty quid, coom on luds, fifty quid.' A lot of these blokes didn't have good jobs and fifty pounds was a lot of money to them. Pretty soon they're all up on their feet shouting and carrying on about the fifty quid. I've never seen anything like it in my life.

"It was funny in a lot of ways but in other ways it was a lot more professional over there. You'd get paid every Thursday in a pay packet, with tax taken out, just like it was a real job, and they had a fulltime gear steward. After training you'd just leave all your muddy training gear there and the next night you'd come back and your gear would be washed and in your locker and your boots would be sitting there all shiny. All you had to worry about was getting yourself there."

Not that that changed Vautin's outlook on training. Just like in Sydney he much preferred to play the game as a way of getting fit. Training was something to be avoided if at all possible. "Every Tuesday night we used to have a long road run," he said, "and one night when they announced the route I realised we were going right past my joint. I told Snoz and we dropped back until we were dead last and when we passed my house we ran straight up the path and in the front door. We sat there having a cup of tea and watching *The Munsters* and when the boys came jogging past we joined back on the end and no-one was the wiser."

Unfortunately Vautin wrote of the scam in his column for *The Manly Daily* and one of Murphy's friends living in Sydney posted it back to him. The coach took the appropriate action. He didn't mention it to either Vautin or O'Connor, but simply plastered copies on every notice board in the club.

Their fellow players were not amused but soon got over it — especially as Vautin continued to show great form on the field. In the 22 games he played for St Helens he said he was unhappy with only two.

"Paul was one of those players who goes a lot better in a game than he does at training," Murphy said. "But I'm not opposed to that. There are some players who can pull out that little bit extra when they're playing and Paul was one of those. There was never any question he gave 100 percent on the field. He never lacked commitment and he was as consistent as most. O'Connor never lived up to his name. He was supposed to be the number one in the world but he never showed that for us. As far as Vautin is concerned, he did alright. I would have liked to have him a few years earlier, but his stay was a success."

"It just suited me," Vautin said. "It was open football and I was fit and injury free. I was still able to do my usual number of tackles but with the game being less defensive over there I was able to get through some gaps too. It was probably the best five-month period of my career."

If Vautin needed confirmation, it came from Brisbane. He bought a video of every match the club played and sent them to his parents each week. "That was the best football Paul ever played," George said, and he is not one to give compliments easily.

St Helens developed into a close-knit and successful side. Vautin and O'Connor fitted in well with a team which boasted its fair share of stars and characters. There was Veivers who went to the club with Meninga in 1984 and stayed to become one of the most consistent players in the country; goalkicker Paul Loughlin who remains the best kicker Vautin has ever played with, and the two halves Darren Bloor and Neil Holding.

"I don't know how fair dinkum Darren was about his footy but didn't he love a drink!" says Vautin. "We'd have training on Saturday morning and he'd turn up blind, run through the moves and head straight to the pub for a pint. He could play a bit too.

"Neil was a funny little bloke. He used to do Aussie impersonations. He'd come up and say, 'G'day mate. How are you mate? Okay mate? How's that boomerang of yours mate, come back yet?' There was plenty of them like that. Real characters and real good blokes."

Murphy said Vautin was very popular with the locals. "They made him feel welcome," he said, "they are very friendly people and they took Paul to their hearts."

When it ended, it ended all too fast for Vautin and O'Connor. The side had made the semi final of the Challenge Cup — just one step away from Wembley. St Helens was up against Widnes who they had not managed to beat all year. With O'Connor and Vautin in the side they were considered outsiders. Without them they weren't given a hope. The two Aussies rang Manly asking if they could stay an extra week but Doug Daley remained firm. "We need you back here for a match on the weekend," they were told. Vautin scratched his head. "What match?" he asked.

"A trial against Souths."

No amount of argument would change Daley's mind. Manly had players guest-starring with clubs all over England and they wanted them home. Vautin and O'Connor reluctantly bade farewell to their teammates and Murphy and climbed on a plane.

At 3am the following Monday morning the phone rang at Wheeler Heights. It was a group of his St Helens teammates crowded around the receiver.. "Futty lud, we woon!"

A call from Murphy followed later in the week. St Helens wanted to fly the Manly pair back for the cup final. This time the club did not stand in their way. "I was going to be captain of one of the most famous clubs in the world at Wembley," Vautin said. "I'd watched on TV as my mate Graham Eadie had done it, and Sterling and Kenny, and now I was going to do it. I was over the moon. I felt great, fit, ready to go. I was dreaming about it every night."

Unfortunately the game didn't live up to the dreams. "We were on a hiding to nothing," O'Connor said. "We were up against Wigan who were the best team in the world and we just had nothing to throw at them. We had one move all year at St Helens, just one. By the end of the season everyone knew exactly what we were going to do before we did it. Fatty went up to Alex at our first training run before Wembley and said: "Alex, this is a pretty big game, mate, shouldn't we be working out a few new moves?' and he said, 'Futty, this is no time to be trying anything fancy, lud.' He just had no idea."

Paul and Kim and the O'Connors arrived at their hotel in Cobham, just outside London, a few days before the rest of the team, and settled in. When training started it didn't take Vautin long to realise their preparation left something to be desired. "We were sort of in camp for a week and Alex didn't know what to do with us," he said. "He just did exactly what we'd been doing all year. Wigan coach Graham Lowe's no dummy, he had us worked out.

"There was a lot of interest in the game and a lot of it centred around me and Snoz. The cameras used to come down to training and Alex would show up and shout out, 'Come on, Futty, you're not in Australia now, lud, roon 'arder.' And that was about it.

"We were playing on the Saturday and on the Friday we finished pretty early. I said, 'That's a pretty light run, isn't it Alex?' and he said we all had to get dressed and on the bus because we were due at Sandown races. Well, that was the worst thing we could have done. Day before the biggest game of our lives and we're on our feet all day watching the horses run around. It was ridiculous."

The preparation was shocking, but the pageantry of Wembley far outshone anything Vautin had expected. "Grand finals, State of Origin, it was up there with all of them," he said. "There's so much tradition, so much emotion. When we arrived everyone was singing. They have this conductor out the front and all the speckies sing those Pommy songs they have. The sound of it is unbelievable. Then they have this tradition where both teams go on a walk around the ground and wave at the crowd. Our bus was 45 minutes late so we got there at 2.15 for a 3 o'clock kickoff. I said, 'We're not going to do that lap of honour business are we? We've got to get in the room and start switching on' but they all did it anyway. Snoz and I didn't, we just started getting ready but all the Pommy boys did and you can't blame them. It was the biggest day of their lives and they absolutely loved it. Good luck to them, but when we ran out we had no game plan, nothing. Alex just hoped that if we went out and ran hard and passed the ball things might happen."

They didn't. Not for St Helens anyway. After three minutes Wigan's nuggetty Test halfback Andy Gregory put up a kick which Saints' rookie fullback Gary Connolly dropped. And that set the scene. Although a good player who is now an international, Connolly was overawed and out of his depth that day. He was in good company. Second rower Roy Haggerty, despite the huge bonus on offer, dropped the ball six times.

"The only players who could hold their heads high were our hooker Paul Groves and half Neil Holding," Vautin said. "I went okay in the first half but pretty ordinary in the second. Poor Snoz had the shits something shocking. All year he'd been in the centres then they flew him back 20,000 kilometres and put him on the wing. He wasn't impressed."

With 15 minutes to go, St Helens was down 17-nil when they received a penalty 35 metres out in front of the posts. Vautin decided to call for a kick up the line followed by the team's one and only tap move. Before he had a chance to instruct his team a runner was at his side. Murphy wanted him to take a shot for goal.

Vautin looked to the sideline. Murphy was signalling frantically towards the posts. Take the shot. 'You're kiddin' thought Vautin, 'What good would that do?' He took the ball and kicked for touch himself.

"I later found out that in the modern era of limited tackle football no team had ever been beaten to nil in a Wembley Challenge Cup Final," Vautin said, "we lost 27-nil and Alex hasn't said a word to me to this day."

Not directly, no, but he did pass on a few choice words when the team drowned their sorrows at the hotel later that night. As a few drinks softened the blow of defeat and the players relaxed by dancing with their wives, Murphy stormed among them and declared that they were all on the transfer list.

"What did he expect, to get a pat on the back for ignoring instructions?" Murphy demanded. "Alright, he was the on-field captain, but nobody likes sitting on the sideline watching a team getting beaten to nil. I don't think Paul was aware of how much getting points on the board can lift a side. A captain has to be the eyes and ears for a coach on the field and he ignored me. Of course I was angry."

In the next day's newspapers Murphy laid the blame for the loss squarely on the shoulders of Vautin and O'Connor. "A complete waste of time and money," he said of bringing the two Aussies back for the match.

It's an opinion he still holds. "I'd never do it again," he said. "Play Australians at Wembley, yes, but never bring them back after they've already gone home. The thing is that Wembley is more than just a football game, it's spectators and kids and people coming to London for the week. It's tradition. The Australians don't understand that. They've got nothing like it. They've got their grand final, but it's nothing like Wembley. For English lads to play at Wembley is lot more than just playing a game, it's being part of history."

In total appearances as player and coach Murphy has been to

Wembley more times than anyone else. "And it's still exactly the same as it was the first time I was there," he said.

"That's the thing you see, very few Australians can handle the occasion and certainly not if they've already gone back home. To have any chance of playing well they have to be part of the whole build up. If Paul and Michael had gone home for good and never come back to play at Wembley I would have said they'd done well for St Helens. The Wembley experience was unfortunate."

Vautin refuses to accept full responsibility for the loss. "We were only two blokes, what could we do? The problem went a lot further than us, but I suppose Alex had to try to protect himself.

"The day after the match they all packed up and headed back to St Helens. Snoz had decided to stay in London but as captain of the side I felt I should go back with the boys and face the music so Kim and I went back with them on the bus.

"When we were about 20 minutes out of town we were met by this open top double decker bus and everyone started getting off our bus and onto the top deck of this thing. I asked what was going on and they said we had to wave to the crowd. I said, 'Wave to the crowd? We lost 27-nil. They'll bloody well stone us!'

"Well, it started in the outer suburbs of St Helens. I was surprised how many people there were but as we got closer I realised they weren't there to cheer. The first thing I heard was this low growl and as we got nearer I realised they were chanting: "You are a loada roobish ..." As we went past they were all yelling out insults — and they had even made up placards like 'Murphy's Morons Do It Again' and 'Saints Are Shockers'. But the boys were all waving with these big smiles on their faces as if they'd won. I was that embarrassed I sat there quietly hoping no-one would see me but the boys weren't having it. 'Coom on, Futty, up you get lud.' Then they started throwing things at us, rotten fruit, old bananas and apples. And the boys just kept smiling and waving."

But when the bus reached St Helens there were 5000 people jammed into the Town Square. And not a boo to be heard. They cheered themselves hoarse as their heroes arrived home.

"It was one of the most emotional moments of my life," Vautin said. "Here we were, thrashed at Wembley and all these people had come out to say 'well done' for doing your best. They had a few speeches and more clapping and cheering. It went on for a while and then we had a few beers with the boys and headed home and I haven't been back to England since."

No, but Vautin has thought of it often. "I wouldn't have missed that trip for the world," he said. "I went over there not knowing what to expect and it was one of the most rewarding and rich experiences of my life. I liked the football, I liked the people and I liked the place.

"In later years when things mightn't have been going too flash, when I was feeling down, I'd think of the time I had there. I'd put on the video of one of the games and pretty soon I'd be smiling.

"You know, if someone was to say to me, even now, if I could be doing anything I wanted, anywhere I wanted, what would it be — you know what I'd say? I'd tell them I'd like to be back in St Helens playing footy with Alex and the boys."

CHAPTER 14

Trouble At Brookvale

If thinking of the days playing and living in St Helens was something Vautin did when times got tough, he must have been doing it a hell of a lot in 1989. Thing have rarely been tougher for the player, or Manly club in general.

The move of Fulton from club coach to coaching director of the junior league opened the door for the popular Alan Thompson to take over the top job. Thommo had proved a winner as reserve grade coach and was looking forward to a long career at the helm of first grade. It didn't take him long to realise the odds were against it.

"It started to become clear to me as early as February that I was going to struggle," he said. "There seemed to be hurdles there, hurdles that just got bigger and bigger. Even before our first game I could sense something was going on. I tried to keep the players out of it. I didn't want them involved, but eventually the hurdles just got too big.

"The season had only just begun and the rumours were already started. I don't know when Graham Lowe was appointed. For all I know he was appointed before our first game. All I knew was that I wasn't going to be around for a second year."

Vautin believes Thompson was never anything but a caretaker coach. Fulton had made some serious enemies in his time in the job and the likeable, easy-going Thommo was the one who paid for it. "Fulton has a very strong personality," Vautin said. "We had a saying when he was coach — 'What Bozo wants, Bozo gets'. And he did. Anything Bozo thought was in the best interests of the team, he made sure we got, whether certain people in management reckoned it was the right thing or not. You've got to remember Bozo had friends in very high places, people like Arko and Packer. When Bozo left it was almost like the blokes on the committee sat up and said, 'Okay, Fulton's not here any more, we're back in charge — and just because Thompson wants something doesn't mean he's necessarily going to get it.' That was in the beginning. By the end Thommo wasn't getting any back-up at all. It had developed into an 'us versus them' situation. The coach and the players versus the committee."

But that was still months away when Vautin and O'Connor returned from St Helens. O'Connor was nursing an injury, courtesy of his stay in England, but Vautin had never started a season fitter. "I thrived on it," he said, "I got fit the way that suits me best — by playing football. To me that's the easy way. Ask me to run around an oval for 20 minutes and I'm on the first bus home. Ask me to play 80 minutes of hard footy and I'll do it and ask for another game. That's just the way I am."

Vautin had started the 1987 season weighing 95 kilos, or 15 stone. After his stint in England he played the first match of 1989 against Parramatta at 91 kilos, or 14 stone 2.

"A lot of our players had been in England," Thompson said, "O'Connor was crook, so was Cleal. Lyons and Paul Shaw came back stale and out of form but Fatty was our best player early on. We just got off to a bad start. We lost our first two games by a few points and never recovered until it was too late."

The first match saw Manly score four tries to two but the Eels took the match 22-20. Next week Brisbane won by four points. Those two losses could be deemed unlucky, but when Newcastle scored a 14-nil win over the Sea Eagles, the knives were out.

"It snowballed," Vautin said. "Everything went against us. It was the wettest winter ever and Brookvale Oval was a sea of mud. You'd be playing there and you couldn't see your feet. It was filthy, the drainage had gone and the place stunk. It got so they wouldn't let us train there. It was our home ground and we weren't allowed on it.

"Out of our first 10 matches we only won two. We lost to Balmain by a field goal. The rumour mill was going berserk. Everyone was going after Alan and he was getting less and less support in the right circles."

Thompson continued trying to raise team morale but didn't have much luck. A trivia night he planned for players and their families was okayed by management then abruptly cancelled. Requests for specialised equipment were turned down. "That team just wasn't supposed to be successful," Thompson said, "it wasn't in the script."

But one person on whom Thompson could depend for support was his captain. Vautin has always been one to stick up for his mates — even to his own detriment. Add that to a healthy dislike for authority, and you have a recipe for disaster. In State of Origin camps the concept of sticking together and hang the consequences is a blueprint for success. That's all very well in the hit and run atmosphere of interstate series, but the closed shop of a football club, with all its political intrigues, jealousies and rivalries, is a different story.

Throughout 1989, Vautin made no secret of his support for two of his colleagues, Alan Thompson and Dale Shearer. Within a matter of months all three were gone from the club in sensational circumstances. A betting man, such as Fatty is, would say he backed the wrong horses, but for Paul, there was no choice.

Thompson never said much about what was happening at Manly until it was over. Vautin, with his access to the media, was not so reticent. It didn't take a Rhodes Scholar to know that there was a major split going on at Manly and Vautin left no-one guessing about which side he was on. He was producing two newspaper columns a week that season, plus appearing regularly on television. At every opportunity he voiced his support for Thompson. In the backrooms, where the decisions are made, the decision makers were seething and Vautin didn't make them look hard for signs of his contempt.

When Manly were playing Canberra at Brookvale, Doug Daley approached Thompson in the dressing room before the match. "Alan," he said, "it has come to our attention that some of the players aren't running through the sponsor's banner when they go on the field. Please ensure that all players run through the banner today."

Thompson replied, "Doug, I've got a few other things to worry about," but passed the instruction on to Vautin. It wasn't met with a great reception.

"You can imagine how that went down," Vautin said. "We were a million to one to do it after that. It was the worst thing they could have said to me."

With all the respect of an eight-year-old refusing to use his counting rods, Vautin called the team together. "Okay fellas," he said, "we've got the word to run through the ADT sign. Here's what we're going to do. No-one runs through it, right? No-one."

The team, led by Vautin, ran onto the field and straight past the sign as Daley and the other directors stood alongside their sponsors, fuming. It was an obvious act of defiance which worsened the already poor relations between captain and management.

"We felt like we'd been abandoned," Vautin said, "cut off and left to die. Thommo never stopped trying. Even at the end he was working out new moves, showing us where we were going wrong on the video but it was no good. He was trying to raise our spirits but he wasn't getting any support. We'd win a match here and there, then lose two or three on the trot. We couldn't get out of the slump and then it was too late."

Morale within the team was at an all-time low, with players openly critical of club management. Perhaps the player suffering the most was Phil Daley, the big prop who had played such a big part in the 1987 premiership win. As the son of Doug Daley, Phil was in an intolerable position. "I'd walk up to a group of players and they'd stop talking," he said. "They'd be saying things about my father and look at me as the enemy. I never had any friends in that team, only acquaintances.

"They all thought Dad and I talked about what was going on in the club. They thought I knew things that they didn't but the truth was we never talked about it at all. The only things I knew was what I read in the newspaper like everyone else."

Noel Cleal said of Phil Daley's dilemma: "If I heard people say things about my father like they're saying in front of Phil, I'd want to bash them."

Understandably, Daley's form dropped way below that which had seen him play for Australia. Finally he quit the club and headed for the Gold Coast. "I just want to go somewhere where I can be one of the guys, not son of the boss," he said.

The relationship between father and son had suffered over the period but improved in the ensuing years. "It was particularly hard for Phil, hard for us all," Doug Daley said, "but he has bounced back."

Phil Daley returned to Manly in 1992 but other victims of the 1989 purge weren't so lucky. On the eve of the team's second-round match against Canterbury, Thompson called them together before a training run at North Head and told them Doug Daley would like a few words.

Daley's address would shock the rugby league world. "Basically he said if any players weren't happy with the club they could leave," Vautin said. "He said he'd been getting feedback that players weren't happy at Manly and they had been critical of the club management. He said if anyone wanted a release they should come and see him and they'd be free to go. Thompson was stunned. He had no pre-warning of the chief executive's offer."

As the rocked players headed off for their pre-training warm-up, Dale Shearer jogged alongside Vautin. "Hey Fatty," he said, "what do you reckon he meant?"

"Well, Rowdy," said an exasperated Vautin, "he meant if you don't like it here you're free to go."

"Beauty," said Shearer, as he jogged off with a smile on his face.

This conversation sealed Vautin's fate. Shearer approached Daley later in the season wanting to take advantage of the club's offer. But Daley maintained the deal had been a oncer. Had Shearer taken Daley up on it that night at training, Daley would have been as good as his word, he said. When no-one acted immediately, he added, the offer was revoked.

Shearer persisted. Backed by the Brisbane Broncos who he planned to join, he took Manly to court. Vautin gave evidence in the case which embarrassed Brisbane and was a hollow victory to Manly. The court was told by the NSW Rugby League that the contract lodged by Brisbane for Shearer was far below his accepted market value. No worries, said Shearer innocently, the extra is going to be made up by a club supporter — a flagrant beach of the league's salary cap rules. The court found in favour of Manly but Shearer had made it clear he would be of little value to the Sydney club. He was released and played two seasons with Brisbane before joining Wally Lewis at Gold Coast.

Shearer eventually got what he wanted, but Vautin was a casualty. "They saw him as a troublemaker because he backed me up," Shearer said. "He saw things the way I did and he said so. I suppose they thought that made him a trouble maker, but they were forgetting how much good he did in the club. I know when I came to Sydney from Queensland he went to a lot of trouble to help me settle in. One of the reasons I did so well when I got down there was because he made me feel at home."

Helping newcomers feel at ease was just part of the job, but any success Vautin had had as team captain earlier in his career was very much ancient history in 1989. Nor were the efforts being made by him and Thompson throughout the year enough to save them.

"Fatty was the captain and he tried to turn things around the best he could," Thompson said, "but it didn't really matter one way or the other. We didn't know, but decisions had been made in the backroom and nothing we did on the field was going to change that."

The simmering relations between Vautin and Daley came to the surface on the eve of Vautin leaving for New Zealand as vice-captain of the Australian team. Vautin had partially dislocated his elbow in the second State of Origin win at the Sydney Football Stadium. He had recovered to play a club round against Canterbury and the third Origin match, but with Manly heading north to play Gold Coast the day before the Australian team medical, felt he could not give 100 percent.

At Saturday morning training at North Head Vautin approached Thompson and told him of his decision. "It's that bad I think I'll be falling off tackles," he said, "I think I'll have to rest it."

"Good as gold," said Thompson. "I'll bring up Owen Cunningham."

Vautin offered to fly to the Gold Coast with the team to give any support or encouragement needed, an offer quickly accepted by the coach.

Standing in the background watching training were Daley and team doctor Bob Higham. As Vautin walked off the field he was called over by Daley. The following conversation took place:

"What's wrong Paul?"

"My elbow's crook, I've had to pull out."

"I see. How long have you had this injury, Paul?"

"About a month. I told Thommo about it."

"Show me."

Vautin offered his elbow to Daley who called the doctor to come closer. "Bob, check that elbow please. Is there any chance of putting a needle in before the game?"

Vautin pulled away. "Listen, I'm not having any bloody needle.

I've told you, I can't do my best and if I can't play, I can't play. I'm out."

Daley persisted. "Bob, the elbow. Is he out? Officially out?"

The doctor ruled Vautin out of the game. Daley continued. "Paul you realise the Australian side is undergoing its medical on Monday."

"Yes Doug, I am aware of that."

"And how do you think you'll go with this elbow of yours?"

"With some physio I think I'll go okay. I've told Thommo I'll go and give whatever support I can."

"Good ... no, wait. Don't you go. You stay here. We'll take a fresh man who can get on the field."

With that, Vautin turned and walked away. His career with Manly was effectively over. He did pass the Australian team medical and made the trip to New Zealand. Maybe if he hadn't, things might have turned out differently. He would have been available to talk to Daley and the committee, perhaps sort out their differences. Instead, they were separated by the Tasman Sea and their battle was fought second hand, through newspapers and television cameras. As Vautin puts it: "The shit hit the fan. I'd done my dash with Doug."

Vautin has never been one to walk away from a reporter with a notebook or microphone in his hand and in New Zealand there were plenty of them around. The lot of a journalist on tour with a sporting team is not an easy one. Editors expect copy every day but teams play only twice a week. Usually it is a case of reporting injuries and selection dramas. In 1989, unlike on the previous New Zealand tour, there weren't any. What there was, was the Fatty versus Manly story.

"For the time I was over there I had no direct contact with Doug," Vautin said. "All I knew was what people told me. I'd be ringing home and get told someone at Manly had said something like, 'Vautin is 31, we have to decide whether it's worthwhile re-signing him or looking to the future ...' and the reporters on tour were telling me that Doug said this and Doug said that and trying to get my reaction."

For much of the tour Vautin remained tight-lipped. The journalists knew there was a story, but until Vautin opened his mouth, it was going to remain simply innuendo. Channel 7's John Brady showed Vautin videotape of Daley talking about the situation in order to get him to break his silence. Finally it was *The Daily Mirror* pair of Peter Frilingos and Tony Adams who cracked the story.

Frilingos in New Zealand and Adams in Sydney put together the two sides of the story and it was splashed over the back page: "Manly Don't Want Me." The article, which was later to win the NSWRL media award for best news story, was similar to many which surface at the end of every season when players are looking to attract interest from other clubs and thus up their marketability. What was different in this case was that it was true. Manly didn't want Vautin, and if he felt going public would change their minds, he was sadly mistaken.

At the same time, Lowe's appointment as coach became official. Vautin, who says he knew it was coming, was still surprised when the announcement was made. "I thought they should have let Thommo finish the year before they went public," he said. "They'd hired the man to do a job. At least let him finish the job before sacking him."

Thompson's fate was now out in the open. Vautin was still in the dark about his. After the third Test at Mt Smart on the Sunday afternoon, he saw Lowe and approached him. "What's happening?" he asked the incoming coach. "Am I going to be playing next year or what?"

He recalls Lowe's answer as, "Fatty, I know there have been some problems there between you and the club but my priority is to sign great players and I believe you to be a great player. As far as I'm concerned, you'll be there next year."

"I'll wait for you to ring me, then?"

"Yeah, I should be back on Monday or Tuesday. I'll call you."

Vautin says those were the last words he was to hear from Lowe for several years.

The Australians returned home on the Monday afternoon. That night Doug Daley rang. "Paul," he said, "I'd like you to be at my office tomorrow at 10am."

It was a sleepless night. For the first time in his long career with Manly, Vautin had not been approached by the club before his contract was up. It had always been a case of the club chief executive, be it Arthurson, Tenison or Daley, congratulating him on his form and asking him to drop in for a talk. Not this time. He was out of contract and the signs were there that Manly were in no hurry to rectify the situation.

Only one year earlier, along with Cleal, Vautin had become the highest-paid forward in the club's history. The two players had waited outside Daley's office together. Cleal had gone in first and when he came out soon afterwards, Vautin asked how he had gone.

"Ninety-five grand," the big man had smiled. Vautin knew he wouldn't get more, but was more than happy to accept the same amount when it was offered: $95,000 plus $400 a win. Daley also said the committee would look at giving Vautin a testimonial year in the future. Things looked rosy.

It was good money. Combined with Vautin's media commitments, it made him one of the best paid players in the game. It had also bought the Vautins a lifestyle they intended to maintain. They had just sold their Wheeler Heights home and bought a larger house at Cromer Heights to accommodate their growing family. Kim was pregnant with the couple's third child.

And now, Manly looked like pulling the rug from under them.

"I was lying there wondering if Manly wanted me," Vautin said. "I was thinking about whether I should try to go back to England. I was keen but I knew Kim wouldn't be too excited about it. She hated the cold and with a new baby on the way it was the last thing she wanted to think about. There was a lot going through my mind."

At five to ten when Vautin arrived at Manly Leagues Club he walked into a media circus. There was no doubt he was the biggest story in rugby league that day. Every major newspaper and television station was waiting.

He walked past them, gave a cheeky "Wish me luck" and bounded up the stairs to Daley's office.

The Big Split

There were no handshakes, no smiles. Vautin walked in to find club president Gordon Willoughby sitting behind Daley's desk. Daley sat alongside him, Vautin facing them. Vautin recalls the meeting this way:

"Paul," Willoughby said, "we, the Manly club, are going to make you an offer ..."

"Beauty," thought Vautin, "it's going to be alright. I'm going to finish my career here ..."

"The offer," continued Willoughby, "for one year, is for $50,000 sign-on and $200 a win. This is our final offer, and it is not negotiable."

Vautin looked from one impassive face to another. "You blokes are kiddin'."

"Mr Vautin, that is the final offer ... and by the way, Graham Lowe knows of the offer and is aware of this meeting."

"I can't take that," said Vautin. "It's half what I'm earning now."

"Are you saying you don't accept the offer?"

Vautin's voice was rising. "That's exactly what I'm saying. I can't accept it, no way. Why are you doing this to me? You're forcing me out of the club."

"We're not doing anything of the sort," Willoughby said, "we're giving you the opportunity to play for the club next year ..."

"I'd be an idiot to take it. You don't want me."

"Yes we do want you."

"Look," Vautin said, starting to feel desperate, "let's cut the crap. This is me you're talking to here. You're saying you don't want me. You want me out of the club. Okay, that's your decision, so what's the story on the transfer fee?"

Willoughby looked at Daley, who spoke for the first time. "We assess your current value at $50,000, therefore that is the transfer fee we would expect."

Vautin blew up. "Come on," he said, "who's going to pay that? You're kiddin' aren't you? I'm at the tail end of my career. You're forcing me out of the game."

"No we're not. We've made you an offer, the rest is up to you."

"What about reducing the transfer fee then?"

Willoughby thought for a moment. "You've been very well paid here," he said, "we won't be reducing that figure. We want to get as much back as we can."

"No chance at all?"

"No."

Vautin got to his feet. "Well, that's it then," he said, "it's over for me here. Thanks for nothing."

He turned and walked out of the office. As he climbed back down the stairs, the enormity of the moment started to hit him. Out in the sunlight the reporters swarmed. For once he brushed them aside, got into his car and drove home.

Some of the journalists followed. Others stayed and waited for Willoughby to appear and make a statement. "The Board felt in its wisdom that the offer was adequate for the club form he's been showing at this stage in his career," he told them.

Typically blunt, when Vautin was later interviewed on television and told of Willoughby's comment, he replied without a moment's hesitation: "That's crap."

The battle lines were drawn. Neither side was willing to back down.

When Vautin arrived home, he walked in the front door and broke down in front of his wife. Five minutes later there was a knock on the door. Channel TEN's Rebecca Wilson had followed him home. Could she have an interview? Vautin asked Kim to send her away. Half an hour later it was David Peters from Channel Nine. By now he felt composed enough to talk. He later had to apologise to Wilson, an outstanding league reporter whose doggedness had for once let her down. "Sorry Rebecca," Vautin said, "you were just too quick."

The competition between the two TV journalists was typical of the furore which would erupt over the next few days. If, as Andy Warhol once said, everyone has 15 minutes of fame, Vautin used up his quota many times over that week. Every night the TV sports bulletins led with the latest in the saga. Newspapers dissected the situation from every angle. Everyone had an opinion — and few of them were opposed to Vautin.

Even Fulton, whose ties with the Manly club were every bit as strong then as they had been two years earlier, was critical of the way the situation had been handled. "For a start, I don't think it had much to do with Paul Vautin," he said. "I think it had a lot to do with the fact that Fatty had supported Dale Shearer in his fight with the club. Shearer was desperate to get away and Fatty stuck by him and stuck by Alan Thompson as well. It didn't help that he was away in New Zealand when it all blew up either.

"It was all very disappointing. From a personal point of view I thought it was all handled very badly. Manly is a professional club and it should have been handled in a more professional manner. I thought Fatty deserved to finish his career with the club. He wanted to finish there and he should have been allowed to."

Ex-players like Eadie were shocked. "If a club can't find a place for the current Australian vice-captain there has got to be something wrong."

There was. It was a lot more than Vautin's club form being considered sub-standard by management. It was more than him supporting Thompson and Shearer or being in New Zealand. It was a combination of all those things, plus perhaps the most damaging of all — a clash of wills between a number of very strong, single-minded men.

As Alan Thompson puts it, "I don't know whether it was because he supported me like people said or whether it was just because he was Fatty. He's a bloke who speaks his mind and isn't afraid to make enemies. He is also a person with access to the media. It's one thing to have an opinion, it's another to voice it in public.

"He's an outspoken person but I think he always had good intentions. The fact is that Manly had every right not to re-contract him, that's their prerogative. The problem was the way they went about it. It was handled so badly it was unbelievable."

Once the media picked up the issue, it ran out of control. To the public's mind there was a good guy and a bad guy. The good guy was Vautin. The bad guy — because the committee remained largely faceless — was Doug Daley.

Daley was inundated with letters from furious club supporters, many of whom said they would no longer attend Manly matches. Others even sent back their club membership badges. Triple M sports director David White, the most avid of Sea Eagles fans, called on disgruntled listeners to phone the club and voice their anger. They did by the hundreds. A petition was circulated at Brookvale Oval and attracted 300 signatures in a matter of half an hour — including that of Paul Vautin. Daley was vilified in the press, on talkback radio and on television.

"Manly have a new coach — perhaps they need a new PR man instead," offered Channel 7's Mike Raymond.

Daley said even he was surprised at the amount of criticism levelled at the club and him personally. "There is a lot of jealousy about Manly," he said. "We have our enemies but we run a tight ship and people don't have many chances to have a go at us. When this happened they saw it as a way to attack the club and they made the most of it."

One of the few to take Daley's side was former Manly player and now radio caller and columnist Peter Peters. Peters, once a Vautin supporter, remained true to the club. "He started giving it to me then and he's been giving it to me ever since," Vautin said. "I'll cop a serve from anyone if I deserve it but I considered his payouts a personal attack. In the beginning it used to get to me, the constant bagging on radio and in his column, but after a while I thought, 'Hey, it's only Peter Peters.' If it had been coming from someone in the game who everyone respected and admired I would have been worried. I listened to him once, counted 576 ums and ahs in half an hour — then turned off. He can bag me all he likes in the future, to me he means nothing and I don't really care what he says."

The furore reached the Vautins' oldest daughter Kylie. "She asked me what a traitor was because a boy at school said that's what her father was," Kim said.

In the background, shaking his head, stood Ken Arthurson, powerless to intervene but horrified by what was going on. "I'd have to say it was one of the biggest regrets of my life. I'm always delighted to see blokes I've brought to the club do well and have loyalty to each other. It's been my good luck to have seen many Manly blokes kick on and that's why this came as such a big disappointment to me.

"The bloody thing went too far. Now I'm not saying that Paul was blameless and I'm not saying Manly handled the thing terrifically either. What I am saying is that a rift developed and harsh words were said and it never should have got that far.

"The spoken word is very hard to withdraw. That rift grew wider and wider until it passed the point of no return. Neither side was willing to give in, and it was a shame. A crying bloody shame."

And if Vautin was suffering, at least he had public support. Daley did not. "At the time we believed it was a decision the club had to take because of financial considerations," Daley said. "We asked Paul to take a pay cut based on his club performance. Unfortunately, it backfired.

"What followed was very bad for the club and very disappointing to me personally. I'd been the first person to welcome Paul to the club. When he and his parents walked through the front door for the first time, I was there to greet them. I'll never forget that.

"The whole thing was very distressing for me and my family. There were some unkind words said but looking back on it now, I think Paul and I both consider it just one of those things. There is no animosity there now. When we see each other, we shake hands and say hello."

Back in 1989 though there were few handshakes or hellos. At one stage it seemed the only place Daley and Vautin would meet would be in a courtroom. After a column appeared in the *Sunday Telegraph*, Daley sought legal advice. "I was told things could be bad for Paul if it went to court," Daley said, "but the newspaper printed an apology and I accepted that. It was just part of everything that was going on at the time that we were all caught up in. There was a lot of public opinion on the matter — opinion that Paul whipped up himself largely. He wasn't the only one asked to take a pay cut. Noel Cleal was another one, but all the publicity went to Paul. Suffice to say, it was very upsetting.

"At the time I had been with the club 35 years. It was, and is, my life, and I believed what we did was the only responsible thing we could have done from a financial point of view.

"Paul had been with the club for 11 years and served Manly very loyally. He gave good service but at the same time he had been paid handsomely. There comes a time in everyone's career when they must bite the bullet. Everyone reacts differently when that time comes."

Daley stresses he never once criticised Vautin or his form publicly during the dispute. The fans didn't give Daley the same respect. Creative sign writing became the order of the day. "Fans Favour Fatty — Don't Deserve Daley", "Save Fatty. Sack Doug Daley", "Do To Doug Daley What They Did To Fatty" and "The Committee Are Morons, Not Maroons" were among the dozens which covered Brookvale Oval grandstand and hill.

As he arrived at Brookvale the first Sunday after the offer to watch the lower grade matches against Newcastle, Vautin was met with a standing ovation and chant of: "We Want Fatty ..." A longtime supporter walked up to him in the grandstand and introduced himself. "Listen Fatty," he said, "we've never met, but I've been watching you since you came to the club. This is an outrage ..." He reached into his pocket and pulled out a wad of 50 and 20 dollar notes. "Look, here's 500 bucks and I reckon I could go around here today and for the rest of the season and raise that extra 50 grand. Would that keep you at Manly?"

Vautin was stunned, and moved. "Put your money, away mate," he said. "It's a kind offer but they don't want me. I've run my race here. Fifty grand, 100, it wouldn't matter. They don't want me here and that's all there is to it."

Vautin was resigned. It wasn't an issue of money, he knew that. He only had to think of the reaction of his former team- mates, now committee members, Max Krilich and Terry Randall. "They were two blokes I'd played with, gone to the wall with, and they didn't want to know me," Vautin said. "For the whole two weeks after the meeting they never came near me once, never rang or approached me. That was one of the most upsetting things."

One time Vautin went up to Krilich at a game. "Thrower," he said, "what's going on?"

"I'm on the committee now, Fatty," Krilich said, "I can't talk about it."

"Thanks very much," Vautin said as he walked off.

Similarly, he approached Randall. One rainy night the Manly players were working on a weight circuit. Vautin's group was supervised by Randall. Vautin stayed behind as the session ended. "Hey Igor," he said, "let me ask you one question. How would you have liked it if the club had treated you this way after 11 years."

Randall gave Vautin a straight answer. "I wouldn't have let it get to this, Fatty," he said. "I wouldn't have hung on as long as you. I would have got out. Look at you, you're nearly gone."

The Australian vice-captain, team player of the tour only weeks earlier, was aghast. "What? As a player? You reckon I'm gone?"

"You're not the player you were, Fatty," Randall said. "You're not recovering like you used to."

"Are you sure you're watching the right player?"

As always, Randall stayed firm. "That's my opinion," he said, and walked off.

Teammate Ian Barkley, standing nearby, walked up. "Fatty," he said, "I heard that and I can't believe he said it. If not for you and Des Hasler I hate to think how we would have gone this year." Vautin thanked him for his support.

"I was hurt," he said, "but at least Randall was being honest. He said what he thought and he didn't lose any of my respect for that. To me he was one of the greats, and always will be."

If Vautin needed any further confirmation that he was through at Manly after those brief exchanges with his old teammates it was provided by his treatment on the day of the Newcastle match. In a monumental piece of bad timing, Vautin was made the token offer five days before his 200th first grade match for the club. It was a milestone few players had reached and one which was traditionally recognised at Brookvale.

"In all the years I'd been there if a bloke played his 200th game it was a very big deal," Vautin said. "All the players would stand there and applaud and the guy was given a plaque and his wife was given a big bunch of flowers. It was something I'd aspired to in my time with the club. I'd imagined myself doing it and when it finally happened I didn't get a thing. The ground announcer made some half-hearted comment as we ran on but that was it.

"I took it personally. Everyone else had been honoured by the club and the crowd, I got nothing. It hurt a lot."

But if Paul was hurting, Fatty hid it the way he always did, with a laugh. When the reporters approached him after the match he gave his cheekiest smirk and offered, "I got here early for the presentation but the other bloke didn't show up."

Other than that attempt at humour, the jokes were pretty few and far between over those couple of weeks, but so were the tears. Vautin faced facts and did the only thing he could — looked for another club. During the tour of New Zealand he had received a call from St Helens, asking how much he would require to play a full season at Knowsley Road. He told them 50,000 pounds, the same as his money with Manly.

"They said they'd get back to me but hadn't," he said, "so I was tossing up whether to get back in touch with them. The problem was Kim was three months pregnant and going there meant either having the baby in England, which she wasn't happy about, or having her fly back halfway through the year to give birth here. With two other kids to think about it wasn't an ideal situation."

There was also that offer from Peter Moore. The Canterbury boss rang during the week and was true to his word. "Fatty," he said, "love to have you here, Matey. I know what you're on at Manly. We'll match that."

Vautin promised to get back to Moore but was reluctant to move to Belmore. "At the time they were going through their own troubles," he said. "There were some troubles at the club and I felt like they were in as much strife as Manly. I didn't want to find myself back in a similar situation to what I'd just been through."

The most attractive option looked to be Brisbane. The thought of playing on a weekly basis alongside the likes of Lewis, Miles and Langer would be like a dream come true for Vautin. All the ingredients were there: no-one was a prouder Queenslander than he, some of his greatest achievements had been on Lang Park, and the local population loved him.

The only problem was getting a start and as with all clubs interested in Vautin's services, that transfer fee remained the biggest hurdle. "One day they said they'd reduce it, the next they wouldn't. It was hard to make any plans because nobody was going to pay $50,000 for a player my age," Vautin said.

Brisbane radio station FM-104 tried to solve the problem. The station, which employed Vautin's State of Origin teammate Peter Jackson, started a Bring Fatty Back To Brisbane campaign, with listeners pledging money to be used to pay the transfer fee. For a while it seemed the appeal would be successful. When it fell short Wally Lewis offered to take a two-year pay cut of $10,000, but even that — and Manly's decision to halve the transfer fee — wasn't enough.

Vautin had rung Brisbane chief executive John Ribot and asked what the likelihood of him joining the Broncos had been. Ribot was blunt. "To be perfectly honest, Fatty, we don't needed a player of your age," he said. "But if the appeal raises the money, you're more than welcome here."

It is unknown how much the appeal did in fact raise, but Ribot finally rang Vautin to say he could not offer a contract. Wayne Bennett says Vautin's age was the overriding factor. "At that stage of his career he wasn't the type of player we wanted," he said. "We were top-heavy with blokes who were getting to the end of their careers, guys like Dowling, Miles, Lewis. What we needed was youth. If we had been starting up the Broncos five years earlier and Fatty had been available he would have been the first player we signed. He would have been just what we wanted, a bloke who always arrived ready to play. It wouldn't matter to Fatty were the game was, whether it was Bourke, Alice Springs or Timbuktu, he'd just ask what time you wanted him and he'd play his guts out. At that stage, though, he just wasn't right for us."

There is another theory too. The Broncos were just about to take the captaincy from Lewis, the first step in him leaving the club. Providing him with a readymade ally in Vautin would have been the last thing club management would have wanted.

Lewis refuses to speculate. "It just seemed to me that there were people there who didn't want him. Why? You'll have to work that one out yourself."

Brisbane out, St Helens unsuitable, Canterbury undesirable, the options were dwindling when Vautin received a call from Arthur Beetson who had just coached him in the Origin series. "Fatty," said Beetson in classic understatement, "bit of drama there, eh? How'd you like to play with Easts?"

It was an offer that came out of the blue, but one which very much interested Vautin. "For some reason I'd always admired Easts," he said. "They always gave us a good clean game and there was the fact that Bozo and Beetson had both coached them. I told Arthur I was keen to talk and he said he'd get Nick Politis to give me a call."

It was not the first time Vautin had spoken to Politis about joining Easts. The boss of City Ford and major sponsor of the club had been involved in some wildfire negotiations late in the 1986 season. Vautin and winger David Ronson were on the road together as sales reps for Wormalds when they found themselves near Easts Leagues Club at lunchtime one Friday. Vautin suggested they drop in for a bite and the first person they bumped into was club general manager Ron Jones.

"Paul Vautin," he said, "how do you do? Step into my office for a moment will you please?"

Taken aback, Vautin introduced Ronson and asked if he should come too.

"Er, no, not for the moment, this won't take long."

They walked into the biggest office Vautin had ever seen and Jones got straight to the point. "How would you like to join us?" he said, writing down some figures on a pad.

"Well, I'd have to see what you were offering, Mr Jones," said Vautin, who had yet to re-sign with Manly.

Jones reached for a phone and rang Politis. "Nick," he said, "you'll never guess who I've got in my office. Paul Vautin. He's interested in joining us. How much can we offer him?"

Jones looked up and offered Vautin a substantial amount of money, then handed him the phone. Politis reaffirmed the offer and said he would be happy to see Vautin in an Easts jumper the following season.

"Righto," said Jones, after Vautin had hung up, "shall I draw up a contract then?" Vautin sat in the big chair stunned. He'd come in for schnitzel and been offered a block of flats and Tasmania. "Well, I can't just sign up like that," he said.

Jones looked shocked. "Why not?" he said. "I can't wait all day."

"But Mr Jones, I've got to think about it, I've got to talk to Manly. I have to do the right thing."

"I'll give you until 7 tonight."

"I don't think I could give you an answer in that time."

"Alright," said Jones, shrugging and getting to his feet, "I'll tell you what. Why don't you go and have a big lunch on me. You and that other fellow, what's his name? Hodgson? Order whatever you like, and get back to me by noon tomorrow. Nice to meet you."

After lunch Vautin drove straight to Fulton's home and told him of the offer. "Gee, that's good money," Fulton said. "You'd be mad to pass it up. You'd better tell Doug."

They rang Daley from Fulton's home. "Paul," Daley said, "any decisions like this have to be made by the club board. This is Friday afternoon, we can't call a committee meeting now. You'll have to wait until next week."

"But Jones wants an answer by noon," Vautin had said.

"Well, that can't be helped."

By the time Vautin arrived home, the phone was ringing. It was Daley who had contacted Jones and taken him to task for negotiating with a contracted player. Jones denied ever having spoken to Vautin but obviously Daley hadn't bought it. At 7pm Vautin was in his office signing a new contract worth more than that offered by Jones and Easts.

Three years later Easts got their man. Politis rang back five minutes after Beetson and asked Vautin what sort of money he was after. Vautin told him of his $95,000 contract with Manly. Politis said he doubted the club would go that far and rang Jones. When he called back 15 minutes later the offer was $70,000 plus $500 a win.

"But Canterbury have offered a lot more than that, Nick."

Politis said he'd try again. A few minutes later he was back on the phone. "They won't increase the sign-on but they'll give you $1500 a win." Vautin agreed on the spot. The entire deal had taken half an hour since Beetson's first call. Just under three weeks after the meeting in Daley's office, Vautin signed the contract with Jones and drove straight to Channel 7 where he announced on Sportsworld that he was a Rooster. "Cock a doodle-doo," he told the viewers.

All he had to do was play out the last few games with Manly, a task that was a lot easier said than done. "On the Thursday night after the meeting with Doug and Gordon Willoughby I went up to training and called the guys around," he said. "I told them there had been a blow up and I wouldn't be around the next year but the main thing was that we should keep going and win the rest of our games for Alan.

"From then on it was bedlam. I lost count of all the letters and phone calls I got and there was all that stuff in the papers and on TV every night. Everything was pro me and anti the club. It was embarrassing really, but more than that, I felt bad for the club. I still loved the joint, I really did.

"I know they must have seen me as a troublemaker but the truth is I never wanted to make trouble. I know I'm portrayed as a bloke who won't suffer fools and someone who speaks my mind and all that, but I'd never just say something for the sake of it, I'd never say anything to hurt the club. I just try to be honest that's all, and there were things that happened to Alan and some other things which happened which I couldn't let go.

"All I ever wanted was for Manly to win games and for the players to be happy. That's all."

Vautin missed the third-last game of the year against Penrith through injury. When Michael O'Connor led the team out he realised with sadness that O'Connor would be captain for the coming year.

He was back the next game for his final match at Brookvale. It was a game Balmain were expected to win easily but the crowd was still out in force to pay its respects to Vautin and lifted the Sea Eagles to an unexpected 10-all draw. The spectators rose to cheer the old warrior off the field. He gave a quick wave to the grandstand and disappeared down the tunnel.

"All these years later I think back on that with disappointment," he said. "In all the years I played I was never one for the victory lap or the big salute. I told the other guys to put me down when they picked me up after the '87 grand final and if ever you saw me at the end of an Origin victory, I'd always be in the background. It wasn't my scene. But now I wish I had done one of those laps, mainly to thank everyone for their support over the years. It was a once-in-a-lifetime thing. Wayne Pearce got to do it, so did Ray Price and Mick Cronin. I guess it's like Peter Sterling said when he was forced out of the game, you can't always go the way you'd like to."

Vautin's last match for Manly was against Wests at Campbelltown, certainly not the farewell he'd dreamed of. As the players warmed up before running on he joked to Dale Shearer and Cliff Lyons that he wanted to go out with a try. They promised to accommodate him. He played his heart out as he had so many times before in a Manly jumper and was chosen as the team's best by several judges. He reminds you with great pride that he was Manly's best player in both the first game he played for them in 1979, and the last, 11 years later.

With 15 minutes to go Shearer made a break close to the tryline, with Vautin outside in support. Shearer threw a poor pass down around Vautin's ankles, but somehow it hit his boot and trickled over the tryline. He ran through and fell on it for the try. Even Wests' notoriously anti-Manly crowd gave a cheer. "Told you I'd set you up," said Shearer.

When the game was over, Vautin jogged off the field, sat down in the dressing room, put his head in his hands and started to cry.

Terry Randall walked up and patted him on the shoulder. "It's been a pleasure, Fatty," he said. "You've been one of the best. Sorry it had to end this way."

Gordon Willoughby came too, and the other committeemen. Through his tears, Vautin looked up and saw Doug Daley at the other end of the room. Neither man took a step towards the other.

The sobs took over. Tough guy Mark Pocock sat beside his long-time captain and put his arm around him. "You'll be right, Fatty," he said. "Just let it all out, mate, let it all go."

Big Jack
And The Roosters

When Vautin walked out to play his first game for Easts at the start of the 1990 season — a trial against the Gold Coast — he caught sight of himself in the dressing room mirror. "I looked at myself in the red, white and blue jumper and thought, 'What the hell am I doing here?'" he said. And that's how it was all season.

"It wasn't that I didn't want to play for Easts," he said, "it's just that I still wanted to be playing for Manly. I'm not making excuses, that's just the way I felt. I should have been strong enough so that it didn't matter but I guess you're only human. I was wearing an Easts jumper and playing at Henson Park but my heart was back at Brookvale.

"It wasn't Easts' fault. Ron Jones couldn't do enough for me. He was ringing up all the time to make sure everything was okay, and when our son Matthew was born he sent a huge bunch of flowers to the hospital. Russell Fairfax was okay too and I had mates there like Gillmeister, Dave Trewhella and Trevor Paterson but it just never seemed to work."

Even the off-season was a disaster. Vautin had been invited to accompany Easts on the end-of-season trip to Hawaii, via a match in New Zealand. He went to New Zealand but media commitments prevented him from going to Hawaii. "I played in the match in New Zealand for about 20 minutes and thought everything was going to be okay," he said, "but then things started going wrong."

Soon after the team began pre-season training Vautin accompanied Bob Fulton on a pig-shooting trip to Quambone. The first morning they got up at 5am and jumped on motorbikes for the trip further into the property. After riding on dirt tracks for about an hour, their rifles slung over their shoulders, they came to a fork in the road. Fulton turned to take the fork, Vautin rode straight and their wheels clipped. The next thing Vautin knew Fulton was slapping him on the face, trying to make him regain consciousness.

"He reckoned I'd done three somersaults and landed on my scone," Vautin said. "I'd been out for about 45 seconds and my first words were, 'Is my gun alright?'." Fulton, keen to bag some pigs, told Vautin to get back on his bike. He tried, but couldn't move his leg. "I couldn't kick-start the bike, Bozo had to do it for me," he said. "He kept telling me I'd be right, but by the time we were heading back all I could think about was how crook my knee felt."

Back in Sydney Vautin couldn't train. After a few days he saw the team doctor and was referred to a specialist who diagnosed a spur on the knee. The operation was to put Vautin a month behind training.

"I never told them how I did it," he said. "I just let them assume it was an old footy injury. Somehow I don't think they would have been too excited if they knew I'd done it pig-shooting with Bozo."

In retrospect that month on the sideline put Vautin behind the eight ball for the whole season, although Easts soon had more to worry about than their latest import's slow start to the year. For Vautin it was a case of deja vu. He'd come straight from a club where management and coach were on different sides ... to a club where management and coach were on different sides.

Unlike Thompson, Russell Fairfax wasn't even given the chance to see out the season, although the year started out quite reasonably.

"When I signed with Easts I'd never spoken to Fairfax," Vautin said, "everything was done through Jones and Politis but during the off-season I rang him to say I was looking forward to playing. I told him while I didn't know what his plans were about the captaincy, I was available if he was interested.

"He thanked me for the offer and said he'd bear it in mind. Hugh McGahan was the logical captain but it didn't take me long to realise he and Fairfax didn't get along. Fairfax had dropped him to reserve grade the year before and Hugh never had a good word to say for him. Whenever Fairfax said anything Hughie would shake his head and mumble under his breath."

Needless to say, Fairfax didn't appoint McGahan captain, instead giving the job to Trevor Gillmeister. Three weeks into the season the coach called Vautin aside.

"Gilly's not handling the job," he said, "you're captain."

The next two matches, against St George and Gold Coast, were wins for Easts and then the team travelled to Canberra to take on the Raiders.

"It was a nightmare," Vautin said, "we bussed down and back on the same day which wasn't a great start and then they absolutely smashed us. It was 66-4, the biggest hiding I've ever been involved in. Mal Meninga just toyed with us."

After Meninga had scored his third try of the day without a hand being laid on him Vautin addressed his team as they stood under the goalposts. "Okay fellas, what's the story, has he got AIDS or something?" he asked.

After try number five to Big Mal it was: "Is he covered in funnel webs?"

The captain's repartee was the only highpoint for the tricolours during a humiliating afternoon in which Meninga scored a record 38 points.

As Vautin put it: "We were calling touch but they weren't stopping."

On the bus heading back to Sydney there was no alcohol, no songs or jokes. After 15 minutes Fairfax got up and put on a video.

"Oh well," thought the players, "at least we'll have some entertainment."

"I want you all to watch this," Fairfax said.

It was the replay of the match.

"We all had to sit there and go through the whole horror show again," Vautin said, "as you can imagine it went over real well."

That afternoon, the biggest loss by an Easts side for 82 years, was the beginning of the end for Fairfax. Easts was a club run largely by three powerful and influential men: Jones, Politis and Harry Phipps. Word soon reached the players that the big three weren't impressed with the way things were going. Vautin, as a newcomer to the club, was not overly involved with the internal politics but felt Fairfax had a lot of good qualities as a coach.

"When I signed with Easts I contacted Gilly and he said Fairfax went okay," he said, "then when we went away to New Zealand I was pretty impressed. Even as the season progressed I didn't have too many complaints. He encouraged ball play and had plenty of ideas. If Russell had a problem it was that he talked too much.

"Rugby league is basically a simple game and you shouldn't try to change that. Russell felt he had to be working things out all the time, planning moves and talking, talking, talking. One time we're in the dressing room getting ready to run out and he's got the blackboard in there showing us moves for 15 minutes before the game. By the time we ran out some of the blokes were more confused than when they walked in."

One time, after the team had lost three matches in a row, Fairfax decided to try some psychological motivation.

Calling the team together minutes before they ran out against Penrith, he said: "Fellas, I want to tell you the difference between commitment and involvement. Now take the case of bacon and eggs. Just simple bacon and eggs fellas. Now the chicken is involved ... but the pig, now the pig is very much committed. Got it? Now when you go out there today fellas, I want you to think about that. Just remember: bacon and eggs."

As Vautin led the team onto the field, hooker Trevor Paterson was behind him. Vautin heard Paterson whispering something under his breath as they walked down the tunnel. Turning around he saw Paterson clenching his fists and chanting over and over: "Bacon and eggs, bacon and eggs."

It didn't do much good. At half time Easts were on the end of yet another hiding. As the players slumped onto the benches Fairfax implored: "Fellas, what's going wrong out there?"

Only Paterson spoke up.

"Hey Russell, "he said, " that bacon and eggs thing ... how did it go again?"

A week later the side played host to Manly at Henson Park. It was a game Vautin desperately wanted to win. Before the match he spoke to the players about his desire for a good showing. He even took Trevor Paterson aside for some one-on-one psyche-up.

"Hey Trevor," he said, "how tough are you?"

"I'm tough Fatty."

"Yeah, but how tough?"

"Real tough."

"Yeah? How tough's that?"

By this time Paterson's fists were clenched, his teeth grinding and eyes spinning.

"I'm this tough!" he shouted, then ran across the dressing room and threw himself head first at the wall.

The stunned Easts players stood there in shock, then recoiled in laughter as Paterson's head not only went straight through the flimsy Henson Park wall, but got stuck there.

As his teammates fell about in laughter Paterson's voice could be heard coming faintly through the wall: "Get me outta here, get me out."

When they were composed enough to move, Vautin and a few others grabbed Paterson by the feet and pulled him clear. The laughter stopped abruptly when the next head to appear, from the other side of the wall, was none other than Ron Jones.

That proved the best part of the day for Vautin. It was one of those games when the harder he tried, the worse things went. His former Manly teammates greeted him like a long lost friend before kick-off, but once the ref signalled time on, they were giving away no favours. The ultimate embarrassment came when Vautin tried a quick kick-off and regather. It fell three centimetres short of the ten metres. Penalty Manly.

At least he could go home after the match and forget about it. Not Paterson. He was summoned to the club and presented with a bill for repair of the wall.

"From then on we lurched from bad to worse," Vautin said, "we lost ten in a row and Russell's head was very much on the chopping block."

One Tuesday night after training, when all the other players were heading off home, Fairfax called Vautin aside.

"Fatty," he said, "got a minute?" They went into the office. "Fatty, I've been hearing some things. Nick Politis tells me you've been bagging me behind my back."

Vautin spluttered an insistence that he had not been doing anything behind the coach's back.

"I might have passed comment, but I was one of the few blokes who had stuck up for him," Vautin contended, "in the papers, on TV, any chance I got I tried to support him. When I drove home I was racking my brain. Then I remembered a conversation I'd had with Nick some months earlier. He'd asked me what I thought of Fairfax as a coach and I said he wasn't too hot in my view, but his heart was in the right place." Vautin was surprised that a private conversation had now surfaced publicly.

The next morning he rang Politis and asked him whether he had told Fairfax of their conversation. Politis was typically blunt: yes, he had told Fairfax, and no, he wasn't apologetic about having done it.

Said Politis: "It had come to the point where Fairfax had lost the respect of his players. He had lost control. I told him that even his own captain was bagging him. There was no point in pussy-footing around. Yes, I did use Vautin's comments, and I make no apologies for that. I did what I did to try and stop the club self-destructing."

Three days later Fairfax announced to the team that he had been sacked, and wished them well for the rest of the season.

"There were plenty of people in the team that didn't like Russell but I was never involved in it," Vautin said, "I was one of the few blokes who tried to stick up for him, still his record spoke for itself and he was out. I've always had the impression he thought I was one of the people behind it."

When word was out that Fairfax was headed for the chop, Vautin had approached Jones and officially applied for the position of captain-coach in 1991. It was also known that Hugh McGahan had done the same thing. Eventually Fairfax was replaced by caretaker coach Bunny Reilly, a member of Jack Gibson's 1975 premiership winning team, and a week later a new face was seen at training and around the club — Jack Gibson.

Gibson and Vautin had had a mixed relationship. At one stage Gibson felt highly enough of Vautin to offer him a place at Parramatta. Later they were at loggerheads over the "battleship mouth, rowboat brain" comment. When Gibson arrived at Bondi Junction some players had cause for celebration. Vautin was not amongst them.

"You're either on or off with Jack," he said. It took exactly 55 minutes for Vautin to realise that in 1990, he was off. Only 15 minutes into the second half of the match against Illawarra, Vautin was replaced. Although captain of the side at that stage, he would not play another first grade game that season.

"Bunny was coach but Jack was pulling the strings," he said, "the next week Hugh McGahan was appointed captain-coach for the remaining six games but Gibson was still in charge."

His first day in the job McGahan called Vautin into the office. "Fatty," he said, "this is the old back to second grade talk."

"What?" said Vautin, "I've gone from captain to reserves?"

"Look, when I heard Paul Vautin was coming to Easts this year, I thought 'you beauty'. I've always admired you as a player Fatty, but it just hasn't happened ..."

McGahan was reiterating what several commentators had been saying throughout the season — that Vautin's form in a losing team had been a shadow of his performances in the maroon and white over the previous decade. One of the most scathing attacks had been by *Rugby League Week's* "Man On The Hill" Clive Galea. Galea, a lifelong Easts supporter, pulled no punches as he took Vautin to task for his efforts. The two came face to face at the Wally Lewis testimonial breakfast in 1990 when Vautin intercepted Galea as he headed for the lifts. They were last seen in animated conversation as the rest of the crowd abated.

So McGahan's words came as no shock. Vautin knew he had struggled, but he wasn't alone.

"Hugh," he said. "It hasn't been a good year for any of us."

At least those were the words that came out. "What I wanted to say was 'you're not exactly in the running for the Rothman's Medal yourself Hughie' but I thought it might not go down too well," he said.

"I asked him whose decision it had been and he said his in conjunction with Bunny. I asked if I'd get the opportunity to get back into the side and he said I would.

"There was nothing to do but accept it. It summed up the year. I'd been dumped as captain of Queensland, now I'd been dumped as captain of Easts. It wasn't the highpoint of my career."

A few days later Vautin came down with 'flu and with 15 minutes of reserve grade training left asked the coach if he could leave early. As he left the field he passed Gibson, standing on the sideline.

"What's the problem Paul?" he asked.

"Jack," said Vautin, falling into Fattyspeak, "I've trained the house down. I've absolutely killed 'em and the coach has given me an early mark."

Gibson gave what Vautin described as a "funny look".

The next week he played reserve grade against the Gold Coast, tried hard and sat on the bench for firsts. Next round it was Souths. After the game the reserves jumpers where handed out. There was no jumper for Vautin.

"Where's mine?" he asked the trainer.

"Jack doesn't want you," he was told.

The next training run McGahan asked Vautin why he hadn't been on the bench. He had wanted to use him.

"I wasn't given a jumper," he said, then went on with it, "how the hell am I supposed to get back in first grade?" He looked around and saw Gibson. "Jack," he shouted, "got a minute?"

Gibson walked over.

"Hey Jack," said Vautin, "how come you didn't want me on the bench last week?"

Gibson looked him in the eye: "Well kid," he said, "I just didn't think you played well enough."

"If that's what you think then how am I going to get back?"

Gibson's voice rose: "Well let's just go back to a few weeks ago eh? That smart arse comment of yours when you came off the field — 'training the house down, coach gave me an early mark'. You're not doing a bloody Lowes ad now kid."

"You don't want me here do you?" Vautin asked.

"It's not a matter of that," Gibson said calmly, "you've got a contract and we've got to play you. Don't worry, you'll get your opportunity."

The next week Vautin did get a reserve jumper but by that time it was immaterial. He injured his shoulder in the reserve grade match and spent the remainder of the season on the sideline. As he approached his final season with the club, the news wasn't good. Even players from other clubs asked him what he had done to Gibson. The word around town during the off-season was that Gibson wanted no part of him. He was told Gibson had called for a full report on his shoulder injury to check for breach of contract. Another friend said Gibson had told him Vautin would be playing "in the park" during 1991.

Vautin went as far as phoning Gibson and asking for a release from his contract.

"I've heard I could be playing park football next season," he said, "it's obvious you don't like me and I haven't got a big wrap on you.

How about paying out my contract and letting me go."

"That's not my caper," Gibson said, "you just keep turning up and we'll see what happens."

Easts appointed Mark Murray coach for the season, with Gibson remaining football manager. One of Murray's first tasks was to call Vautin into his office for a quiet chat. Vautin says his former Queensland teammate pulled no punches.

"Mateship is a thing of the past when I'm coaching," he said, "you'll get no favours from me. If you're playing well enough you'll get into first grade if not, so be it.

"Look, I love Fatty Vautin, everyone loves Fatty Vautin, but that doesn't come into it. You've got to set yourself some goals and work hard. Friendship is over, it's business now. If I drop a bloke and he whinges about it, he's got the problem, not me."

Vautin says Murray made it clear he would have to work for whatever he got in 1991.

"I wasn't going to get any favours, but I didn't expect any," he said, "it was decision time for me. I had one year of my contract left and I was at the bottom of the heap. I could either stay there or head back up. I made the only decision I could, I wanted to play the type of football I could be proud of."

The pre-season started with an eight lap time-trial, not Vautin's favourite form of exercise. He finished second last, in front of Steve Hardy but with a time of 14 and a half minutes — the best he had ever recorded.

"Murray gave me a 'well done, let's see you do better' but it was a start," he said, "I decided to get fair dinkum."

Vautin headed back to the hill at Narrabeen National Fitness Camp which had nearly killed him when he was making his bid for the 1986 Kangaroo team.

"I married myself to that bloody hill," he said, "I'd be out there every day running up there or going around the running track. I'd time myself on those eight laps every day, always by myself. Sometimes I'd train twice a day. I was more committed than I'd been for years."

At the last training run before Christmas, Vautin beat his best time for the eight laps by a minute and a half.

His fitness was good, but his weight remained a problem. "At the end of 1990 I weighed 95 kilos," he said, "and Jack was very big on weight. The first question he'd ask you was 'how's ya weight kid?' and I'd tell him it was fine.

"I was going okay but then we had a break over Christmas and that looked like being the end of me."

The Vautins had decided to stay at a resort in Guam for two weeks. When they checked in at the airport they bumped into Vautin's old Manly teammate, Mal Cochrane.

"Mal asked us where we were going and when I told him, he looked sick," he said. "He'd got married the night before and he and his wife were going on their honeymoon to the same place as me and Kim. I don't think having us tag along was what they had in mind.

"As it was we had a pretty good time with them but after a week of eating out every night and drinking non-stop I blew out. I told Mal I had to lose some weight and he told me about this super diet he had. He told me it was veggies one day, then fruit and veggies the next, then just bananas, then steak, then steak and veggies and then brown rice. It sounded pretty crook, but he told me it worked."

Vautin drove straight from the airport to training where he weighed in at a whopping 97 kilos.

"Have a good holiday did ya kid?" asked Gibson.

As soon as he got home, Vautin went on the diet. "The big thing about it was this cabbage soup you had to eat all the time," he said, "Mal reckoned whenever I felt hungry I shouldn't have a pie or some chips or something, I should have this cabbage soup. I was getting up at seven in the morning that hungry I could eat a horse and hopping into this soup.

"Well it made me lose weight, but didn't I do some horse and carting. I'm a pretty fair horse and carter at the best of times, but eating this cabbage soup all the time put me in gold medal class. The kids were walking around with pegs on their noses. One night Kim had to sleep in another room. It was ferocious stuff."

But it did the trick. After ten days Vautin weighed in at 90 kilos — and stayed there all season.

"I even won a 400 metre race once and I'd never done that in my life," he said.

As Vautin made the effort, he started getting the support of Murray and Gibson.

One night at training Vautin jogged past Gibson who was resplendent in a new blue shirt.

"Nice shirt Jack," he said.

"You like it?" asked Gibson.

"Yeah, get it at Lowes?"

The next night at training Gibson arrived with the shirt freshly laundered and ironed and handed it over to Vautin.

"What's this?" asked Vautin.

"The shirt, you said you liked it, it's yours."

It was Gibson's way of saying Vautin was getting back on-side.

The first pre-season match came around and he was selected. Wests were favoured to win but Easts scored an upset, with Vautin just pipped as man of the match. As Gibson walked into the dressing room after the game the first person he spoke to was Vautin.

"Paul," he said, "you should feel very proud."

For Vautin, it was the ultimate seal of approval. "I felt better than I had for a year," he said, "it meant I'd done it, I'd turned it all around."

The season began as a triumph for Vautin and the Roosters. With McGahan out of the first game agains Souths, Vautin was appointed captain. "Don't read too much into it," said Murray, "just go out and lead them."

In Vautin's personal evaluation book the coach wrote of the match: "An outstanding game. I am very pleased for you, to see you fight back to that level. You're on the way forward — maintain your momentum and who knows what the year holds for you. It is going to be tough but that's why we enjoy the game so much."

Although they lost that first match the team's confidence grew. They developed into a tight-knit group and beat Cronulla and Balmain and drew with Newcastle in a three-match sequence. Vautin was playing with vigour, tackling hard and off-loading — the best start to a season by him for years. State of Origin beckoned.

Murray urged the selectors to not to overlook him and Vautin primed himself for a big match against Newcastle prior to selections. In the end it was Mike McLean and not Vautin who got the nod after a hard drawn match in which Vautin damaged his ribs.

"That's their mistake, not his," Jack Gibson said of the selectors on radio.

Vautin came back for the Saturday game against Brisbane at Lang Park. Murray pulled him aside before the match.

"Don't give up hope." he said, "you're not in the Queensland side but you're still a vital member of this side. Forget Queensland, get out there and play well for us."

If there is a game which Vautin would like to be remembered for in his last year, perhaps it is this one. Easts were at long odds but thrashed the Broncos in an open match in which centre Terry Hill ran riot. Vautin gave the long pass for one try and kicked through for another. It was his last performance on Lang Park and one which he could be proud of.

"We were really travelling well then," he said, "that win against Brisbane put us on a four-match winning streak and those were four of the best games I'd played in years. We beat Brisbane, Norths, Gold Coast and Wests in a Friday night match to go into the five.

"Spirit in the club was fantastic and we had some really good performers. Blokes like Craig Salvatori and Dennis Beecraft were in great form. The one who could have been anything that year was Brett Papworth. He was brilliant but he just kept getting injured. We'd shake our heads when he got hurt. He could play, there was no doubt about that, but the poor bastard never had a chance. I guess he wasn't destined to play rugby league."

Vautin won $1000 for the televised match against Wests and was looking forward to continuing with that form as he returned to Brookvale Oval for the first time since leaving Manly. George and Leila made the trip down to Sydney to be there.

As they had so many times in the past, they drove straight to Manly Leagues Club to buy their tickets. It was a rainy day and they were anxious to sit in the grandstand. Just as they arrived at the desk Doug Daley walked past on the way to his office.

Daley stuck out his hand and welcomed the Vautins to the club.

"Got your tickets yet?" he asked.

"Just getting them," said George turning to the girl behind the desk, "two in the stand please."

"I'm afraid there are none left," she said, "I can only give you two in the outer ground."

Daley stepped forward. "Give them my seats," he said, and walked off.

The match didn't give Easts supporters the result they had wanted, but for Vautin it was a happy homecoming. He played his heart out in a game which Easts led 12-10 at one stage before Geoff Toovey ran amok.

With 39 tackles — including two "quads" of four consecutive hits, Vautin was rated the team's best player by his coach. He also rated ten minutes in the sin bin — the first time he had ever been sent from the field.

"I'd done a tackle and was lying there dazed," he said, "it was close to the line and I looked up and thought 'Cliffy Lyons will run the blind here for sure'. I'd seen him do it so many times over the years. I wasn't part of the play but when Cliffy got the ball I just stood up and knocked him over." Referee Graham Annesley was sympathetic, but firm. "Sorry about this Paul," he said, "you can't do that. You're in the bin for ten minutes."

Coach Murray continued to spur Vautin on with his evaluation reports. "Obviously the Manly game offered special circumstances for you," he wrote "I know you are tough enough to maintain that spirit in the important weeks ahead."

Physically tough enough, yes. Mentally tough? After 12 and a half years in the game, perhaps not. After that Manly match the wheels started to come off the Easts campaign. Murray looked to his experienced campaigners like Vautin and Hugh McGahan to pull the younger players through. It didn't happen, perhaps the Manly game had been Vautin's last attainable goal. Whatever the reason, from that match on something was missing and the close relationship between Vautin and Murray started to fall apart.

"We got beaten 25-14 by St George with Martin Offiah scoring three tries," Vautin recalled, "he was the difference. He was that quick once he got an opening he was gone. I remember playing against his Widnes side for St Helens and it was the same story. After one try he jumped up on the fence and started waving to the crowd. It was the same that night at he Football Stadium. He was a lair but he was a bloody fast lair.

"From there on the rot set in. We beat Canberra but then we got thrashed by Parramatta. They were behind us on the table and we were expected to win but something was missing. There was no team spirit, training had become repetitive and we hadn't changed our tap moves from the start of the year. You could just feel the intensity drop off."

Murray singled out McGahan and Vautin for a blast in front of the team. Afterwards he called Vautin aside.

"I gave you a serve there because you are a leading player. I need more from you," he said. The next week Murray called both Vautin and Steve Hardy to his office for a further talk. Was Vautin still setting himself goals, was the commitment there? He asked both men about their friendship.

"I don't know what he was on about," Hardy said, "maybe he thought we were setting a bad example at training. We didn't mind a bit of a joke here and there but when the job had to be done, we were serious about it. I got the impression Murray was intimidated by Fatty — sort of in awe of him a bit. They'd been close mates but as the season went on they drifted further and further apart."

Late in the season Gibson asked Vautin his plans for the coming season.

"Better make a time to come and talk," Gibson said.

"At that stage I was keen to go around again," Vautin said, "I was fit, I thought I was playing well, I thought 'why not?'." The match against Cronulla was to make things clearer. With McGahan out, Vautin was appointed captain. He now knows something was gone from his game.

"My form had tapered off a little," he said, "I knew that. My fitness was okay, I was still training hard but mentally, maybe I was off a little. I was still trying but I wasn't doing the things I'd been doing during that winning streak of four games earlier in the season.

"We played Cronulla and it was my worst game of the year. The intensity just wasn't there. We got beaten 48-14. I knew I hadn't played well and the next day I started asking myself those questions. Had the rot set in, did I really want to play again? Training hadn't changed since the beginning of the season. It was really getting boring and I wondered if I wanted to go through it all again. I'd have to say I found Murray an uninspiring coach. He was repetitive, and, in my view, had become a Jack Gibson clone. I started talking to Kim about it, saying I wasn't enjoying myself and maybe I should give it away. There comes a time when you have to ask yourself if you want to keep getting out for training, keep getting smashed every weekend on the field."

Subsequent events were to force his hand. The following match against Balmain, McGahan was still out. Murray rang early in the week to tell Vautin he had appointed Salvatori captain.

"At this stage I think it will do his career more good than yours," he said.

Easts went into the match still a chance to make the final five. Murray tried some innovative strategy by choosing not to talk to his players before the game. He did not go with them to the pre-match warm-up and stood silently in a corner prior to them running on. The move back-fired. Easts were beaten 34-18 and with three matches left, were out of contention for the season.

The following Tuesday Vautin was preparing to leave home for training when the phone rang. It was Murray. Vautin recalls the conversation this way:

"Muppet here Fatty. How do you think you went on Sunday?"

"Not too good but we'll come back. We'll beat Newcastle this week."

"Yeah, well that's what I'm ringing about. You're not in the side. As far as I'm concerned you're gone. You won't be playing first grade again this season."

"What? You're saying I'm no chance to get back in?"

"The way I look at it Fatty, you're a leading player in this side. When you go well the whole team goes well. When you don't, you're like a cancer. When you're bad everyone is bad."

"So I'm in reserve grade?" "No, I wouldn't do that to you Fatty. I won't let you go out in reserve grade. Don't come to training tonight. I'm telling everyone, all the other players, the press, that you're injured and out for the season."

"What about using me as a fresh reserve."

"Sorry, that's not an option. Now what sort of injury do you want?"

Stunned, Vautin muttered something about his ribs.

"Ribs it is. Listen, nothing personal, it's a business decision, that's all."

At that moment Vautin made his own snap decision.

"Listen Muppet," he said. "I was in the throes of making up my mind about my future, you've done it for me. I'm retiring, this is it — after this season I'm gone. Any chance of letting me go out on a high note? Can I play the last game against Penrith in first grade?"

"That's your decision about retiring," Murray said, "as far as the other thing is concerned, I'll think about it. No guarantees."

To the press and public, Vautin was out with damaged ribs. To Vautin himself, it wasn't quite that simple.

"The thing was I never expected any favours," he said, "but there are just some things you think a bloke you've known for a long time would do. Muppet had changed a lot from the happy-go-lucky bloke I'd played Origin football with. I don't know what it was — maybe he'd changed, maybe I had, but under the old mates act he could have come up to me and said: 'Fatty, you're struggling. There's three games left, just give us your best.' In the end he made a business decision and stood by it and I respect him for that but that stuff about being a cancer in the side hurt. Later he reckoned he'd never used that word, but it's not a word I would be mistaken about. The meaning was clear, and I don't think I deserved it."

On Thursday night Vautin went to training and was approached by Hardy who asked why he wasn't playing.

"What I could I do?" he said, "he asked me and I told the truth. I can't look a mate in the eye and lie to him."

"I was shocked," Hardy said, "Fatty was a different player to what he had been the year before. He turned things around and this was how they treated him. It was a disgrace. He wasn't playing that badly. He was playing like the rest of the team was playing and I felt he deserved more. I wasn't the only one to think it either. It didn't help matters within the team. We were going badly and that made things even worse. It wasn't so much the older blokes like me, we'd seen plenty. It was the younger guys who were thinking 'what's going on?' It was a funny year, that's for sure."

Bob Fulton was shocked when he heard what had happened.

"They couldn't have known the bloke very well if they asked him to do that," he said, "Fake an injury. That's not Fatty. That's not the way he played, that's not the way he wanted to go out."

Within days the story was around the club. When Vautin bumped into Gibson at the next training he was furious.

"You've let the cat out of the bag have you kid?" he asked.

"What could I do Jack?" Vautin said, "I couldn't lie."

Vautin knew he was on the outer with Gibson but asked for the chance to go out on top.

"Jack, I've been around a long time and I know my time's come. I just want to play that last game in first grade. In 30 years time I want to be able to say I went out in first grade."

"You'll be right kid, " Gibson said, "we'll look after you."

Vautin was also approached by Murray. "What I said to you I said in confidence," the coach said, "now it's all around the club ..."

By that time relations between Vautin and management had deteriorated to what they had been the previous year. Gibson is still furious about Vautin's end to the season.

He refuses to comment on any aspect of the year. "I want no truck with that jerk," he says of Vautin.

"I really don't know what happened," Vautin said, "the thing with Jack is once you disagree with him, that's it, you're gone. He's a reasonable bloke and I quite liked him as a person. In that last year at Easts I got along well with him, we played some golf and talked a fair bit. When it comes to talking about life in general, Jack is tops. You could talk to him for hours. When it comes to football, many people have set Jack up as the guru of rugby league, but I never saw any sign of that in my time at Easts. Comparing football knowledge of the game as it is today, my opinion is that the distance between Bob Fulton and Gibson is from here to Mars and back. Occasionally Jack would come onto the field at training, talk to us for five minutes or so in that distinctive style of his, and then depart. I can't vouch for all the rest of the blokes, but these little talks left me nothing but confused.

"Word was he was disappointed that I wasn't being a leader but you just have to look through those evaluation reports. What was I, a ham sandwich? He was that keen to sign me halfway through the year he was asking me to come and see him every week. The next thing I'm on the outer. They reckoned they were giving me an out but I didn't want an out. I just wanted to play and I was going well enough to be in the team. What did he expect me to do, thank him?"

"When searching for the reasons why Easts went from being semi-final contenders mid-season to winning only three from our last 11 games, the Murray-Gibson combination looked at the players and said that they weren't putting in. Maybe this was so, but why weren't they putting in? Maybe they should have had a good look at themselves. They might have found one of the reasons.

I've got no beef with Jack. He obviously has one with me, but to coin a Murrayism, that's his problem, not mine.

"As far as Easts go they cop a pasting from critics for being the Transit Lounge and all that and while the junior league in the area isn't the strongest that will probably always be the case, but they are a good club and have been well run over the years by Ron Jones and his offsiders. They have had the best sponsor in the game in Nick Politis and a great bunch of players in blokes like Salvatori, Russell, Hall and Marshall and I wish them every success in the future.

Before he announced the team for the final match, Murray called Vautin aside.

"You're in the side," he said, "good luck. I hope you have a good game."

The match was at the Sydney Football Stadium and Penrith won 42-8. East were a far cry from the cock-a-hoop outfit which had barnstormed their way into the final five a few months before. Of their last 11 matches they had won only three. It was to be no fairytale ending for Paul Vautin. His team didn't win, he didn't score the winning points or make the victory lap with a trophy held high. He went out wearing a jumper he had never thought he'd wear, in front of a crowd who knew him best as a former star from another club.

But he went out in first grade and he went out knowing that when the chips were down and he'd put his mind to it, he'd climbed back from the scrapheap if only to be beaten by age in the end.

"That last game, when the full-time siren went I didn't feel any sadness or bitterness," he said, "it was like I'd felt in 1987 when we won the competition. We were the best team then, we had the best coach, we had to win and when we did, all I felt was relief. Well, that was exactly how I felt after that last game. Relief that it was all over."

He walked from the field and a supporter reached down to shake his hand. As he headed up the dark tunnel to the dressing room for the last time the words came clearly to mind.

"Well," he thought, "I've done my duty. I've paid my dues.

CHAPTER 17

Multi Media Personality

"It's like Vietnam here at night because when I get up in the wee hours of the morning my wife's new dog — and I use the term loosely — has always deposited at least three or four landmines in my path ..."

With those words, the character of Fatty, media superstar, was well and truly launched upon an unsuspecting public. It was May, 1985, and *Manly Daily* sports editor Warren Sim was going through Vautin's column for the following Friday. He took one look and hurried in to talk to editor Gary McGay. For the two men the column confirmed what they had suspected when they hired Vautin a few weeks earlier: he was a natural.

The column, with its headline "Nothing To Do With Football", was a description of Kim Vautin's dog — a Lhaso Apso named Muffy. As Vautin wrote of the exotic breed: "It looks like a toilet brush with legs ... About the only enjoyment I get out of it is every Saturday when Kim and I get involved in a bit of Muffy diving — giving the dog a bath."

In the long history of rugby league there have been many players who have pursued a career in the media, yet there has been only one who has really transcended the ex-player syndrome: Rex Mossop. As one television insider said: "They start off as famous players who are bad TV commentators. Then the fame wears off and they're just bad TV commentators." Yet Mossop went beyond that. In over 20 years on television his outrageous dogmatism and sense of the controversial or humorous saw him gain fame as a personality which far outlived memories of his prowess as a footballer. Vautin, starting with that innocuous column in *The Manly Daily*, followed Mossop's lead.

"We were looking around for someone to write a column for us and Fatty seemed to be the logical one," said Sim. "He was Manly captain at the time and he was starting to get known as a pretty outrageous sort of guy. The beauty of his column was that he had the ability to be himself in print. He was a character off the field and he was able to write just like he is. His writing took that larrikin image that one step further."

Then, as now, the majority of columns written by footballers — or more often their ghost writers — followed a pretty standard form. The week before a game against the competition easybeats it would be: "No way we're going to take the River Rats easy this Sunday. There's no such thing as an easy game in this comp and we'll be giving them the respect they deserve ..."

Closer to representative games it would be: "I can't understand why the City selectors don't look at our young prop Jimmy Johnson for next week's big game. He's been absolutely braining them lately. His hit on Billy Black last week shook the foundations of the stand ..."

Often the players whose names and photographs appeared on the top of the column wouldn't even know what it was they had "written". Veteran league writer Geoff Prenter was known as "The Ghost of Broadway" when he put together a column for a different player every day of the week at the now defunct Sydney *Sun*. One of his most famous efforts was under the byline of Souths' male model winger Mike Cleary who often copped a hard time from opposition crowds. Without Cleary's knowledge, Prenter decided it was time to hit back. Cleary picked up his copy of *The Sun* to see the banner headline on the back page: "Don't Call Me Michelle." It took an awful lot of fence-mending before Cleary would speak to Prenter again.

More recently — on the eve of a State of Origin match in 1989 — the Sydney *Sunday Telegraph* decided to use its two columnists, Maroons' star Vautin and NSW and Australian selector Johnny Raper in tandem, each giving a one-eyed look at the match from opposite sides of the border. Not wanting to give the Blues ammunition to fire back at his team, Vautin was remarkably restrained, pointing out the strengths of the NSW players and in classic reverse psychology, virtually announcing it would be a miracle if Queensland scored a point, let alone won.

Raper on the other hand had no such reticence. Not that he knew it. He was racing out the door to catch a plane to Queensland when his ghost writer rang, the last words spoken being: "Chook, trust me."

The column began: "Dream on you cane toads ..."

The Queensland camp jumped on it. The column was reprinted on the front page of the Brisbane *Courier Mail*, causing an outcry that an Australian selector should be so biased. The Maroons used the comments as part of their pre-match build-up, NSW were thrashed and Raper was carpeted by the Australian Rugby League and threatened with the sack.

So much for ghost writers. Vautin never used one, in fact he steered clear of the well-worn path of player columns altogether. After the success of the Muffy column, he wrote about things that went on inside the club or around his home. The sort of things that made him laugh and, as the *Manly Daily* editors soon learned, made everyone else laugh too.

"That one about washing the dog was a classic," said Sim. "It was so completely different to what everyone was used to and the readers just loved it. The Fatty column was easily the most popular column we'd ever run. The number of phone calls and letters we got was amazing."

With the newspaper under the control of what Sim terms "a very conservative general manager", the column took a short time to find its niche. The boss didn't follow the game, didn't care much for nicknames and wasn't sure how the readers would react. Sim and McGay suggested the title "Fatty on Friday" but it was vetoed. The column started its life as "Vautin on League" but after its runaway success, "Fatty on Friday" it was.

"He had a go," Sim said. "He was prepared to get offside with people but generally we never had to change a word. He was working in our sales department at the time and he'd bring it in every week, all typed and ready to go. Sometimes we'd think, 'You can't say that', but more often than not Gary would let it go."

That policy gave the green light to items such as: "I overheard a conversation between two players the other day. It went like this:

Player 1: "Look at those blokes dipping their hands and cups into that bucket and drinking out of it. They shouldn't do that, they could get AIDS."

Player 2: "Wouldn't worry me."

Player 1: "Why not?"

Player 2: "I wear a condom to training."

When filing from the State of Origin match in LA, Vautin reported: "It's so bloody hot over here the chooks are laying hard boiled eggs."

And of an opposition player: "I've seen better heads on carbuncles."

For four years "Fatty on Friday" became a much-enjoyed part of the local newspaper, arriving each week, double typed and right on time — although Sim remembers one week the copy was quite understandably late. "Our office was on one side of a council car park and the beer garden of the Steyne Hotel was on the other. On the day after Manly won the grand final the boys were celebrating at the Steyne and I looked through the office window to see Fatty weaving through the carpark after an obviously hard session."

Vautin stuck his head through the office door with a "What's happenin'?"

"Well, I know your column is due in," said Sim.

"Okay," blithered Vautin, staggering in and sitting down at a typewriter, "I'll do it now."

Sim recalls it as one time Fatty on Friday required a fair bit of editing before publication. "Generally, though, it was just as Fatty wrote it, and the readers couldn't get enough of it," Sim said. "Some of the things he said you wouldn't get away with anywhere but in a suburban paper. It wouldn't be the sort of thing you'd be able to put in the big metropolitan papers."

Prophetic words. When Barry Grove, sports editor of the Sydney *Sunday Telegraph*, was looking for a columnist, Vautin's name was suggested by a reporter who had read *The Manly Daily*. Grove went ahead and hired him. The decision cost him his job.

During the 1988 State of Origin series Vautin wrote a column telling of a trip in the team minibus after a big night at Jupiters Casino. It started: "I thought Big Artie Beetson was in a class of his own when it came to those internal explosions but a very keen rival was discovered during Queensland's recent camp: none other than bustling Sam Backo ..."

The column continued, introducing the *Sunday Tele's* reader — more used to Charlie Chuckles and Don Burke's gardening tips, to such literary gems as: "Being early in the morning it was obvious there'd be a bit of gas floating about and with Sam sitting in between Wally Lewis and Gene Miles up front it was like a symphony orchestra as we puttered along in the bus. Big Sammy was only getting warmed up though and all of a sudden he let rip with one that had oxygen masks falling from the seats and tears pouring out of many pairs of eyes.

"Five minutes later there was another minor explosion in which he nearly blew the door off the bus..."

And finally, the big finish: "It was a fun journey but thank our lucky stars Beetso wasn't on the same bus for what I can politely describe as a Battle of the Sounds. That wouldn't be a bad promotion, you know. One can see the billboards now: Baked Beans Backo v Beef Curry Beetson. What a contest."

Grove, sports editor for six and half years and a veteran of 22 years with the company, okayed the column but two days after publication was called to the office of editor Ian Moore. After being told the column had been unsuitable for a family newspaper, Grove was removed from his job and transferred to the production department of another paper within the group.

He remains philosophical. "I view it as one of the things which happen in this industry," he said. "I'm no martyr, I thought the column was okay. To me it was just an honest example of the way footballers are. There was no foul language. In the end it boiled down to a difference of opinion. I thought it was alright, the bosses didn't, and those are the arguments you always lose."

While the column cost Grove his position on the newspaper it didn't hamper the rise of Fatty. He stayed with the *Sunday Telegraph* and branched out into television as a regular panellist on the Big League segment of Channel 7's *Sportsworld*.

Earlier forays into television had been of varying success. Vautin had developed from a nervous guest of *Sportsworld*'s original host Rex Mossop into an accomplished speaker in front of the cameras.

He had appeared as a guest commentator on the ABC on several occasions but once suffered the anguish of a mental block. As he stood sideline with chief caller David Morrow prior to kick-off of a Canterbury-Cronulla match, Vautin launched into a summary of the two team's strengths and weaknesses. All was going fine as he ran through the Canterbury side, but it fell apart as he turned his attention to their opponents.

He couldn't remember who they were.

After Vautin had stared blinking mutely into the screen for a few seconds, Morrow summed up the situation and jumped in — which might just have saved things if Vautin hadn't forgotten there were no commercial breaks on the ABC.

As Morrow finished speaking Vautin said to him — and everyone else in Australia who was watching: "Geez, I stuffed that one up, didn't I?" Except he didn't use the word "stuffed".

As the screen went blank Morrow apologised for a "slight technical problem".

Little wonder then that when Vautin joined Channel 7, *Big League* producer Owen Dally admits to being "scared stiff."

"He gave me heart attacks," Dally said. "Doing live television with Fatty was a nightmare. You just never knew what he was going to say, but to be honest he never went too far. I think he saved the really bad stuff for the commercial breaks.

"Probably the closest he came was the time he said: 'Opinions are like bums. Everybody's got one.'

"He was totally unpredictable, but that was part of his charm. He said what he believed. He wasn't like these stereotyped cardboard cut-out characters whose image is to sit there, read an autocue and look pretty. He was totally removed from that and that's what made him a success. When we were talking to him about being a regular on the show he said, 'Look, I'm a certain way and I'm not changing. If you want me warts and all, great. If you don't you'd better get someone else.' That suited us fine."

And it suited Paul Vautin fine too. Vautin is no dummy. His alter-ego Fatty might appear that way every now and again as he gets dressed up in funny clothes or lets someone throw a custard pie in his face — but don't be fooled. Sure Fatty is real, he's no stage character, but it's not always easy to be yourself in front of a camera. Paul worked very hard to make sure Fatty wasn't pushed to the background as he learned more about this media game. Became, God forbid, professional. As Owen Dally said, the temptation is there to become just another talking head reading an autocue. Vautin resisted that every inch of the way. For him to lose that larrikin wit, that spontaneity, in order to become as slick and

as polished as some of those he worked with, would
Jimmy Durante getting a nose job. He'd be just like ev
He stuck to his guns — and it worked.

"One of the things we always tried to do on the show ....
fun and Fatty provided that element," Dally said. "It was the same
with Rex Mossop. When Rex did the show he'd do anything for a
laugh. I remember once he arranged for the cameras to stay on him
when we were supposed to be going for a commercial break.

"Rex pretended he didn't know he was still on air and started
yelling out 'make-up, make-up' then when nobody came he pulled
out a handbag and started powdering his nose from a little com-
pact. That was how he was and Fatty was the same. Television can
take itself too seriously and we tried to get away from that. Fatty
was perfect for us."

One of the more memorable moments of Vautin's time with the
show was when Manly made the semi-finals in 1991. Early in the
season, speaking on radio, Vautin had said: "If Manly make the
semis I'll spend a week in a phone box with Darrell Eastlake." With
Eastlake the huuuge volume commentator for Channel 9, the
comment gained wide publicity when the Sea Eagles finished in the
five — and Dally made the most of it.

"We were actually on our way into the studio when I noticed this
red phone box sitting outside the door. It was a prop for *A Country
Practice* and it must have been there all year without anyone
realising. It was just one of those things. I saw it and it clicked.
Fatty!"

The phone box was brought into the studio and Vautin banished
there for the duration. The segment started with a close-up of host
Jon Harker. Dally, in the control room, rang the phone on Harker's
desk and the camera pulled back to show a chastened Fatty making
the call from the booth.

Another time Dally and the panellists conspired over the highlights of an Easts game in which Vautin scored a try. All other tries
in the match had been shown when Harker started to end the
segment for the day. "Hey hang on," blurted an angry Vautin,
"what about my try?" It was only when Harker and the others
started laughing that Vautin realised the gee-up.

He got his own back many times. When Steve Mortimer once
commented that a player who had copped a stiff arm to the head

ₗooked in bad shape Vautin replied: "Oh, sorry, Tom Cruise." There was the time Michael O'Connor came onto the show after suffering severe facial injuries in a State of Origin match. After O'Connor had his say and a deathly serious Harker called for the league to take further action, Vautin piped in with: "Fair dinkum, Snoz, can you put a paper bag over your melon — I think I'm going to have an upp'n."

Fatty didn't always get the last word though. On one notable occasion he was left very much speechless. One of the biggest controversies of State of Origin football blew up after the second match on 1991. The Sydney Football Stadium was the venue for the game in which Penrith tough guy Mark Geyer ran amok, taking on the Queensland side virtually on his own in an awesome display of barely-bridled aggression. It was Origin football at its most fearsome, with Geyer walking the finest of lines between control and madness. The consensus in Sydney the next day was that Wally Lewis, seeing the effect Geyer was having on his team, decided to tip the giant second rower over that line.

At halftime, referee David Manson, fearing an eruption, called captains Lewis and Benny Elias over to ask them to calm down their players. Unfortunately for Manson he also invited Geyer for a chat, bringing him eyeball to eyeball with Lewis who immediately launched into a shouting match with the Blues' trump. Their animated discussion degenerated into pushing and shoving with Manson and Elias trying manfully to get in between, before Geyer allowed himself to be pushed away and up the tunnel, Lewis continuing the invective behind him. It was vintage Wally. Had he succeeded in pushing Geyer over the edge, there is little doubt Queensland would have won the game but Blues' halfback Ricky Stuart, many judges' man of the match, said the halftime blow-up had little effect.

"We couldn't see what was happening because we were already in the dressing room so there was no effect on us at the time," he said. "And by the time MG came into the room he was pretty calm. If there was any yelling I think it was coming from the Queensland room. They were the ones going on about it, we didn't give it a thought until it all blew up the next day. When I saw the replay it seemed obvious to me that Lewis was trying to get Geyer off his game and you could see why. I reckon MG was the reason we were going so well. He was taking it to them. Wally knew the best thing he could do was get MG to stop thinking about the game, maybe get him sent off or binned, but it didn't work. I thought Mark handled it well. He was the one who walked away."

With Geyer seeing out the match, the Blues won, courtesy of a Michael O'Connor kick from wide out in the dying seconds. Geyer and his team had won the battle, but eventually lost the war. Despite being congratulated by NSW officials immediately after the game, later that week Geyer was cited by the same officials over an attempted high tackle on Maroons fullback Paul Hauff. He was suspended for six weeks, ruling him out of the Origin decider, won narrowly by Queensland, and the First Test against New Zealand, won by the Kiwis.

The following Sunday Seven's panel discussed the issue from every possible angle. Was Lewis as guilty as Geyer? Was the Penrith player being victimised, had he in fact shown restraint for walking away from the halftime set-to? Was the League bowing to pressure from a scared Queensland? As would be expected from a predominantly NSW panel, the weight of opinion was firmly behind Geyer and anti-Lewis. Just as predicably, Vautin was right behind his mate and former Queensland captain.

"He was doing what any good captain would do," Vautin told the panel. "He was protecting his players. Geyer was out of control. Wally was looking out for his team ..."

The panellists agreed to disagree, then crossed live to a park in the outer Western Suburbs where Mark Geyer was standing ready to be interviewed. Geyer had heard the previous debate and gave his side of the story, telling of the pain he felt knowing he would not have the chance to play in the decider or realise a lifelong ambition to play in a Test for his country. The effect on his club side would be equally disastrous. He answered questions from panellists Jon Harker, Roy Masters, Steve Roach and Steve Mortimer for close to five minutes before Harker brought the segment to a close.

"Well Mark," he said, "thanks for your time and we look forward to seeing you back on the field. You did a great job for your State on Tuesday night ..."

"Yeah okay," said Geyer, but before the cameras could cut to a commercial break he looked straight into the screen, as if searching around the studio. "But what about Fatty?" he said.

"What's that?" asked Harker.

"How come I haven't heard from Fatty," Geyer repeated. "Is he still there? What's he got to say for himself? I want to hear his question."

In the control booth Owen Dally, not believing his luck, immediately cut back to a shot of Vautin, looking very much put on the spot. Geyer's voice could still be heard. "Where are you, Fatty? Still there?"

"Yeah," Vautin said, staring straight ahead, "I'm here."

"How ya doing?"

"Good, how you doing?"

"Pretty good, how ya going, alright?"

"Yeah, pretty good."

The two enquired about each other's health for a few seconds before Dally brought it to an end. The menacing hulk of Geyer, even through a television monitor, had obviously shaken Vautin, and co-panellist Roy Masters was beside himself.

"Hey, he got you there, Fatty, he put you on the spot. You've got to admire him for that ... Ha ha, he really had you there ..."

Vautin nodded back, not amused. "Yeah right, good Roy," he said, giving the impression he would very much like to work Masters over with a blunt instrument. The tension in the Geyer encounter was very real. Nothing scripted about it, it was live television at its best and the most compelling viewing moment of Vautin's time with the panel. It was also one of the last.

During that State of Origin series, Vautin was driving home from Easts training when he received a call on the car phone in his four wheel drive. "Paul," the caller said, "this is Gary Burns, executive producer from the Ray Martin *Midday Show* ... we'd like you to be one of our guests tomorrow ..."

Knowing the Queenslanders were in camp preparing for the upcoming game, Vautin immediately suspected a gee-up. "Yeah sure," he said, "who is this? Wally? How stupid do you think I am?" Burns chose not to answer the question and eventually convinced Vautin he was indeed needed for an Origin preview alongside NSW glamour player Andrew Ettingshausen.

"We originally had Peter Sterling lined up but he had to go out of town," Burns recalled. "For some reason I decided to give Fatty a call. I knew he handled himself well on *Sportsworld* so I spent the entire day trying to track him down. I finally got him when he was driving out of Henson Park carpark."

The first Midday segment Vautin appeared in was not without its drama. Word reached Burns that Ettingshausen's manager Brian Walsh was not impressed that Fatty would be sitting in for Sterling. Burns heard Walsh believed Vautin to be down market, in direct conflict with Ettingshausen's image as the clean-living, boy next door with the movie star looks. Burns ignored the criticism. "I thought he was mad myself," he said of Walsh, "what could make your client look better than sitting next to Fatty?"

The interview went well, prompting Burns to consider more possibilities. "I came up with the idea of putting Fatty together with Simon O'Donnell in a weekly segment," he said. "At first we thought he was under contract to Channel 7 but when we found out he had never signed a contract with anyone, we quickly got his name on a piece of paper. It was an immediate success. Friday is a notoriously bad day for us. It's shopping day, but once we started with Fatty and Simon, the ratings went up. It became a sort of cult thing. Fatty just proved to be the perfect personality for a show like ours. He's non-threatening. With good-looking guys like ET or Dermott Brereton, you run the risk of turning off the male viewers — they tend to feel threatened. Not with Fatty, they love him, he's just like them. And the ladies want to mother him. He's got that cheeky, irreverent style. He's just your typical Queensland larrikin."

Ray Martin said it didn't take him long to realise Fatty wasn't going to be overawed by the thought of appearing on a non-sport show. "He knew he was on trial but he didn't play it safe and sit there acting coy, he actually took the mickey out of me on that first show. I remember I was teasing Geoff Harvey about something and Fatty had a dig at me. I thought, 'This is okay'. I knew then he wouldn't take a backward step. He reminds me of that bloke in the pub, the one who is the funny one in the group. Every pub has one, and every few minutes they'll be the ones who come out with the funny comment that just breaks everyone up. That's Fatty."

The show introduced the character of Fatty to a whole new audience. People who had never watched a game of rugby league in their lives were suddenly fans of the freckled redhead with the easy-going nature. Burns built on the relationship between Vautin and O'Donnell, having them appear as typical Aussie knockabouts.

Mates who would stick up for each other in a blue, but are more then happy to take the mickey, or try to get one up in the betting stakes. Martin calls them "Laurel and Hardy". The betting started with weekly punting tips and progressed to personal wagers for outrageous stakes. One loss meant Vautin had to clean cars at a local service station while dressed in a tutu. Another saw him lowered into a shark pool in Queensland.

"They stopped traffic," Burns said of the stunts. "When he was dressed in that tutu the cars were banked right up Willoughby Road. That shark pool one was a bit scary — for me, not Fatty. He was fine, but I got cold feet. I could see myself telling his wife and kids that there'd been a slight problem, but it worked out fine in the end. It was all a return to the old days when people like Jack Davey and Bob Dyer used to have bets which would end up with one of them dressed as a baby being pushed down the main street of Melbourne in a pram. Lou Richards used to do that sort of thing too, but he's getting a bit old to be diving into shark pools now. There was a void there. There's nothing new about it, but what is new is Fatty. He'll be in anything and the audience laps it up. We know that if ever the segment is dragging or something is not quite working we can rely on Fatty to jump in and save it."

One example was when a fitness instructor came onto the show to see what sort of shape the boys were in. All was going fine until she pulled out the pincers to test body fat and asked O'Donnell to take off his shirt. He refused. The instructor insisted, the crowd started slow handclapping and Ray Martin tried to talk him into it. No go. The excitement started to die and the segment was at risk of following when Fatty piped up with, "I will."

As he started a slow bump and grind to the accompaniment of the band who quickly went into *The Stripper*, the crowd went wild.

"Hey girls," Fatty shouted into the audience, "how'd ya like your old man to look like this, eh?"

It turned into a hilarious spot, Vautin doing his impersonation of Arnold Schwarzenegger while Martin and O'Donnell doubled up with laughter.

As soon as the show ended Burns thanked Vautin for jumping in. What neither man — nor Martin — was aware of, was that O'Donnell had a good reason for not stripping off on national television. In his courageous fight to beat cancer, the Test cricketer underwent several operations, including the removal of a rib. He was understandably reluctant to bare the scars and was quick to thank Vautin for saving him from what could have been an uncomfortable situation.

There was also another side to that particular segment — one not seen nor heard by the audience. The week before had been Valentine's Day and Fatty had made a crack about Kim waking up to find "a big stalk next to her with a red knob on the end". The joke about the single stem rose Vautin had given his wife did not go over well. Martin and Burns expected an avalanche of complaining mail, but it did not eventuate. "The viewers accepted it once, but I don't know if they would have a second time," Martin said. The following week Vautin apologised to Martin.

"My wife thought that was a bit over the top," he said.

"It was," replied Martin.

So when the fitness instructor pulled out her pincers that day, she called for Vautin and O'Donnell to join her. "I just want to measure your fat," she said innocently. As Vautin rose he turned off his microphone and whispered to Martin: "I'm not touching that one!" Martin was impressed.

He'd learnt his lesson. "He knows he can only go so far," Martin said. "There is an image of the footballer as a foul-mouthed thickhead. Fatty gets away from that. He's your kid brother, your mate from the pub, and the reaction was just amazing. I honestly can't think of any other sportsman who cracked it in television so quickly. I would have to say I wouldn't have predicted it. I knew he was going to be good, but I didn't know how good, or how quickly he would get into his stride."

The success of the Vautin-O'Donnell partnership has led to talk of a club act, while Burns believes they have years to run as a TV pairing. "You never know whether something like this will have the legs when it starts off," he said. "We're not a sports show and Fatty isn't a comedian, but if it fails in one area we always have the other one to fall back on. People are interested in sport and Fatty has natural timing and comic flair. Put the two together and it just works. Somehow, it just works."

Fatty also "works" on radio. 2UE sports director Ray Hadley admits he was "desperate" to sign Vautin as part of the station's top-rating rugby league broadcasting team for the 1992 season, but lost him to Triple M. The two have worked together often on radio, in television commercials and at speaking engagements, but Hadley maintains having Vautin alongside you on live radio can be a frightening experience.

"On the Richter scale of good taste he rates about a half," Hadley said. "I was always terrified. I made sure he was always working on five seconds delay. I think he's more responsible now he's working on television, but back in the early days he was likely to say anything. And there would never be any remorse. But I think he's cleaned up his act a bit now. He had to."

Once Vautin asked Hadley for some advice on public speaking. He had been invited to speak at the Brisbane Rothmans Medal presentation and wanted a few pointers. Hadley explained the speech would need structure — a start, some gags, and a strong finish. And the main thing: it shouldn't go for more than 20 minutes. He offered to sit down with Vautin in the week before the function to run through the talk with him. It was an offer gratefully received — but promptly ignored. A few days after the function Hadley asked Vautin how he had gone.

"Terrific," was the answer, "sensational, absolutely blitzed it! They wouldn't let me sit down — spoke for 90 minutes."

Other reports filtering down to Sydney were not so glowing. "Over the next few days I got reports that he'd been dreadful," Hadley said. "Apparently he'd got up there and told all these filthy stories in front of the sheilas, he was swearing and carrying on. There were blokes wanting to fight him and he was yelling back at them and they were trying to get the microphone off him. I heard there were about half a dozen blokes who were laughing along, but they were probably boofhead Queenslanders like him. The others thought he was awful. And 90 minutes? Shirley Bassey doesn't go for that long."

The quintessential after-dinner speaker he might not have been, but radio was a different story. "I think radio is his go," Hadley said. "I think he's good on TV but on radio he's better. He certainly has the face for it! Radio lacks characters, and that's what Fatty is. He's a knockabout. It doesn't matter if the listener is from Rooty Hill or Double Bay, Fatty can get to them. He breaks down the barriers and, most of all, he's prepared to say something, which a lot of ex-footballers aren't. They're too busy staying onside with everyone. I'd always hoped he'd join us when he stopped playing, but when it came to the crunch he stayed with Triple M."

Signing with Triple M was no clear-cut decision. To opt for a spot on an FM radio station ahead of joining the No.1 league team might appear folly, but once again it was the nous of Paul charting the career of Fatty.

By joining UE Vautin would have been further saturating the market he reached with his newspaper columns, TV appearances and commercials but Triple M offered a whole new following: a young, more hip audience than the *Midday Show's* regulars, and different again from dyed-in-the-wool league followers. Once again he proved about as dizzy as an IBM computer. When the offer from Triple M came via sports director David White, he jumped at it.

White, now a current affairs presenter for Channel 7, is one of Manly's most rabid fans. He admired Vautin as a footballer but as they met socially, he could see there was a lot more to the redhead than an ability to tackle. "We used to talk in the dressing room after the games and he'd break me up," White said. "He was just a very funny guy and I thought if he could reproduce that laconic wit on radio we'd be on a winner. To me he was like a footballing version of Paul Hogan. We signed him up to do what we called Fatty's Friday Footy Rap and it worked from day one. He was a natural and the best thing was that he could have fun with it. There were plenty of footballers on radio at the time but there was a sameness to them. Fatty made a production number of it. He didn't take it too seriously and that was the appeal. He could poke fun at the whole thing because he was actually in there. He had all the nicknames and inside info, the listeners loved it. If Fatty was out of town or couldn't do the spot for some reason people would be ringing up asking where he was."

The segment was part of the top-rating breakfast show of the time, headed by the irreverent Doug Mulray. Doug Mulray and his team weren't people to blush easily. But Fatty stumped them. The moment is now part of Triple M folklore, and by chance, White has it immortalised on video. "Mighty Whitey" had just bought a new video camera and, as Fatty was due in the studio to go live and meet Mulray for the first time, he decided to tape the show for posterity. All was going smoothly until Fatty decided to involve himself in the play. "Hey Douggie," he chirped into his microphone, "I've got a joke for you."

Mulray, sitting on the opposite side of the console, gave White an "I'm not going to like this, am I," look, but nodded nonetheless.

"What's the only thing that's hit more balls that Jack Nicklaus's putter," he asked. Mulray, was not sure he wanted to hear the answer but decided to live dangerously. "What?"

"Rock Hudson's chin," came the reply.

"There was deafening silence for about three seconds as everyone's jaws hit the ground," said White. "Andrew Denton was sitting there with this look of stunned shock on his face. Nobody moved."

And then Mulray leaned forward to his microphone and shouted: "TILT!" and pushed the button for a commercial.

As they were walking out to the lift after the show Fatty asked White: "Should I have cracked that joke?"

"Fatty," said White, "it's too late now. It's on its way to Mars."

And a whole new generation of Fatty fans was born.

Not all his ventures into the world of the media were so successful. Late in his playing career Vautin was approached to write a book, along with John Raper and league writer Ian Heads. Entitled *Fatty and Chook*, it was a collection of funny stories about life in rugby league. Vautin threw himself into the task as he had with his other writing. His stories were researched, wittily written, typed and to the publisher on time. He then followed that by making himself available for personal promotions and book signings. The book sold well and Raper and Vautin awaited the royalties. They didn't come. The publisher went into liquidation and any profits went to creditors. Vautin netted $500 for his efforts.

But that was a rare failure in an otherwise profitable career. When his playing days ended, Vautin's experience on the *Midday Show* gave him a headstart into a career as a television commentator. Although Channel Nine had the rights to televise rugby league they did not exercise them, other than State of Origin, until the start on the 1992 season. The timing could not have been better. Nine needed to put together commentary teams for the Friday night and Sunday games, while continuing with the big rep games. Vautin got the nod, and for a while, it appeared Ray Hadley would be joining him. After weeks of speculation, Hadley opted to re-sign with 2UE, but was still hopeful of being part of the Nine Network's commentary team for *Friday Night Football.*

"I told Fatty it looked like it was all set," Hadley recalled. "He told me he was going to have lunch with Nine's sports boss Ian Frykberg the next day and he'd put in a good word for me. The next day Nine rang to say they wouldn't be needing my services. He's like that, Fatty, do anything for a mate."

Hadley might have been left on the bench, but Fatty was very much at the forefront. He hurled himself into the TV fray with a vengeance and immediately won a following with his off-the-cuff comments. "Someone should tell that bloke sideburns went out when Elvis carked it," he said of an English competitor in the Nissan World Sevens, and followed up by singing the Wigan club song.

During a Sunday match when a player shrugged off a suspect tackle around the groin area, he was full of praise: "He's been grabbed by the goulies," he shouted, "and he's still going — what a player!"

But sometimes his enthusiasm got the better of him. Frykberg had to issue a caution after Fatty said of David Gillespie's defence: "The last thing that went through Gillespie was a packet of Laxettes." Alright for around the bar at the club, but not quite the thing for national television, was the gist of it. And then there was the Ipswich controversy. When Kerrod Walters, his brother Kevin and Allan Langer — all former Ipswich boys — combined to set up a try for the Broncos during their Challenge Cup match against Wests in Wellington, New Zealand, Fatty cried out: "You can put that one down to Two Head City." It was throwaway line which he expected to vanish to Mars with Rock Hudson's putter but he didn't count on the sensibilities of the people of Ipswich. Although Langer had laughed when he heard the comment, others weren't amused. The first Vautin knew of it was when Nine publicist Brian Walsh rang his hotel room from London.

"I understand there's some problem about you insulting the people of Ipswich," Walsh said. "The mayor has called for an apology."

"You're kiddin'," replied Vautin who could still not see what the fuss was about. The conversation was shortlived, but the phone was soon ringing again. A reporter from the *Ipswich Times.* By this time Vautin was starting to get a little bit sick of the attention. "Oh yeah," he said, "so tell me, which head are you talking through?"

That aggressive, up-front attitude was repeated in his weekly rugby league segment on Nine's *Sports Sunday*. Poor Brett Kenny, whose Parramatta side was lurching from one disaster to another, was unlucky enough to be first guest on the unscripted spot. "How can you blokes be over the salary cap?" he asked the hapless Kenny. "You're that bad. You and Sterling must be on half a million each, because the rest of those blokes aren't worth peanuts."

No sooner was Kenny over the shock of that one than he followed up with: "Brett there has been some criticism of Parramatta's forwards in the past. You must admit, they turned it up last night."

As he had so successfully in the past, Fatty remained himself, and let the audience decide for themselves. For the most part they responded with a positive thumbs up. By the end of his first year as a professional media star Vautin was calling football three and a half hours each week, had a one-hour segment on *Sports Sunday*, presented Fatty's Friday Footy Rap on Triple M, appeared weekly on the *Ray Martin Show* and was part of the commentary team for one-offs such as State of Origin, minor rep games and Sevens.

And that's not counting the big one — the Lowes ads.

Johnny Gibbs recalls that even when Vautin was still playing, if the two old mates were out in public it was the Lowes ads people would want to talk about. "Nobody ever talked to him about football," he said. "All they'd be interested in was Lowes."

The commercials for the popular down-market clothing stores have been an advertising phenomenon, one that other companies have tried to copy but without success. The brainchild of advertising exec David Andrews, they have succeeded further than even he dreamed possible. Andrews first sold Lowes marketing boss Linda Penn on the idea of using footballers in print ads soon after the stores were taken over by the Manhattan chain. The new owners wanted to change the image to establish what Andrews describes as a "new David Jones" but he and Penn talked them out of it. Using acquaintances from the Cronulla club, Andrews put together the first series of ads but it was not until the combination of Vautin, Hadley, Michael O'Connor and Steve Roach that he really hit paydirt.

"It was the perfect team," Andrews said. "We had the natural comedian in Fatty, Hadley with the gift of the gab, O'Connor who was respected as a dual international and was therefore thought to have a bit of class, and Blocker Roach the big heavy. We started off with solely print ads and catalogues but it was when we gave them a bit of room to be themselves that it really clicked.

"Fatty is a one-off, one of those guys who when he is good he's good, when he'd bad he's better. We must have made 50 ads together. It's like a series."

And one that works. According to Penn, the campaign is successful on two levels: "We sell heaps of product and the corporate awareness is unbelievable. When we shot at a school 500 kids were yelling out 'At Lowes!' with no prompting." Andrews, who writes the ads, says Fatty was "born to be a Lowes man" but at the same time is one of the few people in the media to differentiate between the on-screen Fatty and the off-screen Paul. "I think I know him pretty well now, but he's not an easy person to know," he said, "he reminds me of a young, rough-edged Tony Hancock. Paul can stand in the background quietly until the cameras are rolling and then Fatty comes to life. He's a total professional. He's his own stunt man, he'll do anything to make the shot work. We had a baseball scene once and he dived in the dirt time after time until we got it right. By the time the shoot was over his elbows were bleeding — and that one where he had to slide down the bowling alley, he did that himself, he literally threw himself towards the camera." He has also been Father Christmas, the Easter Bunny, been filmed in the nude with nothing but a stuffed koala hiding the family jewels and worn a cassock and bald patch as Friar Tuck.

Believe it or not, the TV ads are tightly scripted, while the radio commercials are more ad lib, but according to Hadley a lot of the funniest action is when the cameras aren't rolling. "Fatty can break us up," he said. "There was this one where he had to stare into a sheep's eyes. His line is, "I think she likes me", but when the tape wasn't rolling he added, 'I hope so because I'm crazy about her.' We were getting ready for the next shot and I heard him saying to the sheep, "Well, how about if I buy you dinner first?"

The ads give Paul the chance to give Fatty full rein, but never more when the team travelled to a Catholic primary school at Kingsgrove to film a commercial for schoolwear. Hadley played the teacher, while O'Connor and Vautin, dressed in caps and short-sleeved shirts and school ties, sat at a desk in the midst of a class of 8 to 12-year-olds.

It was an exciting day for the children, appearing in a TV ad with their heroes, and their teacher was having trouble controlling them. After she had given them a dressing down, the room returned to order. It was a moment tailor-made for Fatty, one he had waited for almost 20 years for. With the room silent, he lifted one buttock off his seat and let rip.

"The class just erupted," said Hadley. "They were all yelling out 'Aw, gross, Fatty, gross!' The teacher looked at him and said, 'Fatty, how can I be expected to keep control if you can't behave yourself?' He just giggled at her like he was 10 years old." Father Alban would have known just what she was going through.

But despite his obvious enjoyment of the work, Paul will not stand for Fatty to be compromised, as some producers and camera men have learnt. "He has a short tolerance level," said Andrews. "There are some crew who have found him difficult but then I don't know too many people who are good in this business who aren't difficult at times. The thing is, Fatty has an inbuilt sense to know what will work for him and what won't. I like to think I know what not to ask him to do. We've worked out what we can get away with."

Well, almost. Fatty, who had graced more than one back page in his time, finally made it to the front page of the newspaper when a Lowes commercial he and Blocker appeared in was banned. The ad featured Blocker hitting Fatty over the head with a hammer. A mother complained that it could encourage her children to hit each other with hammers. The Broadcasting Control Tribunal took the ad off air.

Most people could see the funny side. Reporter Debbie Spillane, appearing on Andrew Denton's alternative sports show *Live And Sweaty* on the ABC, said she couldn't see what the fuss was about. "Surely everyone knows there was nothing dangerous about it," she told Denton. "It's common knowledge that if you wanted to hurt a footballer with a hammer the last place you'd hit him would be his head."

CHAPTER 18

The Family;
The Future

On May 20, 1992, the Brisbane Capitols beat North Queensland in the final of the State League at Lang Park as curtain raiser to the second State of Origin match. The winning coach was Paul Vautin.

Soon after Vautin retired, his friend John Gibbs said, "There are three things that he'll never get over — being sacked from Manly, not getting life membership of the club, and the fact that he can't play anymore."

It's true, Vautin probably never will get over what happened at Manly at the end of 1989 and whether he gets life membership of the club remains to be seen. As far as not playing again, well, chances are if someone asked him to he'd pull out the boots and be on the field in a minute.

Not that that is likely. When Vautin rang Wally Lewis to tell him of his decision to stop playing, the reaction was one of good wishes for a successful retirement. With Lewis just appointed captain-coach of Gold Coast, the opening was there for him to offer Vautin one final fling.

"I would have liked him to," said Vautin, "in fact I would have loved him to but he didn't and maybe that's the best thing. I could have asked, but I never would have put Wally in the position of having to say yes for friendship alone. If I had asked, and he did say yes, I never would have known whether it was because he felt I could be of use or because he didn't want to hurt me."

But he hasn't given up entirely. In fact, Gibbs says Vautin still rings him from time to time with news of some half-baked offer of a captain-coach job anywhere from north of England to south of

Townsville. "I tell him, 'Fatty, forget it, it's over' and hang up on him," Gibbs said.

But as the offers get fewer and Vautin's desire to play gets weaker the dream of coaching gets stronger. Vautin will never leave rugby league, it's his life, to the exclusion of all else outside his family.

When former Queensland manager Kevin Brasch asked Vautin if he was interested in coaching one of Brisbane's two sides in the State League the answer was an overwhelming yes. At the time he was negotiating a lucrative contract with Channel Nine, yet put the deal in jeopardy by stipulating he must have a month off from calling Sunday games to coach the Capitols. Luckily Nine's sports boss Ian Frykberg agreed.

"Kevin told me that neither of the Brisbane sides had even made the finals the year before and that it had been pretty embarrassing," he said. "I wanted the job and I wanted to do it right."

Do it right he did. Vautin moved to Brisbane for a month, living in a hotel and working for hours preparing his coaching plans. And the QRL did the right thing by him, securing Frank Lind Oval at West Mitchelton — the ground where it all started — as training venue. The combination worked a treat.

"It's all a case of preparation and getting the respect of the players," he said of coaching, and true to his word left nothing to chance. Every training run, every tap move and drill were meticulously worked out and written down in an exercise book, just as he had done as a schoolboy.

To meld team spirit Vautin dropped in to a local Lowes store and bought $500 worth of shirts. One pattern for the backs, one for the forwards. The team called themselves "The Lowes Boys".

The side remained undefeated in its five matches and brought home the trophy in the final, giving Vautin one of his greatest thrills in the game. As he went from the dressing room to the commentary box where he would help call the Origin match — in the seat once occupied by Jack Gibson — Peter Sterling christened him Super Coach.

For Vautin the prospect of some day coaching a first grade side remains one of his main ambitions, despite the fact he is established in the media and no less an authority than Ray Martin believes that is where his future lies. "If he is sensible I see it being a lifetime career," Martin says and Vautin is hopeful that will be the case.

"When I started thinking about retiring I was worried," he said. "I knew my time was up but I didn't know what I would do. I couldn't be a bank clerk or a garbo because there is no connection with the game. I knew I couldn't walk away. I'll never be able to walk away."

The offer from Channel Nine to join the league commentary team provided the answer. A job in the media which kept him involved with the game — and he has never worked harder. "We see him less now than when he was a player," said Kim. "When he was playing every Sunday I'd take the kids and we'd watch him. Sunday is a family day to me and now the kids miss out, they don't see their father as much because he is away so often.

"But I guess that is all part of being part of Paul's family. When I first started watching him play I couldn't believe that person down on the field was the same person I knew. He's so quiet at home, he doesn't say boo but there he was on the field running into people and diving at their legs. It was a shock and it's the same when he is on TV.

"That Fatty character, that's not Paul. The guy on TV never shuts up. At home you can't get a word out of him. In the Lowes ads he's just an idiot isn't he? Just a fool. It's like they stand around and say 'Okay Fatty, do something stupid' — and he does.

"That's not the Paul I know but that's the way Paul makes his living, and that's what makes him happy. Sometimes it's not easy. He's away staying at the Hilton and having someone make his bed and make him breakfast and I'm here with three kids. That makes me angry at times. Still, I suppose he could have got a nine to five job and come home every night but he wouldn't be happy, and what's the point in that?

"It's been a roller coaster. There have been plenty of good times, like when Manly won the premiership and Paul was playing for Queensland and Australia. There were a lot of people around to share in that, but when the bad times came they weren't around. The Manly thing, getting dropped from Queensland and the end at Easts, who was there when it all fell to pieces? Just me and him."

And Paul appreciates it. Kim Vautin is a strong-willed, inciteful woman who, like her husband, does not suffer fools. When she was interviewed on television after Vautin had injured his eye in the brutal Manly-Easts semi-final in 1987, she was asked, "You must have felt bad seeing your husband hurt like that ..."

"I wouldn't like to see *anyone* hurt like that," she said sharply. Ask a stupid question ...

It's not always easy for the wife of a sporting star. Their husband is often away playing, open to the temptations and pleasures of life on the road while she must face the responsibilities of home and children. Then, when he *is* home, she must take a back seat as he soaks up the limelight and tailors his social life around playing a game on the weekend.

"Kim has been fantastic," Vautin said. "She's stuck by me, been a shoulder to lean on so many times I've lost count. I can never make it up to her for all the support she has been."

For Kim, as much as Paul, the prospect of retirement was a daunting one. With three children — Kylie aged 10, Nikki, six, and Matthew, two, the thought of life without the substantial pay from rugby league wasn't good.

A conversation between Kim and *Midday Show* producer Gary Burns provided some hope. "What's Paul doing at the end of the year?" Burns asked.

"He's thinking of retiring," Kim said.

"Good, I think he can be used around here."

And it went on from there, although Vautin says his work in the media will never replace his love for rugby league.

"What I'm doing now is the best job I've ever had," he said, "and I've never been busier, but I still have this dream. I'd hate to wake up in 20 years time and realise I'd never coached a first grade team."

And what team would he like to coach? Take a guess.

"Manly," he says, "I'd love to coach there. I don't think it will ever happen because of everything that went on, but at least you can dream."

And while he may not ever coach his beloved Sea Eagles, there is still a chance that one day he will be rewarded with life membership of the club. Ten years' service and 200 first grade games are criteria for life membership but not a guarantee. Vautin has achieved both but stepped on a lot of toes as he walked out of Brookvale for the last time.

As Alan Thompson put it, "the day I was sacked I walked out of that club and I haven't been back since. I've still got a lot of friends down there but there are a lot of people who aren't my friends. I'd say Fatty is the same."

Perhaps, but the friends that Vautin does have are sticking by him. In 1991 he was nominated for life membership by one Ron Wheatley. Seconder was John Gibbs. The nomination was rejected as it was put in after the due date, but the move to gain life membership has not lost momentum.

Wheatley and Gibbs intend to keep trying and they are gaining support in high places. Fulton believes Vautin deserves life membership and Arthurson is known to be working quietly to mend the last vestiges of any rift. Doug Daley said: "It will be up to the committee. We'll see what happens."

Meanwhile the dream goes on. Life membership of the club he served so well for 11 years, coach of the team and then, who knows, coach of Queensland.

It is a dream shared by Tosser Turner. "Every year I say I'm going to retire and every year I give myself a reason to keep going," he said, "when Wally retired it was to help Mal, when Mal retires it will probably be to help Alfie. After that, it'll probably be to help Wally and hopefully Fatty when they coach the side. That would be a wonderful day for me, to see my boys back in charge."

But that is all very much in the long-term future for Vautin. Short-term he has his media work and his family: Kim and the two girls, and Matthew who he hopes one day will play the game which has meant so much to his father and grandfather. "Of course I'd love him to play," Vautin says, "but I'd love him to do anything except be a ballet dancer."

He was a kid from Brisbane who came to the big smoke and stayed longer and did better than just about anyone else.

There have been brighter stars from north of the border, of course, but they stayed put and made it in their own patch. Vautin made it away from home but never lost sight of who he was and where he came from. Which is probably why they love him up there. Down in Sydney? Well, he's the first to admit he ruffled a few feathers and there are times when he wonders if there is something wrong with him, the way he tends to leave places on the outer. The lament of the extrovert: would things have been different if I could have learned to keep my mouth shut? The answer of course is yes — but then, he wouldn't have been Fatty Vautin.

His mates, like Gibbs, say no, there's no problem. It's just Fatty doing the talking, and Paul the worrying.

"All that stuff he goes on with," says Gibbs, "he never means anything malicious by it. It's just Fatty making mischief."

For all that, he holds no grudges and hopes none are held by others.

"I've got no beefs," he said, "time is a big healer. There were times I was angry — the thing at Manly affected me pretty badly for a while but you can't dwell on things. Really, looking back on it all I wouldn't change a thing. I gave it my best and I did okay. Sure it would have been nice to have a Kangaroo tour or two and it would have been nice to finish my career at Manly, but that's life, you can't change things.

"I've had some great times and met some unforgetable people. As far as friends go — well, throughout life one doesn't come across many people who you can call 'best' friends. Sure there's lots of mates, friends and acquaintances — people whose company you really enjoy and are great to be with but fall just short of the top bracket. Throughout my footballing career I'm lucky enough to have six mates I put in that bracket — John Gibbs, Ian Thomson, Wally Lewis, Phil Sigsworth, Dale Shearer and Mark Pocock.

"These are men for whom I'd do anything and would trust them with my life. I can only thank them for their friendship and support over the years.

"I've needed that support at times, but in the wrap up there are no regrets, no what ifs. Well, maybe one: if there is one thing I think about, it's what would have happened if I had accepted that offer from Manly. Maybe if I hadn't been so rash things would have worked out but there was a principle there and you can't walk away from that. That's what I've based my life on."

And, besides, the good times far outweigh the bad. Vautin has plenty for his time in rugby league: a nice home, a beautiful family and friends.

"There have been lots of times in life — over the last eight years of my career in particular — where I wanted to run to a mountain top and shout for joy and a few where I wanted to crawl into a hole, shrivel up and never come out," he said. "Beside me in all those situations was Kim. Apart from being beautiful, caring, a great mother and all the rest, she has been so loyal and dependable. I must admit I'm more in love with her now than ever before. Love is a funny thing. We all need it but in particular I need someone to give it to. The degrees of love are infinite: love for parents, love for friends, love for the game of rugby league, love for children and love for your wife — they all bring out different emotions in me and they are all fulfilling. My parents, George and Leila, gave me a wonderful headstart in life with the upbringing I received. I owe them so much — so much that I can't really repay and if I'm half as good a parent as they were I'll be doing okay.

"In the end, does it really matter if I didn't make a Kangaroo tour, or that Jack Gibson thinks I'm a jerk or that I didn't finish my career on top of the world? Not particularly. All that matters to me now is my family. There is nothing more important to me, nothing more sacred than Kim and the tin lids. I had some great times in the game but if there is a better experience in life than watching your own children be born then I'm yet to do it. I was there to see Nikki and Matthew come into this world, saw the pain and sheer hard work that Kim went through and saw the babies take their first breath.

"That's what life is all about to me now, to be successful in my work, whether it be at Channel Nine, a coaching job some day or whatever I'm having a go at, and more importantly, to be a great husband and father. I'm lucky to have found Kim. She's a very strong woman, the sort who will stand with you in the trenches when the war is raging and go to the wall with you if need be yet at times be as tender and loving as is humanly possible.

"When I tell her how lucky she was to have married me she just looks me in the eye and says: 'give yourself an uppercut you goose.' As for the children, the three of them are all so special and I've only got to look at them to have my heart filled with pride. They make life worth living and I hope I can do them proud as a father."

So that then is Vautin's future, in his own words. That, and the lifetime of memories he takes with him.

Some are in that room which opens onto his swimming pool. The framed photos, scrapbooks and signed photographs, the library of videotapes. Others, just as vivid, are brought out like old wine when he sits in front of the open fire and talks of the best of times.

At Everton Park there are scrapbooks every bit as packed as those in Sydney, lovingly kept by Leila, the yellowed cuttings pressed and stuck down like a school project. There is the rosette she wore on grand final day 1987, her son's first Origin jumper and the video recorder he won as man of the match in the KB Cup final. There is the program from Wembley and a story from the London *Times*.

And there is something else, something she cherishes above all. The night after Wayne Bennett's last match as coach of Queensland, George and Leila went to the team celebration with Paul. At the end of the night Leila took her program and asked the coach for his autograph. He looked her in the eye and paused, as he does when he wants to say something important. Then he signed.

"Mrs Vautin," he wrote, "thank you for your son."

Epilogue

The reporter walked through Canberra airport and jumped in the cab waiting at the rank. The driver was in his 30s, of European background and eating a hamburger. He drove with one hand, ate his hamburger and spoke, all at the same time. "Where you goin'?" he asked, a small piece of lettuce flying from his lips and landing on the windscreen.

"Queanbeyan Leagues Club."

"Yeah? What you wanna go there for?"

This was getting a little out of hand. "Tim Sheens."

Correction: this was getting *very much* out of hand, but the driver's friendly interest was so open, so free of malice, and such a change from big-city inhibitions, that the reporter kept answering his questions. "I'm a sportswriter," he said, "from Sydney. I have to talk to him about the Raiders."

"Yeah," said the cabbie, "you write rugby league? So tell me, have Manly re-signed Cliffy Lyons yet?"

"Yesterday."

"Well thank goodness for that. Those blokes in charge out there, they've got rocks in their heads you know. Things haven't been the same since they got rid of Fatty Vautin."

Suddenly the reporter was interested. "You like Fatty Vautin?"

"Like him? Mate, I love him. I adore him. I love him so much I call my wife Fatty, what do you think about that, eh?"

The mind boggled. The reporter pressed on. "How long have you lived out here?"

"All my life," he said. "I've lived in Canberra all my life, and all my life I've supported Manly. Funny eh? I was the only one in my school who supported them. Even when Canberra came into the competition, I used to go for Manly. Last year, Manly came down here, remember? I was the only one on the hill goin' for 'em. There was all these people yellin' for me to shut up and I just kept shouting for Manly. End of the game Manly won and I just stood there pointin' at the scoreboard, they couldn't say anythink then, eh."

But back to Fatty.

"Fatty? I just love him, that's all. He never played a bad game. He never stopped tryin', eh. Even when they were getting a flogging, he'd keep trying, right to the end. And they sacked him. They shouldn't have sacked Fatty, they should have sacked themselves, that's who they should have sacked.

"You know his last game at Brookvale? I took my little daughter, I said, 'sweetheart, today we're going to Sydney because I want you to be able to say you saw Fatty Vautin play for Manly.' So we got the train up, just me and her, and we went to my aunty's place at Petersham and caught another train to Circular Quay and then the ferry to Manly and a bus to Brookvale and we saw him play his last game there. At the end we was both cryin', me and my little girl, but at least she can say she saw Fatty play his last game for Manly at Brookie. That's something she'll never forget."

The reporter told the driver that he was writing a book. About Fatty. The cabbie nearly drove off the road.

He pulled up outside Queanbeyan Leagues Club and looked at the meter. The reporter was already writing the story in his head, about how of all the cabdrivers in Canberra, he got Lou, the one who took his little girl to see Paul Vautin's last game for Manly at Brookie, the one who calls his wife Fatty. The one who wouldn't take the reporter's money.

Lou looked up from the meter. "Fourteen dollars, seventy," he said. The reporter rewrote his story slightly.

He was getting out of the cab as Lou leant over, "Hey mate," he said. "Next time you see Fatty, you tell him something for me, willya? Tell him there's a cabdriver in Canberra who loves him."

Just did, Lou, just did.